LANDMARKS OF
AFRICAN AMERICAN HISTORY

American Landmarks

JAMES OLIVER HORTON
General Editor

LANDMARKS OF
AFRICAN AMERICAN HISTORY

James Oliver Horton

OXFORD
UNIVERSITY PRESS

Published in consultation with the
National Register of Historic Places, National Park Service, the National Park Foundation
and the Gilder Lehrman Institute of American History

To the National Park Service and its chief historian.

OXFORD
UNIVERSITY PRESS

Auckland   Bangkok   Buenos Aires   Cape Town   Chennai
Dar es Salaam   Delhi   Hong Kong   Istanbul   Karachi   Kolkata
Kuala Lumpur   Madrid   Melbourne   Mexico City   Mumbai   Nairobi
São Paulo   Shanghai   Singapore   Taipei   Tokyo   Toronto

Copyright © 2005 by James Oliver Horton

Published by Oxford University Press, Inc.
198 Madison Avenue, New York, New York, 10016
www.oup.com

Oxford is a registered trademark of Oxford University Press

Library of Congress Cataloging-in-Publication Data
Horton, James Oliver.
  Landmarks of African American history / James Oliver Horton.
    p. cm. — (American landmarks)
"Published in association with the National Register of Historic Places,
National Park Service, and the National Parks Foundation"-T.p. verso.
Includes bibliographical references and index.
  ISBN-13: 978-0-19-514118-4
  ISBN-10: 0-19-514118-0 (alk. paper)
1. African Americans—History. 2. Historic sites—United States. 3. African Americans—
Monuments. 4. United States—History, Local. I. Title. II. American landmarks
E185.H6444 2004
973'.0496073—dc22   2004002798

Printing number: 9 8 7 6 5 4 3 2 1

Printed in China on acid-free paper.

Cover: *Cedar Hill, the home of Frederick Douglass, and Dred Scott (inset).*

Frontis: *Martin Luther King Jr. rallies for "jobs and freedom" in Washington D.C. in 1963.*

Title page: *The USS* Arizona *Memorial to those who lost their lives in the attack on Pearl Harbor.*

American Landmarks

JAMES OLIVER HORTON
General Editor

LANDMARKS OF
African American History

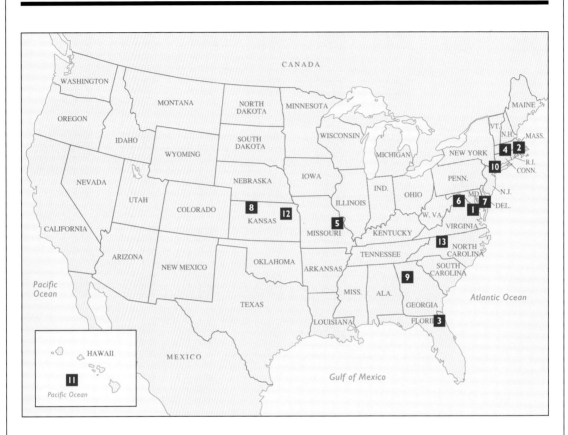

Contents

Page 25
The Old State House

Page 50
The African Meeting House

Page 137
The Apollo Theater

Introduction:
The Power of Place

James Oliver Horton

General Editor

Few experiences can connect us with our past more completely than walking the ground where our history happened. The landmarks of American history have a vital role to play in helping us to understand our past, because they are its physical evidence. The sensory experience of a place can help us to reconstruct historical events, just as archaeologists reconstruct vanished civilizations. It can also inspire us to empathize with those who came before us. A place can take hold of us, body, mind, and spirit. As philosophers of the Crow Indian nation have reminded us, "The ground on which we stand is sacred ground. It is the blood of our ancestors." It is the history owed to our children. They will remember that history only to the extent that we preserve the places where it was made.

Historical sites are some of history's best teachers. In the early 1970s, when I was a graduate student in Boston, working on a study of the nineteenth-century black community of that city, I walked the streets of Beacon Hill imagining the daily lives of those who lived there a century before. Although I had learned much about the people of that community from their newspapers and pamphlets, from their personal letters and official records, nothing put me in touch with their lives and their time like standing in the places where they had stood and exploring the neighborhood where they lived.

I remember walking along Myrtle Street just down Beacon Hill from the rear of the Massachusetts State House in the early morning and realizing that Leonard Grimes, the black minister of the Fugitive Slave Church, must have squinted into the sun just as I was doing as he emerged from his home at the rear of number 59 and turned left on his way to his church. Walking up Joy Street in December added new meaning to descriptions I had read about the sound of children sledding down its slope during the particularly snowy winter of 1850. And twisting my ankle on irregular cobblestone streets made clear the precarious footing for fugitive slaves fleeing at full run from slave catchers empowered by the Fugitive Slave Law of 1850.

Any historical event is much better understood within the context of its historical setting. It is one thing to read the details of the Battle of Gettysburg. It is quite another to stand on Little Round Top, with its commanding view of the battlefield to the north and west, and contemplate the assault of the 15th Alabama Confederates against the downhill charge of the 20th Maine Volunteer Infantry. Standing at the summit, taking the measure of the degree of slope and the open area that afforded little cover to advancing armies is an unforgettable experience. It also bears irrefutable testimony to the horror of that battle, the bloodiest of the Civil War, and to the sacrifice of the more than 50,000 men during four days in the summer of 1863.

The Landmarks of American History series has emerged from this belief in the power of place to move us and to teach us. It was with this same philosophy in mind that in 1966 Congress authorized the establishment of the National Register of Historic Places, "the Nation's official list of cultural resources worthy of preservation." These enduring symbols of the American experience are as diverse as the immigration station on Angel Island in San Francisco Bay, which served as U.S. entry point for thousands of Asian immigrants; or Sinclair Lewis's Boyhood Home in Sauk Centre, Minnesota, the place that inspired the novelist's Nobel Prize–winning descriptions of small-town America; or the Cape Canaveral Air Force Station in Florida, launch site of Neil Armstrong's historic trip to the moon. Taken together, such places define us as a nation.

The historic sites presented in this series are selected from the National Register, and they are more than interesting places. The books in this series are written by some of our finest historians—based at universities, historic museums, and historic sites—all nationally recognized experts on the central themes of their respective volumes. For them, historic sites are not just places to visit on a field trip, but primary sources that inform their scholarship. Not simply illustrations of history, they bring the reality of our past to life, making it meaningful to our present and useful for our future.

How to Use This Book

This book is designed to tell the story of American history from a unique perspective: the places where it was made. Each chapter profiles a historic site listed on the National Register of Historic Places, and each site is used as the centerpiece for discussion of a particular aspect of history—for example, Independence Hall for the Declaration of Independence, or the Woolworth store in the Downtown Greensboro Historic District for Martin Luther King Jr.'s role in the civil rights movement. This book is not intended as an architectural history; it is an American history.

On page 6 (opposite the table of contents), there is a regional map of the United States locating each of the main sites covered in this volume. Each chapter in this volume contains a main essay that explains the site's historical importance; a fact box (explained below); and one or two maps that locate the site in the region or show its main features. Each chapter also contains a box listing sites related to the main subject. For each related site, the box includes the official name, address, phone, website, whether it is a National Historic Landmark (NHL) or part of the National Parks Service (NPS), and a short description. As much as possible, the author has selected related sites that are geographically diverse and open to the public.

Many of the chapters feature primary sources related to the thematic discussion. These include, for example, letters, journal entries, legal documents, and newspaper articles. Each primary source is introduced by an explanatory note or a caption, indicated by the symbol ☙.

At the back of the book is a timeline of important events mentioned in the text, along with a few other major events that help give a chronological context for the book's theme. A list of further reading includes site-specific reading, along with general reading pertinent to the book.

Fact Boxes

Each chapter has a fact box containing reference information for its main site. This box includes a picture of the site; the site's official name on the National Register;

contact information; National Register Information System number (which you can you use to obtain more details about the site from the National Register, whose contact information appears at the back of this book); whether the site is a National Historic Landmark (NHL) or part of the National Park Service (NPS); and important dates, people, and events in the site's history.

Acts of Congress recognize and protect America's 386 National Park Service units, including National Parks, National Historic Sites, National Historic Battlefields, and National Monuments. The Secretary of the Interior designates National Historic Landmarks, of which there are more than 2,300. States, federal agencies, and Indian tribes have nominated the majority of the 75,000 properties listed in the National Register of Historic Places, some of which are also historic units of the National Park Service and National Historic Landmarks.

Picture of site ——————

Official site name ——————

Valley Forge National Historic Park

Contact information ——————
Valley Forge, PA 19482
610-783-1077

Website ——————
www.nps.gov/vafo

National Register Information System number ——————
NRIS 66000657

Site is a National Historic Landmark/
National Park Service owns or maintains site ——————
NHL, NPS

Date built or other significant dates ——————
DATE OF ENCAMPMENT
Winter 1777–78

Architect, builder, or original owner ——————
ORIGINAL OWNER
Laetitia Penn, daughter of Pennsylvania's founder, William Penn

Summary of site's significance ——————
SIGNIFICANCE
At Valley Forge Washington's army struggled to keep warm, overcame a poorly organized supply system, and summoned up the discipline and courage to renew fighting when spring arrived. The winter encampment became a test of the army's ability to survive, and therefore a test of the nation's as well.

Preface

I n the last two generations, racial diversity has become central to an ongoing public conversation in the United States. Americans are coming to understand that the roots of American society are multiracial, and that all Americans have been shaped to some degree by the national response to race and the presence of African peoples in America. This book is meant to give readers an idea of the many African American historical landmarks across the country that tell our national story. Starting with the first permanent British colony in North America at Jamestown, it traces the rise of African America from the arrival of the first bound Africans two years before the *Mayflower* landed at Plymouth to the end of legal segregation in the mid-twentieth century.

Early chapters move from Jamestown and the development of the legal structure of slavery to the Revolutionary era and the leadership role played by Crispus Attucks, the fugitive slave who became the first martyr in the struggle for American independence. These landmarks illustrate the largely unknown and unexpected interracial relationships that span the nation's early history. For example, Florida's Kingsley Plantation tells the story of an African slave woman who became the wife of her slave master and a plantation owner in her own right.

Other sites focus on the African American community in the years before and after the Civil War and how it developed with the coming of emancipation in the mid-nineteenth century. Some sites illustrate major turning points in American history: The Old Court House in St. Louis was the starting point of Dred Scott's journey to the U.S. Supreme Court, where this slave sued for his freedom—his case marking a pivotal point in American legal history. The USS *Arizona,* which was sunk in the Japanese attack on Pearl Harbor, stands as a memorial to those who lost their lives, and to the heroic actions of African American service men and women. And the Monroe School in Topeka, Kansas, which was at the center of the battle to end public school segregation, is a landmark to the historic *Brown* v. *Board of Education* Supreme Court decision.

The African Meeting House in Boston, central to the Underground Railroad and the abolitionist movement, and Nicodemus, Kansas, the black community that arose after the Civil War and experienced the racial terrorism that followed, help tell the story of a people determined to resist racial oppression at all cost. Although many of the sites selected focus on the relationship between black people and the structure of the black community, the giants of African American history are not neglected. Here is also the Washington, D.C., home of the great orator and activist Frederick Douglass and the Sweet Auburn community of Atlanta that nurtured the civil rights leader Martin Luther King Jr.

Spanning time and geography, these historic places encompass the entire nation, for no part of America and no time in its history is without meaningful landmarks of African American history. Some sites will confirm popular expectations, others will confound and surprise. In the South, in New England, in the Mid-Atlantic region, the Midwest, and even in the Hawaiian Islands, the issue of race and the presence of black people have helped to shape American culture and society in significant ways. This is African American history, but African American history is American history, made by Americans in America. These landmarks are part of the heritage of every American.

Jamestown, Colonial National Historical Park

Jamestown, Va.

Slavery and Freedom in British North America

The Jamestown church tower rises above an excavation site in the 1890s. The brick church was built around 1647, and this tower, originally forty-six feet high, is the only seventeenth-century structure still standing at Jamestown. When they first arrived in Virginia, the settlers held their church services outdoors, "under an awning (which was an old saile)," according to Captain John Smith.

It was August 1619, one year before the *Mayflower* landed Pilgrims at Plymouth, Massachusetts, when a Dutch man-of-war dropped anchor at what is today Hampton Roads, Virginia, at the mouth of the James River. The ship brought bound African laborers to the English colony of Jamestown. They were not the first Africans brought to North America. During the mid-sixteenth century, European slave traders transported Africans to work in the Spanish colonies or to serve as soldiers and sailors in the Spanish military forces that pushed through Florida, from Mexico, into what is now the southwestern United States. There is even some possibility that these twenty Africans who landed in Jamestown may not have been the first Africans in the colony, for a census taken several months before they arrived recorded 18 African men and 17 African women living among the 928 individuals then residing in the colony. Still, the arrival of the Dutch ship marked a critical moment in the life of Jamestown, and in the entire history of America. In early January 1620, Jamestown colonist John Rolfe wrote to officers of the Virginia Company in London to report that, "about the latter end of August, A Dutch man of War . . . brought not anything but 20 odd Negroes which the Governor and Capt. Merchant brought for victualle."

When these Africans arrived, the settlement of Jamestown was but a few low structures enclosed in a triangular-shaped fort built along the river. An account by colonial leader John Smith indicates that in 1609 the fort had twenty-four guns of different types set in a defensive pattern along its walls. The strength of

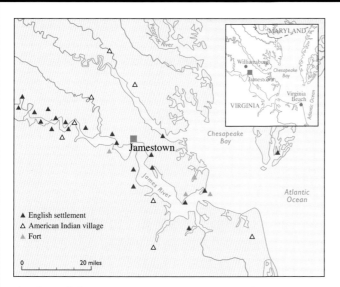

the fort's defenses is, however, uncertain as four years after Smith's account was written, a Spanish prisoner reported that there were only six guns mounted on the fort walls. Most of the buildings were probably wooden with dirt floors, but the most substantial were at least partly brick with tile roofs, large brick fireplaces, brick or cobblestone floors, and wrought-iron door latches and window casements. Beyond the fort, the short grasses and open woodlands of this low-lying peninsula spread out toward the salt marshes and pine woods between the James River and Powhatan Creek. The peninsula was separated from the mainland by a narrow isthmus that eroded during the eighteenth century, leaving Jamestown as a small island. Game was plentiful, as one of the settlers described it in a 1610 letter to the Virginia Company, "The Beasts of the Countrie, as Deere, red, and fallow, do answere in multitude." Apparently large herds grazed just on the outskirts of the settlement. "Next, hard by the fort," he recalled, "two hundred in one heard [herd] have been usually observed." "Further," he continued, "our men have seene 4000. of these skins pyled up in one wardroabe of Powhaton."

The Dutch ship that brought the Africans to Jamestown was fresh from battle with Spanish ships off the coast of Mexico and Peru. It had joined the *Treasurer* an English vessel in preying on shipments of gold that Spanish galleons transported to Spain from the rich gold mines of

Guards in Jamestown watch over African slaves unloaded from a Dutch ship in 1619. The captain traded his human cargo for food and supplies, and the colonists were grateful for the fresh labor force. For nearly two centuries, the slave trade in North America flourished, and as the number of blacks grew, their legal status diminished. By 1705, Virginia had developed its first comprehensive "slave code," laying the legal foundation for slavery in the colony.

Jamestown, Colonial National Historical Park

Western end of Colonial
  Parkway
Yorktown, VA 23690
757-898-3400
www.nps.gov/jame/index.htm
NRIS 66000839
NPS

DATE ESTABLISHED
1607

SIGNIFICANCE
Jamestown is the site of the first permanent British settlement in North America. The landing of African bound laborers there in 1619 marked the beginning of African slavery in the colonies that became the United States.

Latin America. South American gold was making Spain the richest country in Europe and the envy of its neighbors. But there was no gold aboard these Spanish ships. The cargo turned out to be slaves taken from the west coast of Africa, bound for service in the Spanish-American colonies. The Dutch took these slaves as a battle prize, and, by the time the ship made landfall in Virginia, there were at least twenty Africans left alive. The Dutch crew, desperately hungry for food and provisions, traded this valuable cargo to the Virginia colonists at Jamestown.

Within a few months of this Dutch landing, the British ship *Treasurer* arrived in Jamestown bringing an African slave woman, Angela, the first black Virginian whose name was added to the colonial records. After a brief stay, the *Treasurer* set sail for Bermuda with twenty-nine other Africans still aboard. Whether or not the twenty Africans brought by the Dutch were the first to arrive in the colony, it is certain that African life in British North America began in Jamestown and that the Africans' labor was critical to the survival and the prosperity of the colony.

Angela and all those Africans who remained in Virginia quickly found that their colonial captors valued them for their farming skills. When the twenty Africans arrived aboard the Dutch vessel, the Jamestown colonists' need for labor was almost as dire as the Dutch crew's need for food. Founded in April 1607 on a 1,500-acre peninsula in the James River, the colony was the first permanent English settlement in America, and, for its entire existence, it struggled to survive. The British had hoped to find gold in Virginia as the Spanish had in Latin America, but there was no gold, only abundant game and fertile soil that demanded an ever-increasing supply of labor. There never seemed to be enough labor to sustain life on this peninsula of fields, marshland, and forest. The death rate among English colonials was catastrophic. By the end of the first year of settlement only 50 remained of the colony's original population of 105.

New arrivals from England in 1609 boosted the number of colonists to almost four hundred, but that number fell to ninety within a year. During the first fifteen years of its existence, fifteen hundred people migrated to Jamestown, but by 1619, when the first Africans arrived, only two thousand white residents survived. Disease took a heavy toll on European lives and unless something

could be done to provide the labor needed to produce the food, handle the daily work, and cultivate the colony's chief money crop, tobacco, Jamestown would not survive. To make matters worse, the English angered local Indians by encroaching on their lands and forcing many to labor for the colony. The powerful Powhatan confederacy of Algonquian tribes, however, was unwilling to allow its people to be exploited. The Powhatan struck back, taking the lives of many colonists in battle, further reducing Jamestown's population.

In an attempt to shield themselves from further attack, the colonists captured and held hostage Pocahontas, daughter of the Powhatan leader. This did not protect the colony for long, however. Her eventual conversion to Christianity and marriage in 1614 to colonist John Rolfe, with the blessings of both Virginia's governor and her father, brought only temporary peace. By 1619, Jamestown needed more people to defend the colony and skilled agricultural workers to tend the tobacco fields. Within the next two generations Africans provided the labor needed to sustain the colony, and race gradually became the central feature of a caste system that defined status and social place in Virginia society.

In the same year that the Dutch ship traded Africans for supplies, a British ship brought one hundred young English boys from London to work in the colony. These

African slaves who arrived in Virginia were soon put to work on the tobacco plantations. White colonists, struggling with the hardships of life in a new world, were eager to find a labor supply to work the fields and prepare the tobacco, the colony's main cash crop, for market. Here, slaves perform the work, while white owners oversee them.

Pocahontas is dressed in a European outfit with the wide, white collar typical of the well-to-do. Pocahontas met Captain John Smith soon after English colonists landed in 1607, and she remained friendly with the Europeans, despite skirmishes between settlers and Indians. She married tobacco farmer John Rolfe in 1614, and together they traveled to England, where she died in 1617.

poor youngsters had few prospects in Britain and little alternative but to become indentured servants. These boys traded their labor in America for the cost of their passage. As indentured laborers, they signed a contract to serve for a set number of years, after which time they were to be freed. Some newly arrived Africans were also treated as indentured servants and were freed after years of service. In the decades after 1619 both white and black servants emerged from servitude, some to become landholders and even slaveholders, as the slavery system evolved in the first half of the seventeenth century.

The Africans brought to Jamestown in the years immediately after the first arrivals were bound laborers who worked long, hard hours in the fields and in the homes of white Virginians, who increasingly shunned fieldwork. Yet, these Africans were not treated as slaves in the perpetual and inherited sense that later generations would recognize. Anthony Johnson, probably originally from Angola, was one of those Africans who was able to take advantage of opportunities that later generations could never have imagined. He arrived in Jamestown in 1621 aboard the ship *James,* which sailed from Britain. He was sold into service and labored for the next fourteen years. Although the historical record is not absolutely clear on this point, it is probable that Johnson was freed in 1635 after he came to the end of the period of his servitude.

By then Johnson had married Mary, who was listed as a "Negro Woman" in the records of the same household in which Johnson had served. Given the relatively small number of black women in the Jamestown area, Johnson was one of the fortunate few Africans able to marry, but his fortune did not end there. The couple had at least four children, and by the 1640s the Johnson family had become a substantial landholder on the eastern shore of Virginia, breeding cattle and pigs. In 1651 the Johnsons were granted 250 acres under the colony's "headright system," which rewarded settlers for paying passage for servants migrating to the colony. The Johnsons listed at least five servants who worked for them by mid-seventeenth century. In thirty years they had become part of the colony's elite, but few blacks in succeeding generations could replicate this achievement.

There is no slight irony that in 1619, the same year that the first black bound servants arrived in Virginia,

Jamestown signaled its commitment to freedom by establishing the Virginia House of Burgesses, the first representative body in British North America. It is equally ironic that this democratic body, within the next two generation, passed laws that tightened controls on African labor, turning the early treatment of blacks as indentured servants into the perpetual, inherited, dehumanizing system of slavery. Although British Virginians continued to import white servants into the colony, and although their treatment of these servants was generally harsh and even brutal, no white person in the British colonies ever experienced slavery such as that imposed on Africans in America.

By the middle of the seventeenth century, Virginia law began to recognize important differences between white servants and black servants, a process that set the stage for the emergence of a full-fledged slave system by the end of the century. In 1639 colonial regulators providing for the defense of the colony made an important racial distinction when they declared that "all persons except Negroes are to be with Arms and Ammunition." A year later the Virginia court took this distinction a step further when three servants—a Dutchman, a Scot, and an African named John Punch—escaped to the neighboring colony of Maryland. They were captured, and all three were sentenced to whipping. The time of service for the two white men was lengthened by four years, but the court ruled that Punch, "being a Negro," was to serve for the rest of his life.

Service for life was becoming more common for blacks, which explains the higher price paid for their indentures during this period. By the 1660s, sales of African women provided life terms not only for them, but life terms for their children as well. In 1662 the House of Burgesses reversed traditional English law—which decreed that children's status in society followed that of their fathers—making children's status dependent on the status of their mothers. This measure meant that the children of bound African women were bound for life, regardless of who their fathers were. Thus, masters were assured that the children they had with their servant women became their servants as well. American slavery was taking shape.

Sir William Berkeley was governor of Virginia in 1676, when Nathaniel Bacon launched his rebellion against the government. Tobacco prices were dropping, and the governor was granting privileges to the aristocracy while refusing to support the frontiersmen's attacks against Indians. Bacon and his men marched against Jamestown, forced Berkeley out, and controlled the colony briefly before Bacon died unexpectedly.

Events in 1676 convinced the colony's elite that enforcing racial distinctions between unfree laborers—whether indentured servants or slaves—might work to their advantage by promoting racial solidarity among whites. The dangers of interracial cooperation among blacks and whites at the bottom of the colonial social and economic ladder became clear when Nathaniel Bacon, a Virginia planter recently arrived from England, led an interracial army of mainly poor whites, servants, and slaves against the Indians of western Virginia. Bacon was incensed when the colonial governor William Berkeley declared him and his followers outlaws and moved against them with a substantial army. Bacon turned his interracial forces against the governing authority. Before the rebellion ended, Bacon's men forced the governor to flee Jamestown and burned the settlement to the ground.

In the end the rebellion failed, and on October 26, 1676, Bacon suddenly died of what colonial doctors

A Violent Death Rediscovered

Archaeologists have been at work at the Jamestown site since the 1930s uncovering and analyzing an impressive collection of artifacts, including pottery, buttons, musket balls, and human remains. As a result of their work we have learned a good deal about the people of colonial Jamestown and their lives.

In the 1940s archaeologists found two seventeenth-century burial sites just outside the perimeter of Fort James. They discovered fifteen human skeletons, which they photographed and shipped to the Smithsonian Institution to become part of the institution's study collection. These skeletons were classified as the remains of Native Americans.

In the 1990s, Douglas Owsley, a forensic anthropologist at the Smithsonian's National Museum of Natural History, re-examined these remains using techniques and equipment that were unavailable to scholars when the remains were first examined. He found that at lease five of the skeletons are African.

One of these skeletons was an African man between twenty-three and twenty-seven years old who was apparently suffering from the late stages of syphilis at the time of his death. The disease did not kill him, however. The condition of his skull indicates that he had been shot in the head, and that he had apparently been facing his killer when he was shot. Curiously, earlier analysis had not only incorrectly identified the skeleton as Native American, but it completely missed the gunshot wound. Only with modern radiographic equipment could researchers detect the presence of metal, which explained the damage to his skull.

Bacons Epitaph, made by his Man.

Death why soe crewill! what no other way
To manifest thy spſleene, but thus to slay
Our hopes of safety; liberty, our all
Which, through thy tyrany, with him must fall
To its sad caoſs: Had thy rigid force
Bin delt by retale, and not thus in groſs
Griefe had bin silent: Now wee must complaine
Since thou in him, haſt more then thousand slain
Whose lives and saf'tys did so much depend
On him there life, with him there lives must end
If + be a sin to thinke Death brib'd can bee
Wee must be guilty; say twas bribery
Guided the fatall shaſft. verginias foes
To whom, for secrit crimes, just vengance owes
Diſarved plagues, dreding there just diſart
Corrupted Death by Paraſſeelſian art
Him to deſtroy; whose well tride curage such,
There heartleſs harts, nor arms, nor strength could touc
Who now must thoſe wounds, or stop that blood
The Heathen made, and drew into a flood?

identified as the "Bloodie Flux and Lousey Disease,"
probably a form of body lice. His body was never found
and was most likely burned by his men to prevent the
spread of disease. Eventually, Bacon's forces were defeated,
but among those who held out longest were eighty
blacks and twenty English servants.

This incident in the Jamestown area is only one
example of the kind of interracial alliances that were not
uncommon during the colonial period, when race did
not divide the lower ranks of American society as it
would later. After the 1660s the colonial authorities of
Virginia formalized the system of slavery that separated
white servants from black slaves so completely that it
would be difficult for future generations to form the
kinds of alliances that Bacon and his men had formed.
Colonial law removed baptism as grounds for freedom;
prohibited Africans and Indians from holding white
indentured servants; restricted the movement of all
blacks, free and slave alike; and prohibited interracial
marriage. By 1705, when black slaves accounted for

about half of the colony's unfree labor, the colony had set slavery firmly into law.

Jamestown remains one of America's most significant historical sites and a profound historical marker for African Americans in British North America. An archaeological project begun in 1994 has unearthed hundreds of artifacts dating to the first half of the seventeenth century, many of which date to the first years of English settlement from 1607 to1610. Among the most impressive of these are the remains of Fort James. This colonial fort was uncovered in 1996 and identified using a sketch drawn in 1608 by a Spanish spy to aid in an attack on Jamestown.

For decades, historians and archaeologists believed the original Fort James had been washed away as the shoreline shifted over the centuries. During the mid-1990s, however, archaeologists discovered large sections of two palisade walls, a cannon emplacement, three cellars that had been filled in, and a building that had been enclosed within the triangular area of Fort James. English settlers built this fort almost immediately upon their 1607 landing. It burned and was replaced in 1608. A 1614 account by Jamestown settler William Strachey indicated that the river side of the fort was approximately 120 yards long and the other two sides were each about 100 yards long. Originally, a stockade constructed of oak and poplar poles surrounded the fort, which enclosed an area of about one acre. In the fall of 1608, the stockade was extended to enclose an additional three acres, and the fort became five-sided.

Archaeological evidence of both the original fort and its replacement is visible on the landscape. The many artifacts discovered—including metal tools and utensils, pistols, knives, heavy armor with breastplates, and containers of various types—help give a sense of everyday life in colonial Jamestown. There is a church and graveyard dating to about 1617 and the foundations of a number of buildings, including Jamestown's last capitol built in about 1663. After that, the capital moved from Jamestown to Williamsburg, a more healthful location and, at the time, a thriving area of the colony.

Some ten miles from Jamestown is one of the most important sites associated with the 1676 rebellion, Bacon's Castle. Built in 1665, it is one of the oldest brick buildings constructed in English North America. At the

This highly decorated jug, made in Germany, was excavated from Fort James and dates to around 1610. Such stoneware vessels were commonly exported to England in the early part of the seventeenth century, before England developed its own industry. This particular style of jug is called a Bartmann ("bearded man") for the face that appears on the front.

time of Bacon's rebellion it was the home of Major Arthur Allen, a member of the House of Burgesses. The Bacon rebels drove Allen out of the house and occupied it as one of their major strongholds. For four months, this interracial armed force held off Virginia colonial troops. On this site archaeologists have found a seventy-two-thousand-square-foot garden. Dating from 1680, this is the oldest formal garden ever discovered in North America.

Colonial Jamestown was the place where some of America's most basic traditions were founded, traditions that helped to shape American society and culture for the next four hundred years. American democracy and American slavery took shape side by side in Jamestown, forming what would become the nation's most striking contradiction. In a variety of ways, Americans have wrestled with that contradiction and its legacy, but have never successfully resolved it.

The foundation and a few walls are all that remain of a comfortable brick home built in a section of Jamestown that was developed after 1620. By then, the inhabitants had begun to settle into colonial life and to build up the institutions that would define Virginia in the coming decades, among them a two-house General Assembly and a class of permanent black slaves.

Fort Sumter, located in Charleston Harbor, was built on a man-made island of seashells and granite. The opening engagement of the Civil War was fought here, when Confederate forces fired on this Federal fort and secured it for their own use. After the Confederate surrender in 1865, the fort again flew the U.S. flag.

SULLIVAN'S ISLAND, SOUTH CAROLINA

Part of Fort Moultrie National
  Monument
1214 Middle Street
Sullivan's Island, SC 29482
843-883-3124
www.nps.gov/fomo/
NPS

During the late seventeenth century, Sullivan's Island, in the northeast section of Charleston Harbor, became a receiving place for slaves from West Africa and the West Indies. Captives were held in relative isolation on this sandy strip of land to recover from any diseases they may have contracted. Between 1707 and 1799, there were apparently four pest houses constructed on the island, where Africans were quarantined. Although some captains found ways to fraudulently bypass the island, it was the first landing point for perhaps 40 percent of the Africans brought to British North America between 1700 and the eve of the Revolution.

From this island, Africans were exported to all parts of British North America. It became a point of common experience for the countless numbers of unwilling immigrants who had been kidnapped and who would be sold to various locations in America.

FORT MOSE

Anastasia Island
St. Augustine, FL 32085
904-461-2000
www.oldcity.com/mose
NPS

In the early 1700s tensions were increasing between the Spanish settlement at St. Augustine, Florida, and the British colony of South Carolina. The Spanish formed a militia manned by Africans to defend the St. Augustine area against British forays into Spanish Florida. Existing tensions were inflamed when South Carolina slaves began seeking asylum at the Spanish forts built to guard Florida's northern border. Although the Spanish enslaved some of these fugitives, others were freed. In 1738 the Spanish governor granted the fugitives land on a small island in the marsh two miles north of St. Augustine to build Fort Mose (pronounced moh-SAY) and the colony of Gracia Real de Santa Teresa de Mose.

The settlement was a mix of runaway British slaves and an ethnically diverse group of some one hundred Africans and West Indians. The more than twenty households of men, women, and children made up the first community of free blacks in North America. The original fort included a watchtower, a well, and a guardhouse. Its walls were made of earth, stakes, and cactus, and it was surrounded by a shallow moat. The fort was the northernmost outpost of Spanish Florida, protecting the capital of St. Augustine.

Fort Mose remained a major challenge to British slavery to the north and a mecca for runaway slaves. Finally, in the early summer of 1740 the British attacked. Troops from the Georgia colony led by General James Oglethorpe destroyed much of Fort Mose and the settlement, but with the aid of forces from the Spanish settlement in Havana, Cuba, the Africans repelled the invaders. The African community then pulled back to St. Augustine where they built a new Fort Mose. They remained there until 1763, when Florida was ceded to Britain at the end of the French and Indian War. At that point the free blacks of Fort Mose—along with the rest of the Spanish population of Florida, their Indian allies, and British slaves who had escaped to the fort—resettled in Cuba, still under the authority of the Spanish government.

The Old State House

Boston, Mass.

Crispus Attucks and the Boston Massacre

Dwarfed by more modern office buildings, the Old State House in Boston now houses a museum and is one of the stops along the Freedom Trail, which passes by important sites of the American Revolution.

Below the balcony of the Old State House, at the intersection of Washington and State streets, just north of Beacon Hill in Boston, is a circle of cobblestones that marks the spot where the first American patriots died in the struggle that would become the American Revolution. On March 5, 1770, colonists resolved to assert independence clashed with British authorities determined to maintain imperial control. American patriots called it a massacre, and, in the years that followed, that spot beneath the Old State House balcony came to be considered a historic marker of American liberty. It is also a major landmark of African American history and offers further evidence of the interracial nature of the American experience.

Crispus Attucks began his life in slavery, but he did not end it that way. In the fall of 1750, then twenty-seven years old, Attucks escaped from his owners in Framingham, Massachusetts. He was a person of mixed heritage, part African American and part Native American, and at six feet two inches tall, he towered above most men of his day. In freedom, Attucks worked as a sailor, often serving aboard whaling vessels, but he would ultimately be remembered as far more than a common seaman. His life ended in Boston, in the winter of 1770, during a protest turned violent. In the shadow of the Old State House where, during colonial times, the offices of the Massachusetts Bay Colony were located, Crispus Attucks, the former slave, was shot dead by British soldiers. He became the first hero of the American Revolution.

The spot where Attucks died remains outlined in stone and the building still stands as a monument to the nation's fight for liberty and to honor those who died there in its opening battle. The Old State House was not Boston's

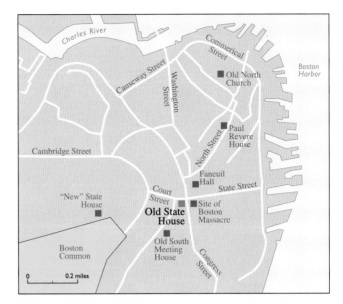

first city hall. Built in 1657–58, Boston's old city hall burned to the ground in 1711. It was a wooden building, which served not only as a city hall but also as a meeting place for Suffolk County officials and for colony-wide functions. Two years later it was replaced by a new brick structure built in the classic British design of the time especially popular for public buildings. With its hipped roof, elaborate window with a central arched section flanked by two narrow rectangular sections, and paneled front doors framed with ornate columns, its building design is known as the Georgian style of architecture.

A nineteenth-century engraving portrays Crispus Attucks as the "first martyr of the American Revolution" as he falls in the Boston Massacre. A former slave, Attucks led a group of angry workingmen in an assault against British soldiers, and he was the first to be killed when the Redcoats starting firing, according to accounts of the time.

A fire in 1747 almost destroyed this new city hall, and burned the records of the hall's original construction. The building was reconstructed the next year and is now the oldest public building in Boston and the oldest Georgian-style building in the country. It is a two-and-one-half story rectangular structure crowned by a three-tiered cupola with a sundial, which was replaced in the 1820s by a large clock, visible from the surrounding area of the city.

In this building Bostonians did the political and economic business of the colony. The Boston merchant and Revolutionary leader John Hancock rented offices in the basement, and colonial merchants did a brisk business in the large hall on the ground floor. The royal governor of Massachusetts met with his council in the most ornately appointed and finely furnished of the three rooms on the upper floor at the east end of the building. From there, windows looked over Boston Harbor, providing a view of the bustling life of the colonial city.

During the height of pre-Revolutionary tensions these rooms rang with fiery and impassioned speeches and heated debates over colonial policy and royal decrees. In 1761, the Boston patriot James Otis spoke out against the Writs of Assistance that allowed British officials to enter private property and search for smuggled goods without the permission of the owner. The Massachusetts Assembly held its meetings in the central area of the second floor. From that space, the assembly—one of the most radical colonial legislatures—condemned the notorious taxes imposed by the Stamp Act and called for representatives of all the colonies to meet in protest.

For many Bostonians assembly debates were the most significant high drama in town. Visitors climbed the spiral staircase from the main level to reach the gallery that opened in 1766 above the assembly meeting hall. Here they observed some of the most inspirational verbal exchanges of the time. Unlike most private citizens in the English Empire, American colonists were able to observe their elected delegates debate the popular issues of the day. These sessions polarized the populace, moving some toward increased loyalty to the Crown and radicalizing others toward American independence. John Adams, the colonial lawyer and farmer who became a leader of the Revolution and the second

Crispus Attucks, Runaway Slave

On October 2, 1750, William Brown placed an ad in the Boston Gazette *attempting to recover his slave identified as Crispus.*

Ran away from his master William Brown of Framingham on the 30th of Sept. last a mulatto fellow about 27 years of age, named Crispus, 6 feet and 2 inches high, short curl'd hair, his knees nearer together than common; and had on a light colour'd beaver skin coat, plain new buckskin breeches, blue yarn stockings and a checked woolen shirt. Whoever shall take up said runaway and convey him to his aforesaid master shall have 10 pounds old tenor reward, and all necessary charges paid. And all masters of vessels and others are hereby cautioned against concealing or carrying off said servant on penalty of law.

Massachusetts artist James Brown Marston painted this view down State Street in 1801, showing the Old State House and the bustling square in front of it. Bostonians played a pivotal role in opposing the British and laying the foundation for a new country, and after the Revolution, their city prospered as a vibrant center of intellectual and commercial life.

President of the United States, believed that the Revolution was born in this brick building. After the Revolution the building became known as the Old State House and was considered one of the most important public structures in British North America.

The Revolution may have been born in its rooms, but the building's exterior also figured prominently in national independence. By 1769, British troops occupied the lower floor of building. And in the area beneath its balcony on March 5, 1770, these soldiers fired into a heckling crowd killing five men. What is now known as the Boston Massacre resulted from an assault on British soldiers by Boston seamen and laborers—an assault led by Crispus Attucks. It was a key incident that became a major symbol of British oppression, elevating a black man to the level of Revolutionary hero.

This "Bloody Massacre," as Paul Revere called it in his engraving of the confrontation, was a consequence of the American struggle against British colonial policy. Angry colonials rebelled against the new tax acts passed in the mid-1760s to raise revenue for the Crown and shore up fiscal control over its North American colonies. The colonists refused to allow customs agents to collect the proscribed taxes. In response, British officials sent an urgent request to England for troops to enforce the laws. Although Britain saw these measures as a legitimate form of colonial management, many Americans vowed to resist what they considered unjust regulation. In the Massachusetts colony, as elsewhere, colonists protested by boycotting English goods, refusing to pay the taxes, and attacking British tax officials who represented the heavy hand of what was increasingly called tyranny. As the British military presence increased in Boston, public resentment spiraled upward, especially among the working people in the city who found themselves in competition with British soldiers, who were willing to perform part-time work at less than customary wages.

Crispus Attucks, no less than his fellow workers, felt the pressure of the British military presence in the city. Sailors were particularly vulnerable to and infuriated by the practice of impressment—the summary, on-the-spot drafting of American men into the British navy. Men taken into service in this way had no recourse to British law. During the mid-eighteenth century, impressment riots had racked several seaport communities as sailors and dockworkers, white and black men, made their anger evident in forceful, often violent, protests.

By the late 1760s, the additional economic pressure imposed by the growing military presence in Boston was becoming unbearable for many of the city's workingmen and women. Some saw Attucks as a natural leader of his fellow workers. He was described in a fugitive slave advertisement appearing in the *Boston Gazette* on October 2, 1750, as a tall, "well set mulatto," with "short curl'd hair" and "knees nearer together than common." Attucks worked on a whaling crew sailing out of Boston harbor, and sometimes, when in port, in a factory making rope in the city's North End. He, like many other workers, blamed England for his economic troubles and hated colonial officials and the British soldiers as symbols of British oppression.

The Old State House

15 State Street
Boston MA 02129
617-242-5642
www.nps.gov/bost/bost_lographics/
   oldstate.htm
NRIS 66000779
NHL, NPS

DATE BUILT
1713

SIGNIFICANCE
Boston's oldest public building, the Old State House is the site of the Boston Massacre, during which Crispus Attucks, a former slave, became the first martyr of the American Revolution.

British officers survey a group of American sailors on the deck of a ship. Before the Revolution, British soldiers had the right to impress American seamen into service in the British navy, and it was one of many practices that angered the colonists and fueled their fight for independence.

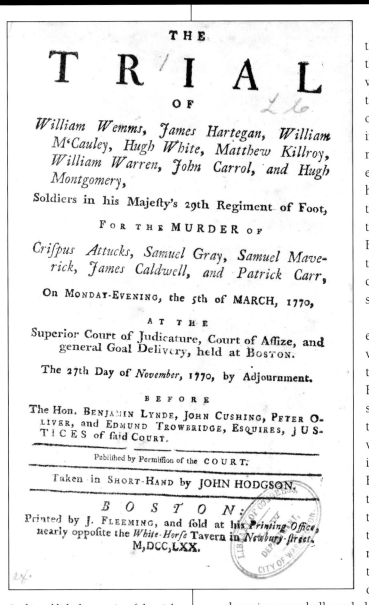

THE

TRIAL

OF

William Wemms, James Hartegan, William M'Cauley, Hugh White, Matthew Killroy, William Warren, John Carrol, and Hugh Montgomery,

Soldiers in his Majesty's 29th Regiment of Foot,

FOR THE MURDER OF

Crispus Attucks, Samuel Gray, Samuel Maverick, James Caldwell, and Patrick Carr,

On MONDAY-EVENING, the 5th of MARCH, 1770,

AT THE

Superior Court of Judicature, Court of Assize, and general Goal Delivery, held at BOSTON.

The 27th Day of November, 1770, by Adjournment.

BEFORE

The Hon. BENJAMIN LYNDE, JOHN CUSHING, PETER O-LIVER, and EDMUND TROWBRIDGE, ESQUIRES, JUS-TICES of said COURT.

Published by Permission of the COURT.

Taken in SHORT-HAND by JOHN HODGSON.

BOSTON:

Printed by J. FLEEMING, and sold at his Printing-Office, nearly opposite the White-Horse Tavern in Newbury-street. M,DCC,LXX.

In this published transcript of the trial of the British soldiers who killed five Americans in the Boston Massacre, the indictment declares that the soldiers, "not having the fear of God before their eyes, but being moved and seduced by the instigation of the devil and their own wicked hearts," fired upon Crispus Attucks and his compatriots with "malice aforethought."

Tensions boiled over in the early spring of 1770. On the afternoon of March 5, when a British soldier entered the tavern where Attucks and other seamen were gathered to inquire about local employment, already heated tempers exploded. One sailor offered his outhouse for cleaning, and the insults and anger drove the soldier from the tavern. For the rest of the afternoon the Americans drank, their complaints growing louder as spirits flowed.

About nine o'clock that evening, several Boston men were wounded in an altercation with British soldiers. Eyewitnesses reported that the soldiers chased the Bostonians through the streets and alleyways threatening and assaulting them. In response, some Bostonians rang the bells of the city to sound an alarm and to call people to confront the troops. At one point eyewitnesses reported that twenty or thirty men (some said thirty or forty) wielding clubs, throwing snowballs and chunks of ice and stone, were taunting the guard at the Custom House on King Street. John Adams told colonial authorities that the group consisted of, "saucy boys, [N]egroes and mulattoes, Irish teagues [anti-British Irish Catholics] and outlandish jack-tarrs [common sailors]." Two accounts given at a trial after the event placed Attucks as the leader of the angry crowd, harassing the sentries, poking one with a stick and calling him a "lobster," a pejorative allusion to the red coat of the British uniform.

In a statement before the Boston Court, John Adams, who defended the British soldiers, described Attucks as having "undertaken to be the hero of the night; and to lead this army with banners, to form them in the first place in Dock Square, and march them up to [King Street] with their clubs...to make the attack." Andrew, a Boston slave, described for the court the escalation of violence. Tempers flared as Attucks, who Andrew referred to, as a "stout man...the mulatto," vowed to declaw the "lobster." The scene was utter chaos, Andrew testified, with "the multitude shouting and huzzaing, threatening life, the bell ringing, the mob whistling and screaming like an Indian yell, the people from all quarters throwing every species of rubbish they could pick up in the street." At a critical moment, when the crowd hesitated, Andrew remembered that Attucks shouted, "the way to get rid of these soldiers is to attack the main-guard...strike at the root: this is the nest."

Apparently, the crowd assumed that the troops would retreat rather than fire on them, and pressed the point. Attucks, armed by one account with "a large cordwood stick," "threw himself in, and made a blow at the officer...cried kill the dogs, knock them over." "This was the general cry," another eyewitness recalled. John

A Hero's Reward

Although General George Washington would later refuse to enlist African Americans into the Continental army, this petition to the Massachusetts Legislature on behalf of the valor of Salem Poor was signed by fourteen officers and testifies to the heroism of black Revolutionary soldiers.

A Negro called Salem Poor of Colonel Frye's regiment, Captain Ames' company, in the late battle at Charlestown, behaved like an experienced officer, as well as an excellent soldier. It would be tedious to go into more detail regarding his heroic conduct. We only beg leave to say, in the person of this said Negro centers a brave and gallant soldier.

The reward due to so great and distinguished a character, we submit to the Congress.

Cambridge, Dec. 5, 1775

More than one hundred patriots of color served the American cause at the Battle of Bunker Hill.

Adams believed that Attucks's aggressive "mad behaviour in all probability" lead to "the dreadful carnage of that night." In his defense of the soldiers, he pointed to their reluctance to use deadly force. Twice the British captain of the guard gave the order to fire into the crowd, but the soldiers hesitated. Finally, in frustration and near panic came the order once again, "Damn you, fire, be the consequence what it will." This time the soldiers answered with a musket volley. Five of the Boston men fell. Three were killed and two wounded. Among the dead was Crispus Attucks, shot twice in the chest, the first to die in what was to become the American Revolution.

At this early stage in the Revolution, the mob action that had led to the Boston Massacre was unsettling to many who would later embrace, and even lead, the War for Independence. John Adams was so disturbed by what he saw as the actions of a lawless mob that he volunteered his legal services for the British soldiers who were charged with murder. In his legal defense, Adams used race and class to identify Attucks and his companions, and argued that the soldiers acted in self-defense. Several times in his statement to the court, he referred to Attucks as the "stout mulatto" at "the head of . . . a rabble of [N]egroes, etc." This self-defense argument saved the soldiers from the death penalty. Two soldiers were declared guilty of

A 1770 engraving by Paul Revere depicts the Boston Massacre against a detailed city backdrop. The First Church appears in the background, behind the Old State House, and the Royal Custom House is located behind the British troops. A poem included at the bottom of the print begins "Unhappy Boston! see thy sons deplore, Thy hallowed Walks besmeared with guiltless Gore."

manslaughter and, after the clergy
interceded on their behalf were branded
on the thumb; the others, including
one officer, were acquitted.

While John Adams was busy sav-
ing the lives of the British soldiers, his
more politically radical cousin, Samuel
Adams, worked to encourage anti-
British sentiment in the colonies.
Samuel made the Boston Massacre a
symbol of British disregard for
American rights and even American
lives. He helped arrange a public ceremony for Attucks
and the others who died, burying them in the Granary
Burial Ground on Tremont Street near Beacon Hill,
where two other Revolutionary notables, Paul Revere
and John Hancock, were later laid to rest. Ironically,
within three years of his defense of the British soldiers,
John Adams would speak very differently of Attucks
and his followers than he had at the trial. In 1773
the lawyer, by then a leading figure of the coming
Revolution, wrote a letter of scathing criticism directed
at the British royal governor of Massachusetts. He
charged the governor with gross offenses against the
people of the colony and threatened retribution in the
name of American patriots. Adams signed the letter not
with his own name, but with the name of a man who
had become a symbol of the spirit of American liberty.
That man—who had become an American hero, even
in the mind of John Adams—was the fugitive slave, the
leader of the crowd that Adams had called rabble,
Crispus Attucks.

Generations later, nineteenth-century Boston
recognized the significance of the sacrifices made in
this first defiant act in the battle for American freedom.
Led by a number of prominent black abolitionists,
black Bostonians inaugurated Crispus Attucks Day in
1858. In 1888, the Crispus Attucks Monument was
erected on the Boston Common, despite the opposition
of the Massachusetts Historical Society and the New
England Historic Genealogical Society, which regarded
Attucks as a villain.

The Old State House continued to be significant in
Boston's political life and, by extension, in the political
life of the nation long after the Boston Massacre. There,

*After the Revolution, Governor John
Hancock of Massachusetts presented
this flag to a company of black soldiers,
called the Bucks of America, to honor
them for outstanding military service
during the war. Thousands of blacks
fought in the Revolution, eager to
support the call for "life, liberty, and
the pursuit of happiness" and hoping
to gain independence both for their
country and for themselves.*

and on the Boston Common, patriots commemorated the anniversary of the Boston Massacre each year, until the start of the Revolution five years later. The celebrations marshaled the discontented ghosts of the victims to stir the resolve of Americans to resist tyranny. On July 18, 1776, the Declaration of Independence was first proclaimed in Boston from the Old State House balcony to the city's jubilant citizens. The building's west wing became home to the Courts of Suffolk County and the Massachusetts Supreme Judicial Court, where in 1783 slavery was declared unconstitutional in the Commonwealth of Massachusetts. The Old State House remained the seat of Massachusetts government until 1798, when the new state house that is used today was built at the top of Beacon Hill.

During the first three decades of the nineteenth century, the city of Boston rented space in the Old State House to several businesses. Contractors removed the interior spiral stairway to enlarge the commercial space, and finally renovated the entire building to accommodate various shops and a meeting place for the city's Masonic Order. Then, after 1830, the building was used as Boston's City Hall. It was during this period that the structure again became important to African American history; it served as a refuge for the white abolitionist newspaper editor, William Lloyd Garrison, one of the strongest voices for antislavery in the nation. Garrison helped to facilitate the national interracial abolitionist movement, and formed the New England Anti-Slavery Society in the sanctuary of the African Meeting House on Beacon Hill. He was a favorite in the black community of Boston and elsewhere for his stands in defense of African American rights. For the same reasons, he was hated by anti-abolitionists, who saw his associations with blacks and his radical positions against slavery as dangerous to the public order.

In October 1835, after an abolitionist meeting, Garrison was pursued through the streets of Boston by a number of prominent businessmen, "gentlemen of property and standing," as they were later characterized in local newspapers. He sought shelter within the Old State House. Aided by some city officials and several black Bostonians, and with a black carriage driver beating off the mob with his whip, Garrison escaped the building and spent the night in the city jail for his own protection.

The next day the black abolitionist John B. Vashon, who had been an eyewitness to the mob attack, visited Garrison, presenting him with a new hat to replace the one he lost in the melee.

In 1879, some Bostonians organized the Boston Antiquarian Club and saved the Old State House building from being moved to Chicago for the World's Fair. Two years later, a museum of Boston history opened in the building. In 1960 the Boston National Historic Sites Commission declared the Old State House the most important public building built in America prior to the Declaration of Independence. The spot under the balcony of the Old State House, marked today by a circle of paving stones, is the place where, on the eve of the American Revolution, black men and white men stood together in the name of liberty.

BUNKER HILL MONUMENT

Breed's Hill
Charlestown, MA 02129
617-242-5641
www.nps.gov/bost/Bunker_Hill. htm
NHL, NPS

In June 1775 the British paid a heavy price to capture Breed's Hill in a battle later mistakenly named for the adjacent Bunker Hill. American minutemen, blacks as well as whites, were dug in on the hill, defending it against oncoming British soldiers, considered the finest troops in the world. "Don't shoot until you see the whites of their eyes," came the order to the minutemen, calculated to put the British within mus-

ket range. It took three frontal assaults before the superior British force pushed the Americans off the hill. British losses were heavy; more than 1,150 out of their 2,500 men were killed, a casualty rate of 47 percent, the highest in British history to that point. African American sharpshooter Peter Salem fatally wounded British commander Major Pitcairn. Salem, who had also served at Lexington Green, was later cited for his actions.

Although most blacks who fought for the American cause during the Revolution served in integrated units, George Middleton commanded an all-black company from Massachusetts called the Bucks of America. After their service at Breed's Hill, John Hancock honored the unit with a specially designed company banner. Middleton lived on Boston's Beacon Hill after the Revolution. His house at 5–7 Pinckney Street is now a site on the city's Black Heritage Trail. Another black soldier, a twenty-eight-year-old veteran of the French and Indian War, Salem Poor, later served with George Washington at Valley Forge. Many of the black men who stood at the Battle of Bunker Hill went on to distinguish themselves throughout the war.

The Bunker Hill Monument is a 221-foot granite obelisk that marks the site of the first major battle of the American Revolution.

BATTLE OF RHODE ISLAND HISTORIC SITE

Junction of Routes 114 & 24
Portsmouth, RI 02871
401-625-6700
www.rihphc.state.ri.us/

At the junction of Routes 114 and 24 in Portsmouth, Rhode Island, is a monument to the African American soldiers who served in the First Rhode Island Regiment of the Revolutionary War. In February 1778, a Rhode Island law emancipated any slave in the state who agreed to serve the Revolutionary cause. That spring the state enlisted more than two hundred blacks, most former slaves, into an African American regiment led by white officers under the command of Colonel Christopher Greene.

In August 1778 Rhode Island's "Black Regiment" engaged British and Hessian— troops from Hesse, Germany— units that were pushing out of Newport, driving American troops before them. Despite three successive British charges, 138 black soldiers held their ground, giving other American units the opportunity to regroup for an orderly withdrawal. The action of these African Americans saved their fellow soldiers from almost certain annihilation. Later General Lafayette described their effort as the "best fought action of the war."

Kingsley Plantation

Jacksonville, Fla.

Race and Family in Spanish Florida

Anna, the African wife of plantation owner Zephaniah Kingsley, lived in the kitchen house (foreground), known as "Ma'am Anna House." In Anna's native Senegal, women and men did not share living quarters, and her husband seems to have respected her traditions. The main plantation house (background) is detached from the kitchen house to reduce the risk of fire.

On Fort George Island, outside Jacksonville in northern Florida, is the Kingsley Plantation, which consists of a main house, an attached second building, and a barn. Almost a quarter mile from the plantation house, arranged in a semicircle—the traditional West African housing pattern, as opposed to the linear European arrangement—stand twenty-three slave dwellings relatively intact, and the remains of several others. Originally there were thirty-two slave cabins, but over time the elements have taken their toll. The buildings that remain are remarkably well preserved given that Africans constructed them more than 150 years ago.

The slave cabins are built of "whole shell tabby," often called coastal concrete, a mixture of sand, lime, and water, with oyster shells added to speed the drying process and increase the density of the mixture. Buildings constructed of this material are solid, able to survive the severe coastal storms that routinely destroyed most other structures. Oyster shells were plentiful on the island, the remains of food consumed by Native Americans who settled in Florida some ten thousand years before Columbus arrived in the Western hemisphere. One of the cabins has been restored to its nineteenth-century form. Its tabby walls are strong and well insulated, keeping the cabin's interior warm in winter, and, more important for the climate of this region, cool in the long, hot summer.

In coastal areas of Florida, whites and slaves alike built their homes using tabby—a mixture of sand, lime, water, and oyster shells, all of which hardened into a concrete-like substance. The raw materials were plentiful, and tabby, unlike wood, would not decay in the subtropical climate.

These buildings were the homes of an African workforce brought to the island in 1814, when sea captain and slave holder Zephaniah Kingsley established a plantation on this site. At that time Florida was a Spanish possession. Throughout the eighteenth century, Spain struggled to secure the area from the Native Americans and from Great Britain, whose colonies to the north posed a continual threat. In 1763, at the end of the French and Indian War, Britain gained control of Florida. Spain regained it in 1784 as a result of the Treaty of Paris, which ended the American Revolution.

In the late eighteenth century, during this second Spanish colonial period, Spain established its seat of local government in the largest town in the region, St. Augustine. In 1791 Spanish authorities granted a heavily wooded area near the mouth of the St. Johns River—not too far from the capital city—to an American, John McQueen. McQueen, a transplanted Philadelphian living in Charleston, South Carolina, was a land speculator whose ventures drove him into such heavy debt that he moved to Florida to escape his creditors. With him he brought his family and more than three hundred slaves who worked his crop of sea-island cotton.

A man with a flamboyant personality, McQueen became a leader in the English-speaking community in East Florida, and was soon socializing with the Spanish elite, including the governor himself. But his prestige, like his financial solvency, was short lived. He was again overtaken by debt that forced him to sell his Fort George Island holdings in 1804. The land passed to another planter who worked it with greater success with an enslaved labor force of almost two hundred. For three generations, slave labor was the key factor that allowed white planters to turn a profit from the land.

Slavery was a central feature of life in East Florida, as it was elsewhere in the antebellum South, but on Fort George Island, the institution, and the racial customs that supported it, took an unusual turn during the first decade of the nineteenth century. It was then that Zephaniah Kingsley and his family came to Fort George Island and founded the Kingsley Plantation. Kingsley was born in Bristol, England, but grew up in Charleston, South Carolina. He was a child of ten when his family brought him to the American South in the 1770s.

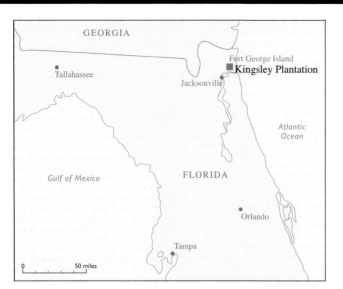

Coming of age in a slaveholding society, like many young white men of that day and in that place, Kingsley found that there was great profit to be made in the slave trade, and he threw himself into the business with a flourish. Not content to manage his business from Charleston, Kingsley took to the seas to participate first-hand at the end of the business that sickened even some of the most hard-boiled slave traders. He traveled to the coast of West Africa and to the Caribbean where he personally selected his human property, purchasing them from European slave traders and arranging their Atlantic transport.

In 1803, Kingsley visited Spanish Florida. Already a man of some means, he bought 2,600 acres of prime agricultural land on Fort George Island on the banks of the St. Johns River. He continued to prosper as did many slaveholders of the period, but then Kingsley's life took a strange turn. On a trip to Havana, Cuba, he bought a slave, Anta Majigeen Njaay, a young black woman born in Senegal, West Africa. He soon became no ordinary slaveholder. He wrote in his journal that he and Anta, whom he routinely called Anna, "married" in a "foreign

St. Augustine, Florida, the oldest city in the United States, was founded in 1565 by the Spanish. In this view of the city in 1740, the Spanish town and the castle are clearly labeled. Spain lost control of Florida to the British in 1763, later regained it, but lost it again in 1821, when the area became a U.S. territory. Soon afterward, Florida adopted the strict racial restrictions and legal codes of the rest of the American South.

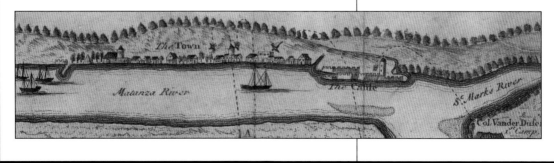

Kingsley Plantation

Part of the Timucuan Ecological
  and Historic Preserve
13165 Mount Pleasant Road
Jacksonville, FL 32225
904-251-3537
www.cr.nps.gov/goldcres/sites/
  kingsley.htm
NRIS 70000182
NPS

DATE BUILT
1798

ORIGINAL OWNER
John McQueen

SIGNIFICANCE
A typical plantation home of
Spanish colonial North America
and the cotton-producing South,
Kingsley Plantation had an
unusual history of racial accommodation.

land" in accordance with the marriage traditions of her
people. It was an African marriage, he said, not one
"celebrated according to the forms of Christian usage."

Anna came from the Islamic Wolof people who
live in the dry, barren region of northern Senegal. Her
family had high status in her native land, and she led
a privileged life until the spring of 1806. Then her
village was raided by Tyeddo warriors, the special armed
force of Amari Ngoone Ndella Kumba, king of Kajor,
who ruled a coastal kingdom that had risen to power in
Senegambia during the eighteenth century. They were
seeking slaves to sell to European traders. These fright-
ening men with long braided hair came at dawn, on
horseback, overwhelming all who stood before them.
They killed Anna's father and many other men in her
family compound before taking her, her mother, other
relatives, and the family servants captive.

Now they were all slaves, and their captors marched
them toward the coast in western Senegal. In the town
of Rufisque, at the foot of the Cape Vert peninsula, the
party was taken to the market where French and English
merchants bid for each of them. Their new owners then
transported them to Gorée Island off the coast of modern
Dakar. There, Europeans had established a fort that
served as a holding place, one of the primary points of
departure for slave vessels bound for the Americas.

Anna could not remember how long she remained
imprisoned in a series of windowless rooms. She saw
light only when guards brought the meager food and
water that kept her alive until European traders placed
her and the other captives aboard a large sailing vessel
that eventually brought them to Cuba. She never saw
her Wolof home again. She could not have known how
much her life would change when, in the summer of
1806, an American trader with a slight British accent
purchased her in Havana.

Kingsley spent three months in Cuba, until October
1806, when he and three of his slaves, including Anna,
sailed for Florida. She was pregnant with their first child
by the time she and Kingsley set up a household at Laurel
Grove (now the town of Orange Park), the large plantation south of Jacksonville that he had purchased in 1803.
Although Anna remained legally a slave, she and Kingsley
lived together as husband and wife. She supervised the
household, including the work of the domestic servants

and slaves, and when her husband was away she managed the plantation. In his memoir, Kingsley explained that "[Anna] has always been respected as my wife and as such I Acknowledge her." In 1811, he filled out a manumission document legally declaring her and their three children free. Anna was then eighteen years old.

Three years later, the Kingsleys moved to the present site of the Kingsley Plantation, which at the time occupied the entire Fort George Island. The main living area was a complex of structures. The plantation house located at the northern end of the island is believed to be the oldest plantation house still standing in Florida. This two-story, wooden-frame building constructed about 1800 has both an attic and a basement, with a wide covered porch and a solid tabby foundation. Another house, built in the 1790s, was Anna's separate residence. It is connected to the main house by a covered walkway. It too has two stories, and has a large central chimney and a fireplace in each of four rooms. It has its own porch and is a combination of wood and tabby construction.

The relative independence with which Anna lived provides clues to her status within the family. She seemed to have been a remarkably equal player in the management of the Kingsley Plantation, which was worked by sixty or seventy slaves. In many respects, she was more than a typical planter's wife for most of the thirty-seven years of her marriage, until Zephaniah Kingsley's death. She was at Kingsley Plantation, as she

A reconstructed slave cabin at Kingsley Plantation forms part of a semicircle with the original cabin ruins. The wooden shutters and roofs of the ruins have rotted away in the humid climate, but the tabby walls remain.

Anna Is Set Free

In 1811, Zephaniah Kingsley freed Anta Majigeen Njaay, whom he had held as a slave since 1806. This is his declaration of Anta's freedom, a document legally setting her free. At this point he was already the father of her three children, and the couple was living as husband and wife, as they continued to do until his death in 1843.

Liberty

In the name of Almighty God, Amen: Let it be known that I, D[on]. Zephaniah Kingsley, resident and citizen of the st. Johns River Region of this province hereby state: That I have as my slave a black woman named Ana, about 18 years old, who is the same woman that I purchased in Havana from a fleet which, with permission of that government, was introduced there; this Negress I have had and have procreated with to produce three mulatto children named Jorge, three years and nine months old; Marta twenty months old; and Maria, one month old. And focusing on the good qualities of the already mentioned Negress and for other causes, I have decided to give her freedom graciously and without any other interest, the same accorded to the aforementioned her three children. And so, to reduce all this to its simplest form., by this document, I grant that I free and liberate the aforementioned Negress Ana and the three children from their subjection, captivation, and servitude, and as a consequence I remove my rights of property, possession, utility, dominion, and all other royal and person deeds, which I have possessed over these four slaves. And I cede, renounce and transfer to each of them so that from today forward, they can negotiate, sign contracts, buy, sell, appear legally in court, give depositions, testimonials, powers of attorney, codicils, and do any and all things which they can do as free people who are of free will without any burden. Declaring them to be free of obligation . . . and obligating me to this statement and to the liberty which I give them through it, it will be certain and assured to the, and that I, and my heirs and successors will not contradict this in any way, and if it so happens that one of them should bring lawsuits or contradicting accounts, we desire that they not be heard nor admitted in a court of law since that which he attempts is not a right which pertains to him; and so it is observed that the approval and validation have been acquired, adding strength to strength and contract to contract, to which resolution I obligate myself with my present and future properties, power and submission to the justice of His Majesty in order that they compel me to its fulfillment as through a sentence granted, and passed in authority of judged affair about which I renounce all laws, privileges, rights of my own volition, and in general in form which is prohibited. In whose testimony is dated in this city of st. Augustine, Florida, on the fourth of March, 1811. I, the scribe hereby give faith that I know the granter of these privileges and that I sign with witnesses Don Juan de Entralgo, Don Bartolome de Castro y Ferrer, and Don Bernardo Jose Segui being present.

Zeph. Kingsley

had been at Laurel Grove, Kingsley's partner, taking on much of the management duties, and at times operating her own business and owning her own property. She was not the only African woman treated as a wife by a white planter in Spanish colonial Florida. The Spanish system of slavery was far less restrictive than the system in the United States. It allowed for interracial relationships and mixed-race families, which were not tolerated in the United States.

Apparently Zephaniah was supportive of Anna's independent ventures and cared deeply for their children, but he was no racial egalitarian. However Zephaniah Kingsley felt about his own family, it did not stop him from owning other human beings. The Kingsley Plantation grew to more than thirty-two thousand acres, attended to by more than two hundred slaves. It was an enormous operation, producing a comfortable profit from crops of cotton, citrus fruits, sugarcane, and corn. Kingsley believed, as did many planters, that African labor was necessary to work the fields in Florida, because he was convinced that whites could never stand the harsh work conditions. In an 1828 essay entitled "A Treatise on the Patriarchal System of Society," he wrote in support of his theory that, "Nature has not fitted the white complexion for hard work in the sun, as it is evident that the darkness of complexion here is a measure of capacity for endurance of labor."

Whole oyster shells protrude from the tabby walls of the plantation barn. The open kettle in the corner was used to boil down sugarcane into a sweet syrup.

Yet, Kingsley was no ordinary slaveholder. Although he did not free his slaves, he did attempt to soften some of the most blatant evils of an inherently evil institution. He employed his slaves under the task system of labor, which allowed them greater control over the pace and schedule of their work. Unlike the gang system common in the cotton-producing South—where slaves worked from sunup to sundown at as fast a pace as the overseer could enforce—under the task system the overseer set certain work to be accomplished. Slaves were allowed time off after their tasks were completed. A resourceful slave might work rapidly to complete the tasks required, leaving time for hunting, fishing, or tending small gardens to supplement the plantation rations. Under this arrangement, slaves built the thirty-two small cabins to shelter their families not far from the plantation's main house.

The term "good master" is an oxymoron, for, as abolitionist and former slave Frederick Douglass argued, the good master recognizes the evil of slavery, frees his slaves, and ceases to be a slave master. Yet, Kingsley did more than most slaveholders to keep slave families together and to allow them to live in family units on the plantation. While he was absent from the plantation, much of the daily management fell to one of the slaves,

Slaves, in a rare moment without work, relax in front of their cabins. In most of the South, slaves did not have the advantages granted to those on Kingsley's plantation—small privileges such as being assigned tasks rather than gang work and time off to tend to their own homes and gardens.

Abraham Hanahan. Kingsley eventually freed Hanahan, who then took the name Free Abraham Hanahan and built his own home and a barn for his animals. As a freeman, he took over many of the responsibilities for a store that Kingsley operated, and made a good living for himself as a trader, a river pilot, and a farmer. Hanahan's case was not unique. Kingsley freed a number of his slaves and allowed others to purchase freedom for themselves and their families.

Kingsley's unconventional slaveholding practices became considerably more difficult, however, after 1821 when Florida was seized by U.S. forces and became an American territory. Race relations that had been somewhat fluid under the Spanish now became more rigid under American rule. In 1823, President James Monroe established a legislative council for the Florida territory to supervise the transition from Spanish to American law. Kingsley was one of those appointed to serve on the committee, and he took a special interest in issues of race. He proposed the gradual abolition of slavery, liberal and unrestricted manumission of slaves, and civil rights for free blacks. His suggestions were not popular among his fellow slaveholders, and the council acted in a fashion more in keeping with conventional American racial policies.

The council refused to abolish slavery, and in fact made it more difficult for masters to free individual slaves. It limited the rights of free blacks, prohibited interracial marriage, and placed harsh restrictions on slaves. The signs were unmistakable. Florida was rapidly taking on the legal and social characteristics of the slaveholding American South. Kingsley would not be allowed to continue his style of slaveholding or to continue comfortably his family's lifestyle. He set forth his objections to these changes in his "Treatise on the Patriarchal System of Society." "Our laws to regulate slaves are entirely founded on terror," he charged, ". . . constructed for the protection of whites, and vexatious tyranny over the persons and property of every colored person."

As racial conditions in Florida hardened and slavery grew more stifling for its victims, Kingsley took steps to safeguard his family from what he termed the growing "spirit of intolerant prejudice." He visited the independent black nation of Haiti and struck a deal with its president, Jean Pierre Boyer, who was at the time attempting to encourage immigration. Kingsley purchased land in Haiti, and in 1837, Anna and their sons moved to the community he established there. Free Abraham Hanahan accompanied the family as did others of Kingsley's former slaves including some that he freed in order that they might join the group.

In 1839, Kingsley sold his Florida plantation to his nephews Ralph King and Kingsley Beatty Gibbs. Here again Kingsley revealed his contradictory attitude toward slavery. Although many of Kingsley's former slaves accompanied the family to Haiti as free people to whom Kingsley promised land in return for nine years of work, he left the plantation's new owner with a considerable number of slaves whom he did not free. Furthermore, on his death in 1843, Kingsley left some eighty-seven black people still enslaved in Florida. Before he died, Kingsley told Boston abolitionist Lydia Maria Child, as she recalled in an 1842 letter, that "the best we can do in this world is to balance evils judiciously." The region of Haiti where Kingsley established his colony is now the Dominican Republic, where some descendants of Anna and Zephaniah still live today.

Before his death in 1859, Gibbs bought out Kingsley's interest in the Fort George Island plantation and became, for a time, one of the largest slaveholders in that region of eastern Florida. Kingsley Plantation went through a number of other owners before the Civil War dramatically changed the lives of all those, black as well as white, residing in northeastern Florida. More than a thousand blacks from the region, free and enslaved, enlisted in the U.S. Army during the war. Some of them became part of the U.S. occupying force, as Confederates fled west toward the interior of the state to escape the advancing Union troops. Some slaves were forced westward with their masters, but thousands fled to freedom in the North.

For a time, some African Americans took control of the land they had worked for their former masters. By the end of the war, former slaves, now free, farmed much of Kingsley Plantation in small plots. Although the federal government officially abolished slavery, it did nothing to compensate former slaves for generations of exploitation and unpaid labor. Thus, former slaves could not control the land their people had made profitable. In 1869, John Rollins, from New Hampshire, acquired the former Kingsley Plantation and employed black workers to grow oranges in return for wages, rent-free housing, and garden land.

Growing oranges, however, could not sustain area landowners in the long term. The cold winter of 1894–95 killed most of the trees, and by the turn of the twentieth century, the orange groves had all but disappeared. Some black people still worked land in the region, but Florida's economy was changing, and a new form of racial control was emerging across the South. The Jim Crow system of codified racial segregation was not as bad as slavery, but it nevertheless deprived African Americans of the rights and protections that Zephaniah Kingsley had sought to maintain. The term Jim Crow comes from a black caricature portrayed by Thomas D. Rice, a song-and-dance man who performed in blackface as "Jim Crow." Rice was said to have copied the moves of an old black man who limped around and sang a little ditty as he tended horses. Jim Crow was the way of life all over the South, and Florida was no exception. Kingsley's interracial family would not have been

A former slave, Mariah Jones Delancy, and her daughter pose for a formal portrait at a Jacksonville studio in the 1880s. When Florida was under Spanish control, inhabitants held flexible attitudes about race and interracial relationships, but those attitudes became less tolerant after Florida became part of the United States.

tolerated, and an enlightened attitude about race, such as Kingsley's, would have been greatly discouraged.

During the twentieth century, Florida became a tourist destination for wealthy and middle-class white workers from the North. Today Kingsley Plantation consists of the main house and Anna's house. The kitchen house also remains as does a garden used to demonstrate the cultivation of sea-island cotton of the type grown by the slaves during the nineteenth century. There is also a barn built of tabby and the remains of the slave quarters. A carpenter's shop and mill, built in the early nineteenth century, no longer exist.

The Kingsley Plantation was in many ways typical of plantations worked by slaves in Florida and much of the cotton-producing South before the Civil War. In other important ways, Kingsley was unique. The slave families here were more secure than most, they had greater opportunities to gain their freedom than most, and they had greater control over their work schedule than almost any other slaves in cotton country. Zephaniah Kingsley's relationship with Anna and their mixed-race children was also unusual. This relationship made his continued ownership of slaves and his support for some modified form of bondage, even while he argued for gradual emancipation, even more striking. In some ways his personal contradictions are reminiscent of one of his contemporaries, Thomas Jefferson.

Jefferson—the author of the Declaration of Independence, which included the lines, "We hold these truths to be self-evident, that all men are created equal, that they are endowed by their Creator with certain unalienable Rights, that among these are Life, Liberty and the pursuit of Happiness"—owned slaves all his life. Unlike Kingsley, he never acknowledged his relationship with Sally Hemings, the slave woman with whom he fathered children, nor did he ever acknowledge the paternity of the children themselves. Certainly he would not have been willing to leave the country in order to keep his family intact as Kingsley had done. Each man had his contradictions and perhaps slaves understood these contradictions better than most. Slavery was no simple institution and bound people survived by understanding its power, its limitations, and its contradictions.

CHARLES PINCKNEY NATIONAL HISTORIC SITE

1254 Long Point Road
Mt. Pleasant, SC 29464
843-881-5516
*www.cr.nps.gov/nr/travel/
charleston/pin.htm*
NPS

The Snee Farm, located on the grounds of Charles Pinckney's plantation, housed up to fifty slaves. Pinckney was one of the founders of the U.S. Constitution. The farm demonstrates the importance of slavery in South Carolina in the early history of the United States and the influence of slavery on the development of rice culture in the low country. An archaeological study of the farm, begun in 1987, has uncovered some 20,000 artifacts, including fragments of fine china; brass tacks and draw handles, which suggest upholstered furniture and desks; wine-bottle glass, English tableware and other evidence of the owners' gracious living made possible largely through the work of their slaves.

OLD SLAVE MART

6 Chalmers Street
Charleston, SC 29401
843-958-6467
*www.cr.nps.gov/nr/travel/
charleston/osm.htm*

Located on one of Charleston's few remaining cobblestone streets, the Old Slave Mart is the only slave market structure remaining in the state of South Carolina. Constructed by slave traders Thomas Ryan

The Charles Pinckney Historic Site currently has 28 acres of the original 715 of Snee Farm. Before the invention of the cotton gin in 1793, rice was South Carolina's most important staple crop, and plantations such as Snee Farm depended on large slave populations to do the difficult work in the wet fields.

and James Marsh in 1853, the Old Slave Mart was part of a complex of buildings that made up the city's most important slave auction galleries. Its large interior room has a twenty-foot ceiling behind the building's façade, which features a high arch, octagonal pillars, and a large iron gate. Sales were held indoors, with slaves standing on auction tables three feet high and ten feet long and spaced to allow buyers to pass between them during the auction. The building was used for slave sales until the late fall of 1863. After the Civil War, the building was used as a tenement house for African Americans until the 1920s, when it became a automobile salesroom. The building is being renovated and will soon house a museum devoted to Charleston's role in America's domestic slave trade.

MONTICELLO

Thomas Jefferson Pkwy
Charlottesville, VA 22902
434-984-9800
www.monticello.org
NHL

Just south of the plantation house at Monticello, the his-

toric home of Thomas Jefferson, is a thousand-foot-long road shaded by a line of mulberry trees called Mulberry Row. In the eighteenth century and the early years of the nineteenth century, until Jefferson's death in 1826, this area was a central location on this working plantation. Along this road were storage buildings, a blacksmith and carpentry shop, a sawmill, a smokehouse and dairy, and other key facilities where slave artisans kept the plantation in good repair. At Monticello, Jefferson held more than two hundred slaves. At the same time, he struggled with his life as a slaveholder and its contradiction with his commitment to human freedom. He was never able to reconcile this contradiction in his own life and in the life of the nation. He considered slavery a danger to America's experiment in freedom. "We have the wolf [slavery] by the ears," he wrote in an 1820 letter. "We can neither hold him, nor safely let him go." Slavery continued to be America's irreconcilable contradiction until the bloody Civil War ended it thirty years after Jefferson's death.

The African Meeting House

Boston, Mass.

Platform for a Community

A mix of unskilled, illiterate laborers and well-tutored professionals gathered at the African Meeting House on Boston's Beacon Hill in the spring of 1863. From the pulpit in the sanctuary, abolitionist, editor, and former slave Frederick Douglass urged black men to answer the nation's call for recruits for the new 54th Massachusetts Infantry. This black unit, commanded by white officers, was organized under the leadership of white abolitionist Robert Gould Shaw to serve the United States against the forces of the southern Confederacy in America's Civil War. Blacks had demanded the right to bear arms for the nation since the start of the war, but for two years, President Lincoln and the U.S. Congress had refused. It was fitting that when the call for black troops finally came, the African Meeting House played a major role. This building, which served as church, school, and political, social, and cultural gathering place, was the hub of Boston's black community.

The African Meeting House was built as a church in 1806 by black workers intent on establishing a place for African Americans to worship with dignity. The building was located on Smith Court, just off Joy Street, a main artery that connected the homes of the city's wealthy at the top of Beacon Hill to the black residences scattered along the hill's northern slopes. Its simple brick façade, with four two-story, arched windows with large panes, was finished in the then-popular Federal building style, named in honor of the period following the Revolution. Buildings in the Federal style are symmetrical and boxy, with oval center entrances on the front and rear, and large oval evenly spaced windows, low-pitched gable roofs, and end chimneys.

The ground level has stairs on either side of the front entrance leading to the sanctuary above. There is a

Prominent Boston abolitionist Lewis Hayden (above) was part of the community served by the African Meeting House, a center of social activism until the end of the nineteenth century.

balcony at the rear of the sanctuary, above the stairs from the ground level. The building's design is typical of early nineteenth-century Boston, and was adapted from a basic townhouse design published in architect Asher Benjamin's 1806 pattern book, *The American Builder's Companion*. Funds to purchase the land at 8 Smith Court and to complete the building were collected by an interracial committee. Although Boston's African American community was not affluent, members gave what they could. African-born community leader Cato Gardner contributed $1,500 gathered from his friends and personal contacts, and white supporters at Boston's First and Second Baptist churches also donated money toward the $7,700 needed to complete the project.

The African Baptist Church was officially organized with twenty members in August of 1805, and took residence the next year in the newly constructed African Meeting House, the first black church in Boston. Above the front door to the church is a commemorative inscription in honor of "Cato Gardner, first Promoter of this Building 1806." Most of the church's original members transferred their affiliation from Boston's First and Second Baptist churches, where white congregations segregated them during religious services to "Negro Pews."

The white congregations also barred blacks from church governance, allowing them no influence over the placid and controlled style of worship unsuited to most African American religious tastes. Dissatisfied, black church members withdrew from the First and Second Baptist congregations in the last years of the eighteenth century and met as an informal church, first in African American homes and then for a time in central Boston's Faneuil Hall. While services were being held in this historic Revolutionary meeting place, Thomas Paul, a black teenager from New Hampshire, joined the group. Reverend Paul, ordained in the spring before the meeting house opened its doors, ministered to the church for more than two decades, until illness forced him to step down in 1829.

The African Meeting House was the religious home for a substantial number of Boston blacks and an unmistakable symbol of racial pride. In this regard, it is significant that African Americans selected the name "African" for this most important structure in the community. These were American people who sought a

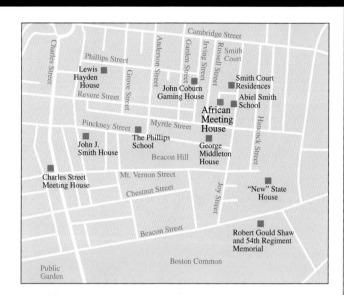

tangible expression of their African heritage. Although, the African Americans established a church that was uniquely theirs, they never completely severed ties with their white brethren. African American delegates represented the church at meetings of the Boston Baptist Association, and whites sometimes attended services at the meeting house. In fact, Reverend Paul's preaching and the choir's music attracted so many white visitors that, at one point, African Americans feared that the growing white attendance might dampen the emotional spirit of their services and threaten the African character of the church.

The meeting house drew members from all over the city, and the construction of the city's first black church building both resulted from and further encouraged the migration of increasing numbers of African Americans to Beacon Hill. They settled on the lower slopes, behind the State House, that faced the Boston Common below. African Americans lived on this back side of the hill from about its midpoint to Cambridge Street at the bottom of the slope and beyond. In the early nineteenth century, Boston was a walking city, and as many blacks served in the homes of affluent

The Reverend Thomas Paul was the first minister of the First African Baptist Church, which was established a year before the African Meeting House was constructed as its permanent home.

white Bostonians, the short distance from the lower slopes to the summit of Beacon Hill was convenient for both black domestic workers and white employers.

The African Meeting House was never simply a religious meeting place. As is traditionally true of black churches, it stands as a landmark to both sacred and secular African American communal efforts to provide mutual aid and to combat racial injustice. Because it housed so many vital community functions, the African Meeting House helped unify a diverse black population. The small size of Boston's black community and the city's residential patterns ensured that churches such as the African Meeting House served a socially and economically heterogeneous congregation.

Customary racial restrictions in Boston forced almost all black people to live on lower Beacon Hill and in the neighborhood across Cambridge Street. An area in Boston's North End characterized by boardinghouses that catered to laborers and sailors rounded out the residential housing open to African Americans. Swift and violent action met any blacks who sought to move into areas beyond these neighborhoods. When Robert Morris, a black lawyer, tried to purchase a grand house in one of the city's fashionable areas, a mob vowed to destroy the house rather than allow a black family to occupy it. The geographic concentration of the black community ensured that, at least in its churches, its laborers and seamen associated with its shopkeepers, skilled workers, and small business owners as well as with the teachers, doctors, and lawyers of its small professional class.

Wherever black people struggled against racial prejudice or slavery, wherever blacks were denied opportunities, the black church offered support, serving a broad range of community needs. In the early nineteenth century, education was one of the community's primary concerns. Massachusetts had only recently abolished slavery, in 1783, and the African Americans who formed the meeting-house congregation were the first generation in Boston of free people of color. They organized one of the earliest educational institutions, the African School, in the home of Primus Hall, the son of a Boston slave and one of the city's early black leaders. In 1808 the school moved into the meeting house.

The African Meeting House was also a community cultural center. Musical recitals and dramatic productions

African Meeting House

46 Joy Street
Boston, MA 02114
617-723-8863
www.nps.gov/boaf/boaf.htm
NRIS 71000087
NHL, NPS

DATE BUILT
1806

SIGNIFICANCE
The African Meeting House was the central institution of Boston's Antebellum free black community and is the oldest African American church still standing in the United States.

were routinely held in its sanctuary and meeting rooms. In April 1833, for example, the Baptist Singing Society gave a concert in the sanctuary. A small seven-piece orchestra, featuring barber Peter Howard on clarinet, opened the program with the overture to Mozart's *Marriage of Figaro.* Mrs. John T. Hilton, wife of a well-known black hairdresser, performed a vocal solo, and she was followed by a vocal trio selection. Musical training and rehearsals occupied several evenings during the week. On Monday evenings, laborer William F. Bassett taught music fundamentals to adults and children. On Wednesdays, the church choir rehearsed, and it sometimes staged public musical presentations. On other nights of the week, the church provided a place for the Social Harmonic Society, various youth choirs, and the Amateur Band, directed by barbers Peter Howard and James G. Barbadoes. Children's choirs and glee clubs, dramatic productions, and debating clubs all found space in the meeting house for their activities. With so much going on at the church, it was little wonder that on several occasions various black literary and debating societies—including the Boston Philomanthean Society and the Young Men's Literary Debating Society—were forced to meet in the basement rooms.

Despite the heavy demands for its space, the African Meeting House was always open to protest groups and community activists. The African Society, a mutual aid organization that provided for widows and orphans, conducted many of its fundraising activities and held its meetings on the ground floor. The sanctuary was frequently given over to antislavery protest meetings, which grew in frequency and size by the 1830s. When the radical white abolitionist William Lloyd Garrison sought a place for a gathering of antislavery reformers, the African Meeting House was the only hall in the city to open its doors to him.

It was in early 1832, on a cold and snowy January evening that a young black boy, William C. Nell, stood outside a meeting house window and watched as abolitionists debated the issue of slavery and the need for its destruction. Nell, who as an adult became a prominent abolitionist, community leader, and historian, never forgot the scene that still inspired him decades later. That

William Cooper Nell was one of Boston's most active black community leaders. He worked to integrate the city's public schools, was a printer for the abolitionist newspaper The Liberator, *and authored some of the earliest accounts of African Americans in the American Revolution.*

This abolitionist flag dating to around 1859 features only twenty stars because it has dropped those that represent the slave states. Almost thirty years earlier, white abolitionist William Lloyd Garrison and others founded the New England Anti-Slavery Society at the African Meeting House in Boston.

night Garrison and other courageous reformers established the New England Anti-Slavery Society. This group brought together black and white reformers and became one of the most effective regional organizations in the crusade against slavery in the decades before the Civil War. It provided the foundation for the American Anti-Slavery Society, organized in 1833.

The African Meeting House is an important landmark not only for Boston blacks, but for African American history generally. It is an important example of how black churches furthered the ambitions of people denied traditional economic, social, and political outlets in American society. For those who could not realistically hope to hold political office, high military rank, or powerful economic position, the church offered a critical, if reduced, opportunity to pursue typically American dreams. If few could be doctors and lawyers, many could be good church-going people, a title that conveyed considerable status in the African American community. Significantly, unskilled and semiskilled workers were among the most active church members.

For young single men and women, the meeting house was a place to socialize with friends and to keep abreast of community affairs. On a given Sunday, one could meet a future mate or make important social and economic contacts. Church suppers were popular social occasions for church members from all segments of the black population, allowing workers and potential employers to rub shoulders in an informal and festive atmosphere. In this regard, the meeting house was especially significant for workers migrating to Boston for the first time. Social relations among blacks of every social station and of various occupational levels were strengthened as they

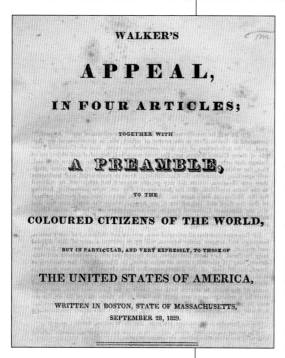

David Walker wrote this appeal in 1829 as a free black North Carolinian living in Boston. In it he condemned the hypocrisy of Christians who would tolerate slavery and called all slaves to bloody revolution.

served on the same committees, held church offices together, and represented the church at regional and national religious conventions.

Boston's black community grew steadily in the decades before the Civil War, and the African Meeting House, joined by new black churches, played an increasingly political role. In 1816, with Kentucky's Henry Clay presiding, a group of some of the nation's most prominent leaders, men such as former President James Monroe, future President Andrew Jackson, Francis Scott Key, who composed the song that would become America's national anthem, and Massachusetts political leader Daniel Webster, formed the American Colonization Society.

In 1820, with the financial assistance of the U.S. Congress, the society founded the colony of Liberia on the West coast of Africa. When the organization aggressively began to encourage free blacks to migrate to the colony, many African Americans suspected that this was a veiled attempt to shield slavery from the vigorous abolitionist activities of free blacks. By 1830, free African Americans across the northern states had rejected the society's colonization plans, which seemed to disregard the fact that black Americans were not African, but Americans whose full citizenship rights ought to be recognized by the nation and their fellow Americans. Despite the racism that seemed so deeply embedded in America, blacks had not yet given up on their faith in their nation. The African Meeting House served as a forum for gatherings of Boston blacks who debated these issues.

The African American dentist and abolitionist John Rock spoke for many when he explained why he rejected colonization. "This being our country," he said, " we have made up our minds to remain in it, and to try to make it worth living in." In Boston and elsewhere black Americans pointed to their service as Revolutionary soldiers and demanded their right to claim an American identity in a land that they had, in the words of David Walker, a militant spokesman for anti-colonization, "enriched . . . with [their] blood and tears." Although the African Meeting House retained its name, the congregation of the African Baptist Church renamed itself the

First Independent Church of the Free People of Color. The congregation explained at a meeting of the Boston Baptist Association that "the name African is ill applied to a church composed of American Citizens."

Throughout the decades before the Civil War, the First Independent Church of the Free People of Color, which continued to meet in the African Meeting House remained steadily active against slavery and on behalf of the black community. It played an important role as meeting place, fundraising center, and as Underground Railroad headquarters, for those who provided shelter for runaways seeking protection in the city. After the Fugitive Slave Law of 1850 strengthened and expanded slaveholders' rights to recapture escaped slaves, the meeting house became the site of increasingly militant agitation. This was the political atmosphere in 1863 Boston, when Frederick Douglass stood in the meeting house's sanctuary beseeching black men to join the war effort to destroy slavery.

Black men answered his call, and the meeting house saw many of its members march off to war as soldiers of the 54th Massachusetts Infantry. In one pivotal battle, at Fort Wagner in South Carolina, at least 116 African Americans died, and another 156 were wounded or captured. Six hundred blacks were among the five thousand U.S. troops who stormed the heavily fortified Confederate garrison in the summer of 1863. The congregation was active during the war years and beyond, donating everything they could for the relief of African Americans emerging from slavery. The volumes in its Sunday school library dipped from five hundred to one hundred as the church sent books to the South to aid in the education of the freedmen.

Meanwhile, due in part to the popularity of the hard-hitting sermons and community activism of Reverend Alexander Ellis, who had come to the church in 1869, the congregation continued to grow. The congregation reached almost three hundred by 1874, more than twice its pre-war membership. By the 1880s the church had changed its name again, this time to St. Paul Baptist Church, and before the end of the century it sought a new location as the growing black population moved out of Beacon Hill into Boston's South End.

In 1898 the meeting house was sold to a Jewish congregation newly arrived in Boston. By 1905 it had become a synagogue and the home of Congregation Libavitz, which remained in the building until the 1970s. As the African Meeting House had served Boston's black community during the nineteenth century, the building served many in the city's Jewish community for most of the twentieth century. In 1971, as a result of determined efforts in the black community, the National Register of Historic Places recognized the historic significance of the African Meeting House and named it a historic site. The following year the Museum of Afro-American History purchased the meeting house with an eye toward restoring the building to its 1855 appearance, a time for which the greatest structural documentation is available.

The African Meeting House is now largely restored. As this old and venerable structure stood, illustrating the dignity of a struggling nineteenth-century black community; as it served and sheltered a significant Jewish community in the twentieth century; it now stands as a symbol of the determination and resilience of all those who struggled for freedom and human rights.

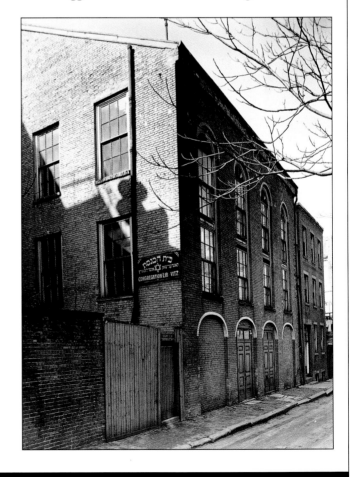

Hebrew lettering and the Star of David announced that the old African Meeting House was now the synagogue of the Congregation Libavitz. Recognizing the importance of the oldest existing black church building in America, the Museum of Afro-American History purchased the structure in 1972.

The Abiel Smith School closed twenty-one years after it opened, when an 1855 Massachusetts law ended segregation in public schools.

THE LEWIS AND HARRIET HAYDEN HOUSE

66 Phillips Street
Boston, MA 02114
617-742-5415
www.nps.gov/boaf/site6.htm
NPS

On Beacon Hill, not far from the African Meeting House is the house, built in 1833, where Lewis Hayden lived in the years before the Civil War. Hayden, born a slave in 1811 in Lexington, Kentucky, escaped—with the assistance of Underground Railroad workers—first to Detroit and then to Boston. He operated a small clothing business in the city and soon became an active abolitionist, connecting Boston's white abolitionists to the black foot soldiers of the movement. With his wife, Harriet, he ran one of the most important Underground Railroad stations in the city. The Hayden house became particularly active after the passage of the Fugitive Slave Law of 1850, which strengthened federal laws guaranteeing slaveholders the right to recover their escaped "human property."

In 1850, William Craft and his wife, Ellen, adopted an ingenious deception to make their escape from slavery. The light-complexioned Ellen posed as a young white man traveling north for medical care, while William played the role of personal servant. In these guises the couple traveled to Philadelphia and then on to Boston, where they contacted the city's abolition-

ists. When the word circulated through the black community that slave hunters had arrived in Boston to recapture the fugitives, Ellen went on north, but William was trapped in the basement of Hayden's house. With the determination that characterized his antislavery resolve, Hayden loaded gunpowder onto the porch of his home and threatened to destroy the house and all who attempted to enter if the slave hunters did not withdraw. His actions discouraged the attempted capture, and a gathering of Boston's black men drove the slave hunters from the city.

The Hayden home sheltered fugitive slaves as they made their way north to freedom. It also provided meeting space for abolitionists and community activists. Hayden recruited soldiers for the Massachusetts 54th Regiment during the Civil War and his only son died while serving in the U.S. Navy. In 1873, Hayden was elected to the Massachusetts State Legislature. By the time he died in 1889, Lewis Hayden was one of the longest serving, most well-known and respected leaders of Boston's black community.

THE ABIEL SMITH SCHOOL

46 Joy Street
Boston, MA 02114
617-742-5415
www.nps.gov/boaf/site13.htm
NPS

The Abiel Smith School was the first public school for

African Americans in the country. The primary and grammar school was named in honor of a white businessman who willed two thousand dollars to the city of Boston for the education of black children. Until the building's construction in 1834, classes were held in the African American homes and on the lower level of the African Meeting House. An effort to integrate the city schools lead to a boycott by African Americans of the Smith School starting in the late 1830s. In a significant school desegregation case in 1849, future Massachusetts senator Charles Sumner and black lawyer Robert Morris brought suit against the Boston School Board on behalf of Benjamin Roberts and his daughter Sara. They demanded that Sara be allowed to attend the school nearest to her home, but the Massachusetts Supreme Court ruled that she must attend the all-black Smith School.

Finally, in 1855, the Massachusetts legislature

instituted a measure that integrated the public schools in the state. As Boston's schools were opened to blacks, the Smith School closed. The building was used to store school furniture until, in 1887, it became the headquarters for an organization of black Civil War veterans. It is now part of the Afro-American Museum of Boston. On its second floor the sword of Robert Gould Shaw—commander of the Massachusetts 54th Regiment—and the print-composing table used by William Lloyd Garrison, the abolitionist editor of the *Liberator,* are on display.

BOSTON'S BLACK HERITAGE TRAIL

Trail begins at Beacon and
    Park Streets
Boston, MA 02108
*www.nps.gov/boaf/blackher-
    itagetrail.htm*
NPS

The Black Heritage Trail consists of fourteen historic sites—including the African Meeting House, the Lewis and Harriet Hayden house, and the Smith School—significant to the history of the nineteenth-century free black community of Boston. The trail begins with the Robert Gould Shaw and the 54th Regiment Memorial at Beacon and Park Streets at the northern edge of Boston Common. The memorial honors the 54th Massachusetts Regiment—the first all-black regiment recruited in the North to fight for the United States during the Civil War—

and its commander, Colonel Robert Gould Shaw.

Just up Beacon Hill, at 5–7 Pinckney Street, is the George Middleton House. Although most of the five thousand African Americans who fought for the American cause in the Revolution served in integrated military units, Middleton commanded the Bucks of America, one of three all-black military companies. After the Revolution, he devoted himself to serving Boston's black community, working for the improvement of education and in the abolition movement. Built in 1797, his house is the oldest standing wooden structure on Beacon Hill. Other sites on the Black Heritage Trail include the Phillips School, one of the first integrated schools in Boston; the home of black abolitionist John J. Smith; the Charles Street Meeting House, the first integrated church in the United States; and John Coburn's Gaming House, the business that allowed Coburn to provide critical funds to support antislavery work in Boston.

HISTORIC WEEKSVILLE

1698–1708 Bergen Street
Brooklyn, NY 11213
718-623-0600
*www.weeksvillesociety.org/his-
    toric/historicweeksville.html*
NHL

In 1838, James Weeks, an African American who moved to New York City from Virginia, purchased land in what is today the Bedford-

Stuyvesant neighborhood of Brooklyn. In the decades before the Civil War, this area became home to a thriving African American community. Its residents spanned the social spectrum from laborers to professionals. Susan Smith McKinney-Steward, New York State's first black female doctor lived there in the mid-nineteenth century, as did a number of schoolteachers and ministers. The community was also home to several needed institutions. The Brooklyn Howard Colored Orphanage Asylum and the Zion Home for Aged Relief cared for the community's youngest and oldest residents. The African Civilization Society investigated the possibilities of West African colonization, and the *Freedman's Torchlight,* a newspaper first published in 1866, kept the people connected to one another and to the wider world.

In 1968, historian Jim Hurley and pilot Joseph Haynes were flying over Brooklyn as part of an aerial research project when they discovered the last remaining section of Weeksville, four frame houses along Hunterfly Road. These houses are the oldest known existing buildings in Bedford-Stuyvesant. In 1970, these building were registered as National Historic Landmarks. Eventually, the Weeksville Society purchased the buildings, and, with a coalition of other local groups restored them. In addition to the restored buildings, the site is also home to the Weeksville African American Museum.

The Old Courthouse

St. Louis, Mo.

Dred Scott, the Supreme Court, and the Struggle for Freedom

"The question is simply this: can a [N]egro whose ancestors were imported into this country and sold as slaves, become a member of the political community formed and brought into existence by the Constitution of the United States, and as such become entitled to all the rights, and privileges, and immunities, guaranteed by that instrument to the citizen?" This was the question, not at all simple, put before the U.S. Supreme Court in March 1857 in the landmark case *Dred Scott* v. *Sandford*. The Court answered "no," supporting the proslavery argument and intensifying the growing national conflict over the institution of slavery. In doing so, it went beyond the original question raised by the slave Dred Scott in the Old Courthouse located between Broadway and Fourth Street in St. Louis, Missouri, on April 6, 1846. The question, when it was first heard, was more straightforward. Can a slave who spent substantial time outside the jurisdiction of slavery claim freedom? The case that began in St. Louis's Old Courthouse ended in the U.S. Supreme Court, with a decision that shook the nation and helped to bring on the Civil War.

Initially, the Old Courthouse was a brick structure completed in 1828. Over the next forty years, as the population of the city of St. Louis grew, it was enlarged and remodeled. Its exterior was made more ornate and a new larger, more impressive dome was added to the central section, expanding the interior rotunda. In 1839 contractors laid the cornerstone in which they placed newspapers from several cities in the region, an assortment of coins, and the names of a number of government officials. The building was not officially declared complete, however, until July 4, 1862. By then it was the grandest structure in Missouri.

Dred Scott (above), whose suit for freedom began in the Old Courthouse in St. Louis, lost his case before the U.S. Supreme Court when Chief Justice Roger B. Taney declared that blacks were "beings of an inferior order."

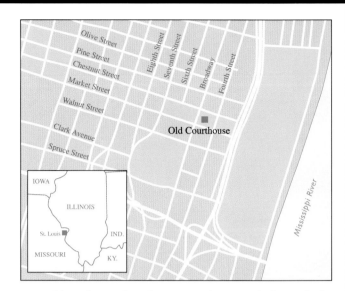

Although it is best known as the court before which Dred Scott and his wife, Harriet, argued for their freedom, the Old Courthouse, as it was called even then, had already played a pivotal role in St. Louis history. Here city offices—once scattered throughout the community in a church, a tavern, and a fort—were brought together, allowing for a more centralized urban administration. As the city became a major trading center, the courthouse was expanded so that its original building became a wing of the new, larger structure. It was in its old west wing that the first Dred Scott trial was held.

Scott was born a slave in Virginia about 1799. He was the property of Peter Blow. When the Blow family relocated to St. Louis in 1830, they brought Dred Scott with them. Shortly after the move, economic pressures forced the family to sell some of its property, including Dred Scott. That sale changed Scott's life, as sales often did for those bound in slavery. He became the property of a military surgeon, John Emerson, who was soon transferred to a military post at Rock Island, Illinois. He took Scott with him, and they lived in Illinois until the spring of 1836. Then another military transfer brought master and slave to Fort Snelling, on the west bank of the Mississippi River, in the territory then known as Upper Louisiana, now Wisconsin.

Before year's end, Dr. Emerson purchased a female slave, Harriet Robinson, from a local justice of the peace, and soon after, he consented to her marriage to Scott. The couple lived in free territories for nine years, even after their master was transferred to Missouri and

Louisiana. Then, in 1838 when Emerson married, he ordered the Scotts to join him. By then Harriet had given birth to a daughter, Eliza. In Missouri, she had a second daughter, Lizzie. Under prevailing law, both the children were slaves, having been born to a slave woman.

When Emerson died in 1843, Scott attempted to purchase his freedom from his widow, but she refused. Instead she hired the Scotts out to work for others, who paid her for their services. Finally, Scott sought freedom for himself and his family through the courts. He was encouraged by his minister, John Anderson, and his case was financed by his former masters, the Blow family. The Scotts' attorney claimed that, as Dred and Harriet had lived for years in the free territory of Wisconsin, they and their children had the right to freedom. There was precedent for this argument. At the time, Missouri courts recognized a policy of "once free, always free," and in similar cases other slaves had attained their freedom using this argument. The case came to trial in June 1847 and was heard in the first-floor, west-wing courtroom of St. Louis's Old Courthouse. The Scotts lost their case on a technicality, but were granted a second trial in 1850, held in the same courtroom. This time the jury granted the Scotts their freedom. Unfortunately, however, this was not the end of their struggle.

By the mid-1840s, when a slave successfully sued for his freedom, it was viewed by most in the South as a dangerous attack on the institution of slavery that had come to define the South and its way of life. Having lost at the local level, there was pressure on Mrs. Emerson to appeal her case, retain her slave, and safeguard slavery from these kinds of freedom suits. Her appeal was successful. The case moved beyond the Old Courthouse to the Missouri Supreme Court, which reversed the lower court decision, arguing that "times now are not as they were when the previous decisions on this subject were made." The court ordered that the Scotts be re-enslaved. Ironically, Scott had lost on another technicality.

Dred and Harriet were not ready to relinquish the freedom that had seemed so close at hand. Their case attracted the attention of the antislavery movement, and a team of abolitionist lawyers took action on Scott's behalf. The team filed suit in St. Louis Federal Court in 1854 against John F. A. Sanford, Mrs. Emerson's brother, who acted for her estate. (John Sanford's name was misspelled

The Old Courthouse

11 North Fourth Street
St Louis, MO 63102
314-655-1700
www.nps.gov/jeff/ocv-dscottd.htm
NRIS 66000941
NHS

DATE BUILT
1828, remodeling completed 1862

ARCHITECT FOR REMODELING
Henry Singleton

SIGNIFICANCE
The Old Courthouse was the site of the initial trial in the *Dred Scott* case, ultimately one of the most important Supreme Court cases and rulings in American history. This center of urban administration was once considered Missouri's architectural showplace.

in the Supreme Court records, and the case has been known since as *Scott v. Sandford.*) As Sanford was a resident of New York, the case could be moved out of the Missouri court system and heard by the federal courts. The trial took place not in the Old Courthouse but in the Papin Building, near St. Louis's present-day Gateway Arch. The court decided in favor of Sanford, prompting Dred Scott and his team of lawyers to appeal to the U.S. Supreme Court.

Dred Scott's legal drama, begun in the Old Courthouse, was a significant part of a much larger national debate, older than the country and dangerous to the Union. Although the founding fathers never specifically mentioned slavery in the Constitution, the shadow of that institution hung heavily over the proceedings that brought the document to life.

The thirteen British colonies and all the original states in the Union had sanctioned slavery, but, starting with Vermont in 1777, most northern states set about abolishing the institution in the decades after the Revolution. The Georgia and South Carolina representatives at the 1787 Constitutional Convention in Philadelphia, however, flatly refused to be a part of any national union that denied protection to slavery. Although South Carolina's representative, Charles Cotesworth Pinckney,

The iron-framed dome of the Old Courthouse dominated the St. Louis skyline well into the twentieth century, and it provided a model for other government buildings around the country. In the nineteenth century, for entertainment, people often attended the debates, speeches, and court proceedings held in the ornate rotunda.

did not get the explicit constitutional guarantees protecting slavery that he demanded, representatives from more moderate southern states, such as Virginia's George Mason, agreed that the federal government should not hinder the maintenance and growth of slavery. Even most northern representatives believed that the Constitution needed to protect slaveholders' right to their human property and thus prohibited Congress from interfering with the importation of slaves into the country for at least twenty years after the passage of the Constitution.

Dred and Harriet Scott were slaves who had lived in a free state and in free territory when they decided to sue for their personal freedom under Missouri state law in 1846. Earlier Missouri court decisions had emancipated slaves who had traveled to free states or territories, and Scott expected his suit to be quick and successful. Eleven years later, however, the U.S. Supreme Court declared him a slave with no right to bring suit before the court.

By the time Dred Scott stood before the St. Louis court, there were more than three million slaves in the United States, and slavery was an important and well-established institution in America life. Even as slavery dwindled in state after state in the North, the institution expanded in the South. It became critical to the southern economy and so significant nationally that the entire country felt its power. Cotton, the major slave crop, played a large role in America's foreign trade. By 1840, it was, in fact, more valuable than all the nation's other exports combined. And the value of the slave population was a major part of the national wealth, greater in value than all of America's banks, railroads, and factories put together. Thus, when Dred Scott asked that the court grant freedom for himself and his family, his request might well have been seen as a threat to an important economic foundation of the nation.

Any challenge to slaveholding in the South was further complicated by the rise of the militant abolition movement then causing a great stir in many regions of the North. The white abolitionist William Lloyd Garrison, editor of the radical newspaper *The Liberator,* joined forces with black abolitionists to attack slavery and lobby the North on behalf of freedom. Although most white people in the northern states were not ready to support the antislavery argument, a few legislatures in Massachusetts and Pennsylvania, for example, passed regulations in the 1840s, called personal liberties laws, prohibiting state officials or facilities from participating in the enforcement of the 1793 Fugitive Slave Law, under which slaveholders attempted to recapture their property.

Missouri was a part of this debate even before it became a part of the United States. It entered the nation in 1821 as the twelfth slave state, balancing the previous year's admission of Maine, the twelfth free state. Slavery was central to the state's economy and to that of its major city of St Louis, where slave trading was big business and slave auctions were sometimes conducted from the front steps of the Old Courthouse. Often these sales were conducted to settle slaveholder estates or to pay debts and fulfill business contracts between local merchants. For the Scotts, as for slaves generally, the courthouse was not simply a hall of legal justice.

By the mid-nineteenth century, the increasing hostility between abolitionist and proslavery activists had become a national concern that some in the Congress hoped to cool with the passage of major compromise legislation. The Compromise of 1850, as the series of bills was called, offered the antislavery advocates the admission of California as the thirty-first state with an antislavery state constitution and the abolition of the slave trade in the District of Columbia. To slavery's supporters, the Congress offered a new, stricter fugitive slave law that did not give an accused fugitive the right of legal counsel, a jury trail, or even the right to speak in self-defense. The new law also required all citizens to assist in the capture of fugitives on penalty of fine and arrest. Black and white abolitionists vowed to resist this law at all costs, and President Millard Filmore, bent on showing resolve to the South, vowed to enforce it.

Meanwhile, Kansas erupted. In 1854, Congress passed legislation that allowed the fate of slavery in that territory to be decided by the will of a majority of its settlers. Almost immediately friction became hostility that gave way to open warfare as proslavery forces and abolitionists rushed to claim political control of the territory. The violence of "Bleeding Kansas" spilled over into northern cities where abolitionists fought to protect fugitive slaves, and even into the hall of Congress, where Preston Brookes, a proslavery South Carolina congressman attacked Massachusetts antislavery Senator Charles Sumner in the Senate Chamber. Sumner had derided an elderly senator from South Carolina, a relative of Brookes, for his support of the proslavery forces in

Kansas. Brookes' attack on Sumner was a part of the sectional violence, and, because it occurred on the floor of the U.S. Senate, it shocked the nation. By the mid-1850s America seemed to be moving toward a major confrontation between pro- and antislavery forces. It was in this atmosphere that Dred Scott and his lawyers came before the U.S. Supreme Court to make their argument.

In 1857, when the high court considered Scott's case, five of its nine justices, including Chief Justice Roger B. Taney, were sons of the South. Two of the northern judges were strong advocates of states' rights policies that favored the South, and a third was on record as being proslavery. Only the remaining northern judge was opposed to slavery. In the political heat of the era, the Court's findings took on immense political significance. It went far beyond ruling on the freedom of one African American family. On March 6, 1857, eighty-year-old Justice Taney read aloud the lengthy majority opinion in the *Dred Scott* case. Seven of the nine justices, all of the southerners and two of the northerners, agreed that Dred Scott should remain a slave, but the majority opinion did not stop there. The Court also ruled that as a slave Dred Scott was not a citizen of the United States, and therefore had no right to bring suit and "no rights which the white man was bound to respect." In a direct slap at the new Republican Party, established in 1854, and its free soil platform, which declared the party's opposition to the expansion of slavery into the free territories, the Court argued that the federal government had no right to prohibit slavery in the western territories. This judgment was a central point of contention in the political powder keg of the 1850s.

The public reacted strongly to the *Dred Scott* decision. Abolitionists feared that the Court's affirmation of slavery's constitutional protection would encourage its unchecked

In the opinion in the Dred Scott case, Chief Justice Taney asked, "Can a negro, whose ancestors were imported into this country, and sold as slaves, become a member of the political community formed and brought into existence by the Constitution?" He went on to answer his own question: "We think...they are not included, and were not intended to be included, under the word 'citizens' in the Constitution."

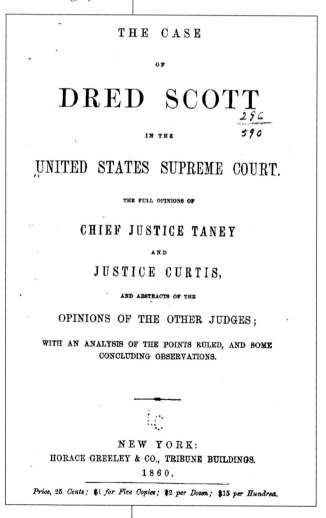

THE CASE

OF

DRED SCOTT

2 9 6

IN THE

5 9 0

UNITED STATES SUPREME COURT.

THE FULL OPINIONS OF

CHIEF JUSTICE TANEY

AND

JUSTICE CURTIS,

AND ABSTRACTS OF THE

OPINIONS OF THE OTHER JUDGES;

WITH AN ANALYSIS OF THE POINTS RULED, AND SOME CONCLUDING OBSERVATIONS.

NEW YORK:

HORACE GREELEY & CO., TRIBUNE BUILDINGS.

1860.

Price, 25 Cents; $1 for Five Copies; $2 per Dozen; $15 per Hundred.

expansion. Many abolitionists now joined the Republicans in a fight to gain control of Congress and the courts. They understood that the Republican Party was not an antislavery party, but they hoped that it might at least be successful in limiting slavery's spread and curbing its power. For African Americans, supporting the Republican Party, which appealed to white voters by declaring itself a "white man party," was especially difficult. Yet, given the practical political choice between Republicans and the proslavery Democrats, there really was no choice. Most African Americans supported the

A Personal Story of the Underground Railroad

William Still's parents were both slaves. His father bought his own freedom. His mother escaped in 1807 with her two daughters, leaving two sons behind. Fourteen years later William was born in the free state of New Jersey. An important abolitionist as an adult, he operated Philadelphia's extensive Underground Railroad network.

In a letter written to James Miller McKim, an abolitionist coworker, on August 8, 1850, he described his encounter with a man from Alabama named Peter Freedman who came to him seeking information about his family who had come North as fugitives years before. Still recognized the story. "My feelings were unutterable," he explained. "I could see in the face of my newfound brother, the likeness of my mother. I told him I could tell him all about his kinfolk." Soon, Peter was reunited with his mother and sisters. "I shall not attempt to describe the feelings of my mother and the family," Still reported, "on learning the fact that Peter was one of us; I will leave that for you to imagine."

The family's struggle was not over, however. For the next five years, Peter and his family struggled to gain freedom for the wife and

In 1872, William Still self-published his book, The Underground Railroad. *The book described the day-to-day workings of the underground network and the deeds of the fugitives. "The race had no more eloquent advocates,"* he wrote, *"than its own self-emancipated champions."*

children he had left behind in Alabama. Finally, with the assistance of William's abolitionist contacts, they gained their freedom in October 1854. By the mid-nineteenth century only 10 percent of African Americans were free. Their personal connections to slavery strengthened their commitment to the abolition movement and the Underground Railroad.

Republican Party, but, as one black abolitionist made clear in the pages of the *Liberator,* "We do not pledge ourselves to go further with the Republicans, than the Republicans will go with us."

Skeptical as they were of Republicans, African Americans were furious at the Supreme Court. They deemed its decision in the *Dred Scott* case to be one of a number of federal assaults on their rights that had occurred throughout the 1850s. Now the nation had spoken through its Court to declare African Americans, some the children and grandchildren of Revolutionary War veterans, non-Americans. For many blacks it was the last straw. In April 1857, less than a month after the Court's decision, at a protest meeting in Philadelphia, the black abolitionist Charles Lenox Remond expressed the rage that so many felt. "We owe no allegiance to a country which grinds us under its iron heel and treats us like dogs," he said. "The time has gone by for colored people to talk of patriotism." At a New York abolitionist meeting, Frederick Douglass said, "I denounce the representation as a most scandalous and devilish perversion of the Constitution, and a brazen mis-statement of the facts of history." In the aftermath of the Court's decision, some blacks left the United States for Canada, but others redoubled their determination to stay and fight for the rights that the Court had denied them. In Boston, Pittsburgh, Cincinnati, and other cities, African Americans formed military companies in self-defense and in anticipation of a coming war on slavery. Meanwhile Republicans, also opposed to the *Dred Scott* decision, set into motion a political campaign that looked toward the 1860 Presidential election.

The *Dred Scott* decision had, by late 1850, moved the country to the brink of civil war. Dred Scott did not live to see the war that finally ended slavery. He and his family were freed in the spring of 1857, after Mrs. Emerson remarried, this time to an antislavery congressman. A year later, on September 17, 1858, Dred Scott died of tuberculosis and was buried in St. Louis. His national story began during the 1840s in a small courtroom in the Old Court House in St Louis. In its time, with its domed roof that sat above an impressive interior rotunda, this building was a marvel of engineering and architectural design. Construction of the final section of the building, its north wing, was begun in 1857 and continued for five years; contractors were hired and fired as the city came under criticism for the slow pace of the work. One newspaper editor mocked the construction as having taken three or four hundred years, and remarked sarcastically that "its first architect has been dead for some two hundred years."

Finally, the building was completed during the Civil War. The impressive structure has four wings with a dome at the center of its axis. In the rotunda under the dome, three tiers of balconies, or galleries, overhang the floor. Stone pillars support the lower gallery, and oak columns support the upper two. Its columned entrance gives a formal and dignified look to the center section, which is topped by a distinctive new dome built in the 1850s to replace the original.The new dome is constructed of a lightweight wrought- and cast-iron skeleton with a copper exterior. The dome features the ornate and detailed architectural style of the Italian Renaissance, popularly employed in state buildings during that period. It was inspired by that of the National Capitol then under construction in Washington, D.C. The dome of the Old Courthouse was, in fact, completed eighteen months before the Capitol's dome. Both were modeled stylistically after the dome of St. Peter's Basilica in Rome.

In this 1860 parody of the Presidential election, Dred Scott—whose Supreme Court case heated up an already incendiary debate about the future of slavery—provides the music that the others must dance to. Four Presidential candidates appear with their constituents; in the upper right-hand corner, Abraham Lincoln is partnered with a black woman.

Even as its remodeling continued, the Old Courthouse remained a history-making site in the volatile years before and during the Civil War. Missouri split over the question of southern secession. Although its governor and other powerful state officials favored joining the Confederacy, Missouri remained a part of the United States. The state itself became a battleground, where antislavery and unionist supporters faced pro-slavery forces, clashing in St. Louis and elsewhere in the state. The Old Courthouse was the site of some of this violence. On New Year's Day 1861, just a few days after South Carolina had seceded from the United States and less than a week before Mississippi followed suit, an antislavery mob of some two thousand halted a slave auction taking place on the steps of Old Courthouse. Their action illustrated the extent of the hostility against slavery, even in this slaveholding city, in this slaveholding state.

The Civil War years were difficult for all of Missouri, a border state that saw its citizens fighting on both sides of the war. The Old Courthouse was a major judicial site in the state through the 1860s. When word reached the city in early April 1865 that the Confederacy had surrendered, the courthouse was quickly decorated for a joyous celebration, but then, just a few days later, came the news of the assassination of President Abraham Lincoln. Black crepe was woven into the red, white, and blue victory decorations and the central rotunda became a monument to the fallen President.

Gas lamps illuminated a bust of Lincoln and a three-foot-high memorial, referred to as a "tomb" in a local newspaper. Guarded by the 41st Missouri Regiment, it was a special place for the black people who came in droves to honor the man most lovingly called "massa Lincoln." He was the President who led the nation out of slavery, and was the only President up to that time to speak publicly in favor of citizenship rights for black people.

Beyond the Civil War, the Old Courthouse continued to be the site of significant moments in history. One of the most important civil rights cases involved Virginia Minor, an officer in the National Woman Suffrage Association. Ironically, this case bore a direct connection to the *Dred Scott* case. During the 1872 Presidential election, the association challenged regulations denying women the right to vote. In 1886, Virginia Minor and her husband, Francis, authored *Women's Legal Right to the Ballot,* a book that argued that the Fourteenth Amendment to the U.S. Constitution—originally conceived to reverse Taney's opinion in the *Dred Scott* decision—did more than broaden U.S. citizenship to include African Americans. They argued that it also made women citizens of the United States, and thus entitled them to vote.

Minor attempted to register for the 1872 national election, but was refused. It was not until the passage of the Married Women's Act of 1889 that a married woman could sue in Missouri courts. Thus, Virginia's husband, Francis, himself a lawyer, brought suit on her behalf. He sued the registrar, Reese Happersett, in a hearing that began early in 1873 in the Old Courthouse.

The Minors lost their case, but appealed the decision to the state supreme court, which also heard the case in the Old Courthouse, this time in its second floor courtroom. But again the judgment went against them. The court held that that the purpose of the Fourteenth Amendment was to extend voting rights to newly freed slaves, not to women. A final appeal to the U.S. Supreme Court in 1874 settled the matter. The Court ruled unanimously in the case of *Minor* vs. *Happersett* that the Constitution of the United States did not confer the right of suffrage upon anyone, and that suffrage was not a right of citizenship. It upheld the right of individual states to decide which citizens could vote within their jurisdiction. This decision was significant for African Americans, for it left their access to the ballot in the hands of the southern states, where in the late nineteenth century, the vast majority of blacks lived.

The Old Courthouse in St. Louis is a fitting landmark of African American history, in part because within its walls Americans have debated the meaning of freedom and citizenship. Because race has so often been at the center of such debates, the rights of black people are always in question, even when the particular case at hand does not directly involve their status.

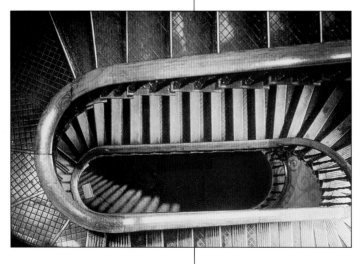

This cast-iron stairway is located in the east wing of the Old Courthouse. Still in use, the stairway was built in 1854 and is supported entirely by the wall in which it is embedded.

This courtroom inside the Old Courthouse is one of two restored rooms on the second floor. Originally, the building held seven to twelve courtrooms for use by the county and city courts.

This historic building has played a significant role in the formation of America's legal and constitutional tradition and its social and political history. In this place Americans disadvantaged by the contradictions of American democracy sought redress and set in motion great forces that changed the nation. Its role is not limited to one case or one time. It was in the Old Courthouse that Louis D. Brandeis, who would later take significant humanitarian positions as a justice on the Supreme Court, was admitted to the bar in 1878. During the 1990s it has served as the site for naturalization ceremonies in which immigrants attained the citizenship that had eluded both Scott and Minor.

The Dred Scott Courtroom in St. Louis's Old Courthouse is no longer in existence. During the mid-nineteenth century, renovations added a new corridor dividing the large room where the Scott trials were heard into two smaller courtrooms. In 1941, the National Park Service installed a new roof and began extensive interior restorations, which were suspended during the war, but continued in 1955. In 1979, the Park Service reconstructed the roof and restored its interior murals. It completed additional exterior renovation in 1985, and the next year it constructed history galleries. Today, the Old Courthouse is home to extensive museum exhibits that tell the building's story, and the history of the Dred Scott family and its struggle to find an elusive American justice.

THE JOHN MERCER LANGSTON HOUSE

207 East College Street
Oberlin, OH 44074

At 207 East College Street in the Ohio college town of Oberlin stands a two-story wood-frame house long associated with African American history and the fight against slavery. Built in 1855, it was the home of John Mercer Langston, the free-born son of Ralph Quarles, a wealthy white Virginia planter, and Lucy Langston, a former slave of African and Native American ancestry. John and his two brothers, Charles and Gideon, were raised by William Gooch, a white neighbor and family friend. At fourteen, John entered Oberlin Collegiate Institute, graduated in 1849, and then earned a master's degree in theology. John read law with an attorney in the nearby town of Elyria. He passed the Ohio Bar in 1854, the first African American to do so. The next year, he moved to the house on Oberlin's East College Street becoming, as he said, "the first colored homeowner on East College Street," which was he recalled, "the most fashionable street in town."

By then John Mercer Langston was already quite distinguished. In 1855 he had been elected clerk of Brownhelm Township just outside of Oberlin, making him the first black man to hold elective office in American government. During the next decade, Langston built his law practice and continued in local politics, serving on the city council and on the board of education. He was deeply committed to the abolitionist cause and he encouraged the Ohio Republican Party to move toward a solid antislavery position. He participated in fugitive slave rescues, supported John Brown's raid on Harpers Ferry, and recruited black troops to serve in the Civil War. When, in January 1863, news of President Lincoln's Emancipation Proclamation reached Oberlin, Langston read the words to a large crowd gathered at the college chapel. He then led a procession down East College Street to his home where they celebrated this momentous event in the history of freedom.

John Mercer Langston lived in this house in Oberlin's fashionable white neighborhood from 1856 until 1871. After the Civil War, Langston moved to Washington, D.C., to work with the Freedmen's Bureau. He later served as minister to Haiti and as a Republican Congressman from Virginia. He published his autobiography, From the Virginia Plantation to the National Capitol, *in 1894.*

The Mother Bethel A.M.E. Church, center of both black religion and activism in Philadelphia, is the country's oldest piece of property continuously owned by African Americans.

MOTHER BETHEL A.M.E. CHURCH

419 Sixth Street
Philadelphia, PA 19147
215-925-0616
www.motherbethel.org

Mother Bethel A.M.E. (African Methodist Episcopal) Church was established in 1794 by Richard Allen, a former slave who became a Methodist minister. In 1787, Allen led African Americans to withdraw from Philadelphia's predominantly white St. George's Methodist Church in protest of their racially discriminatory practices. Black members of the congregation were forced to sit in the back of the church during prayers and were sometimes made to stand. Finally, on July 29, 1794, a wooden building formerly used as a blacksmith shop was moved to a lot on Sixth Street, and was dedicated as Bethel African Methodist Church. The wooden structure was rebuilt several times, and was finally entirely rebuilt in brick in 1841. The structure that stands today is renovated version of the 1889 building.

Through the years Mother Bethel, as the church was called almost from its inception, has served as a major social and political forum as well as a center of Philadelphia's African American religious life. It served as a safe house for fugitive slaves, and it was the site of black community meetings protesting slavery and organizing civil rights activities. Like many black churches Mother Bethel functioned as the heart and soul of black community.

THE JOHN P. PARKER HOUSE

300 Front Street
Ripley, OH 45167
937-392-4188
www.cr.nps.gov/nr/travel/ underground/oh2.htm
NHL

John P. Parker, a former slave, was born in Norfolk, Virginia. While in slavery Parker learned to read and write and became a skilled blacksmith. He purchased his freedom with money he earned in his trade, and moved, in 1835, to Ripley, Ohio, on the banks of the Ohio River. There he established a highly successful foundry business that he used to help finance the town's Underground Railroad activities. His home at 300 Front Street in Ripley became a center for Underground Railroad operations and a hiding place for many fugitive slaves escaping across the Ohio River from the slave state of Kentucky. On several occasions Parker risked his own freedom, traveling into slave territory to guide fugitives to safety in Ripley. In the 1880s Parker dictated his memoirs, entitled *His Promised Land,* recounting his dramatic adventures with the Underground Railroad in southern Ohio.

Harpers Ferry National Historic Park

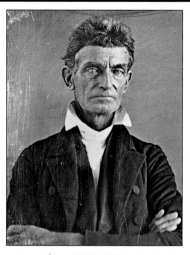

Harpers Ferry, W. Va.

Allies for Freedom

By April 1865, when the Confederacy surrendered to the forces of the United States, more than 600,000 Americans lay dead and countless others were wounded. Officially, fighting in the Civil War began in April 1861, when Confederates fired on the U.S. garrison at Fort Sumter, in Charleston Harbor, but many scholars date the hostilities much earlier. Some historians believe that the Civil War began in Kansas territory in the mid-1850s with the clash of proslavery and antislavery forces. Others believe it started in 1859, when abolitionists attacked Harpers Ferry, Virginia, foreshadowing the violence that followed just a few years later. One name has become synonymous with the fury that brought on the most destructive conflict in American history. Acting with and on behalf of African Americans in Kansas and at Harpers Ferry, John Brown symbolized a refusal to compromise with slavery and a willingness to kill, and, in the end, to be killed in an attack on the slavery that held four million black people in bondage.

At 7:05 on the morning of October 17, 1859, conductor A. J. Phelps of the regular Baltimore and Ohio eastbound train for Baltimore stopped at Monocacy, Maryland, to use the telegraph. The message he sent to his supervisor was to the point:

Harpers Ferry (right) was a small Virginia town, at the point where the Potomac and Shenandoah rivers meet, when John Brown (above) decided to raid a major federal arsenal located there. He hoped that in targeting an arsenal halfway between North and South, he would encourage both slaves and free blacks to join his abolitionist cause. Brown was fifty-six years old in this portrait, taken three years before his raid.

My train eastbound was stopped at Harpers
Ferry this morning about 1:30 by armed abolitionists—They say they have come to free the
slaves and intend to do it at all hazards—It has
been suggested you had better notify the Sec. of
War at once. The telegraph lines are cut East
and West of Harpers Ferry and this is the first
station that I could send a dispatch from.

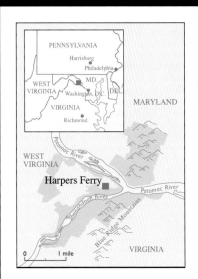

John Brown's raid on Harpers Ferry was underway.
In the mid-nineteenth century, Harpers Ferry was a village of three thousand people situated at the meeting
point of the Potomac and Shenandoah rivers. Almost 12
percent of its population was African American, of whom
150 were slaves and 150 were free people. Many of the
free black men worked as laborers or wagon drivers, but
a few were skilled craftsmen who worked as masons,
plasterers, butchers, and blacksmiths supporting the
town's major manufacturing enterprise—the armory.
President George Washington established Harpers Ferry
as one of two national armories for the production and
storage of arms and military equipment. Earlier in the
century, Harpers Ferry's economy centered around the
armory, which manufactured high-quality muskets, conducted weapons research, and developed firearms.

It was this arsenal that attracted John Brown and his
raiders who, on Sunday evening, October 16, sometime
after 10 PM, descended upon the slumbering community.
They must have presented an ominous picture, Brown, a
gray-bearded man of almost sixty years and eighteen
much younger men, thirteen white and five black, each
dressed in a long gray coat and armed with sidearms
and a rifle. They had been walking for at least two hours
when they crossed the Baltimore and Ohio Railroad
bridge leading a horse and wagon, moving toward the
federal armory building at the eastern end of town. The
sound of the approaching party alerted the armory's

As a U.S. sergeant in Robert Gould Shaw's 54th Massachusetts Regiment, William Carney participated in an assault on Fort Wagner, South Carolina. In 1900, he was first African American to be awarded the Congressional Medal of Honor.

night watchman, who emerged from his office expecting his supervisor. Instead he came face-to-face with the raiders. At their direction, the watchman opened the armory gate and admitted the party, whereupon John Brown announced that he had come from Kansas to free the slaves of Virginia.

The raiders took two watchmen as prisoners and wounded another; then Brown dispatched a party to capture more hostages. Eventually, the raiders held as many as forty prisoners in the engine house on the grounds of the arsenal. By morning, there had been some shooting and the station baggage man, Hayward Shepherd, a free African American, had been killed. Morning also brought resistance from the townspeople of Harpers Ferry. Church bells rang out the alarm and officials sent messengers to alert the militia in nearby Shepherdstown and Charles Town. Some of Brown's men urged that they take what arms they could and escape to the mountains where the plan called for gathering local slaves into an armed force. But Brown hesitated, fortifying his forces inside the armory.

By late morning of October 17, word of the raid had spread to surrounding communities in Virginia and Maryland. Armed men from the town and surrounding area attacked the armory, and the fighting left eight of Brown's men dead or captured. Before noon, the Charles Town militia reached Harpers Ferry, and before the day was over ninety U.S. Marines under the command of U.S. army colonel Robert E. Lee, assisted by U.S. Army Lieutenant J. E. B. Stuart, arrived and surrounded the arsenal. Ironically, both Lee and Stuart later became Confederate heroes. The next morning Lee demanded that Brown surrender. Brown refused, and within minutes marines rushed the engine house. In the end, ten of Brown's men lay dead or mortally wounded—including Brown's sons Watson and Oliver—and five, including Brown, were captured. Five others escaped, but two of these men were later captured in Pennsylvania and returned to Virginia. Each of the captured raiders was indicted for treason against the Commonwealth of Virginia and for murder, and each pleaded not guilty.

The trials were held at the Jefferson County Courthouse in the county seat of Charles Town. Brown was tried first, so quickly that the court would not delay long enough for his lawyer to arrive from Ohio. Instead, the court appointed two local men—both of whom had taken part in foiling the raid—to defend him. Based on a telegraph from A. H. Lewis, who knew the Brown family in Akron, Ohio, explaining that Brown's mother and others in her family had been declared insane, Brown's lawyers attempted to use an insanity defense, but Brown refused. "I reject, so far as I am capable," he told the court, "any attempt to interfere in my behalf on that score." He made his defense on the principles of anti-slavery, pleading that his actions on behalf of human freedom were morally correct.

The Virginia jury disagreed. After three-and-a-half days of trial and forty-five minutes of deliberation, it found John Brown guilty and sentenced him to hang. On December 2, 1859, at 11:30 AM, John Brown was executed for treason. Among those in attendance were future Confederate general Thomas J. (Stonewall) Jackson, then a professor of political science at Virginia Military Institute, and the actor, John Wilkes Booth, dressed in uniform and pretending to be a member of

The Faithful Slave Memorial

In an elaborate ceremony at Storer College in 1931, the local chapter of the United Daughters of the Confederacy donated to Harpers Ferry a rough stone pillar carved with an inscription in appreciation of the loyalty of "faithful slaves," honoring Hayward Shepard, a black baggage handler killed by the John Brown party. Festivities included speeches by leaders of that organization in praise of "faithful slaves." The president of the United Daughters told the white crowd that "loyal black mammies" at the time of the Civil War could be counted on by slaveholding families to show their love for their white masters in moments of crisis. The ceremony also included an unscheduled reply by one of the college's black music teachers who, before leading the college choir in song, took exception to the foregoing speeches. She made it clear that her ancestors had defended the nation in war, had fought to end slavery, and were definitely not "the mammy type."

If the memorial was controversial at its dedication, it was even more so during the 1960s and 1970s. The wording on the memorial, among other things, praises Shepard as a "respected colored freeman" who, it is claimed, remained loyal to the slaveholding South and whose action was a "tribute to the best of both races." In the swirl of racial tension of the modern civil rights period and especially during the rise of the Black Power movement, the memorial was removed from public view, obscured by a wooden cover.

Harpers Ferry National Historic Park

Harpers Ferry, WV 25425
304-535-6298
www.nps.gov/hafe
NRIS 66000041
NPS

SIGNIFICANCE
Harpers Ferry was the site of the John Brown Raid, one of the most important abolitionist actions of the antebellum period and a contributing factor in the South's decision to secede from the United States.

U.S. Marines attack the abolitionists barricaded in the engine house—now called John Brown's Fort—at Harpers Ferry. Brown and his men shot back through holes in the doors before being forced to surrender. The newspaper that printed the picture noted that it was "from a sketch made on the spot by our special artist."

the 1st Virginia Regiment in order to attend the execution. Six years later Booth assassinated Abraham Lincoln.

In his final message, written in jail on the day of his hanging, Brown foretold the bloody future. "I, John Brown am now quite certain that the crimes of this guilty land will never be purged away; but with Blood." He was right, of course. The Civil War that followed in less than two years was bloody indeed, costing more than 600,000 lives. Harpers Ferry became a symbol of that great struggle for freedom. As Brown hoped to destroy the evil of slavery, so the South hoped to protect and expand that institution. The Southerners seceded in part in reaction to the raid on Harpers Ferry and because they believed that abolition would ultimately triumph in the United States. As the former slave and abolitionist Frederick Douglass would later say in this memorable oration on May 30, 1881, on the subject of John Brown at the Fourteenth Anniversary of Storer College in West Virginia,

> When John Brown stretched forth his arm the sky was cleared. The time for compromises was gone—the armed hosts of freedom stood face to face over the chasm of a broken Union—and the clash of arms was at hand. The South staked all upon getting possession of the Federal Government, and failing to do that, drew the sword of rebellion and thus made her own, and not Brown's, the lost cause of the century.

African Americans, slave and free, figured prominently at Harpers Ferry and in the war that followed. Before the raid, Brown sought support from blacks and recruited from among their ranks. In the northern states and in Canada, Brown expected that "all the free Negroes in the northern states would immediately flock to his standard," one witness told a Senate committee investigating the raid. Indeed there were many black people who shared Brown's wish to attack slavery at its root. Black leaders—from the Boston radical abolitionist David Walker in the late 1820s to the former slave and New York antislavery activist Henry Highland Garnet in the early 1840s—had called for open slave rebellion. Black newspapers like the *Ram's Horn* in New York City cried out, "Slaves of the South, Now is the Time!"

In his meetings in the United States and Canada, free blacks encouraged Brown in his project. Many African Americans approved of Brown's intentions, but thought his plan of raiding Harpers Ferry for guns to arm Virginia slaves was doomed to failure. They saw his plan to establish fortifications in the Virginia mountains from which to launch a broad slave attack on the South as impractical. Brown attempted to recruit Harriet Tubman, the famed Underground Railroad conductor, and Frederick Douglass to join him. Douglass turned him down, and Tubman was ill at the time. The five blacks who joined his band were a varied group, but none was as prominent as Douglass and Tubman.

Brown met with his followers at his headquarters in Chambersburg, Pennsylvania, in late summer 1859.

Osborne Perry Anderson: A Survivor

During the Civil War, Osborne Perry Anderson enlisted in the U.S. Army in 1864 and became a noncommissioned officer. He was mustered out of the army at the close of the war in 1865 and died of consumption in Washington, D.C., on December 13, 1872. In 1861 he published A Voice from Harpers Ferry, *an account of the raid. In the book's preface he described why he chose to publish his memoir of the events at Harpers Ferry.*

The only African American to escape from Harpers Ferry was Perry Anderson, a free-born Pennsylvanian. Only thirty at the time of the raid, he escaped to Canada where he had lived before the raid.

My sole purpose in publishing the following Narrative is to save from oblivion the facts connected with one of the must important movements of this age, with reference to the overthrow of American slavery. My own personal experience in it, under the orders of Capt. Brown, on the 16th and 17th of October, 1859, as the only man alive who was at Harpers Ferry during the entire time the unsuccessful groping after these facts, by individuals, impossible to be obtained, except from an actor in the scene and the conviction that the cause of impartial liberty requires this duty at my hands alone have been the motives for writing and circulating the little book herewith presented.

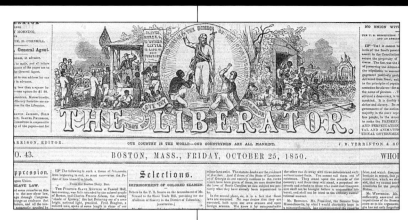

Abolitionist William Lloyd Garrison published the first issue of The Liberator in Boston in 1831 and continued until 1865, after the Thirteenth Amendment abolishing slavery had been passed. Garrison was such an ardent crusader against slavery that he was said to have called the Constitution "a covenant with death and an agreement with Hell" because it allowed the practice.

Among his followers was his first black recruit, Shields Green, a fugitive from Charleston, South Carolina. In his mid-twenties, the Emperor, as Green was sometimes called because of a rumor that he was the son of an African prince, had escaped to Canada after his wife had died in slavery. He was forced to leave his small son enslaved in South Carolina. In 1858, Green had accompanied Frederick Douglass when he visited Brown in Canada. In their discussion Douglass raised serious and legitimate objections to the plan, finally declaring it too dangerous. As he departed, Douglass turned to Green and asked, "Shields, are you coming?" "No," Green answered, "I believe I'll go with the old man." Green committed himself to the raid in the distant hope that somehow he might free his son in the process.

Another recruit was Osborne P. Anderson who, like Green, had met Brown at the Canadian gathering. Anderson was free-born from Chester County, Pennsylvania. He had worked as a printer with the *Provincial Freeman,* a black newspaper in Chatham, Ontario. Anderson survived the raid and returned to Canada. During the Civil War, in 1864, he enlisted, became a noncommissioned officer, and was mustered out at the close of the war in Washington, D.C.

By the time Anderson joined Brown in Chambersburg, Green and Dangerfield Newby, a former slave from Fauquier County, Virginia, were already there. Newby, like Green, had a very personal reason for wanting to join Brown. A blacksmith in his mid-forties, Newby had a wife, Harriet, and six children still in slavery in Virginia near Harpers Ferry. The preceding spring Harriet had written saying that the family was about to be sold into the deep South and begging her husband to come for her and the children, "for if you don't get me somebody else will." A wife's love was a powerful incentive to undertake the dangerous mission. "Their has ben one bright hope to cheer me in all my troubles, that is to be with you…," she wrote, "com this fall without fail." Shortly after receiving this last letter, Newby joined with Brown for the October raid, but he never reached his family. Dangerfield Newby was the first of the raiders killed at Harpers Ferry. Harriet and the children, the youngest just crawling, were sold to a Louisiana slave dealer.

Two other black men rode with John Brown, Lewis Sheridan Leary, and John Anthony Copeland Jr. They arrived in Chambersburg on October 12, four days before the raid. The men were relatives, both living in Oberlin, Ohio. Leary, a saddler and harness maker originally from Fayetteville, North Carolina, had lived in the college town of Oberlin for three years and had become active in the town's black community. He was a member of the debating society and was a vigorous reformer. "Men must suffer for a good cause," he argued in a speech before the young black men of Oberlin before he joined the Brown group. Leary had convinced his nephew John Copeland, a former student at Oberlin College and active abolitionist, to join the raid. Captured at the arsenal in Harpers Ferry, Copeland with Shields Green was tried, convicted, and hanged. Leary was wounded and died during the raid.

John Copeland was captured after the Harpers Ferry raid, tried, and found guilty of treason against the state of Virginia. He was executed in 1859. From his cell, he wrote this letter to his parents, telling them to "remember that if I must die I die in trying to liberate a few of my poor and oppress people from my condition of servitude...."

Harpers Ferry's location, at the convergence of two mighty rivers, and its situation on the Baltimore and Ohio railroad, one of the most important east-west transportation routes in the region, continued to make it a strategic target during the Civil War. In the spring of 1861, after Confederate troops attacked Fort Sumter in Charleston, South Carolina, Virginia troops attempted to take possession of the arms depot, the railroad, and the canal at Harpers Ferry. U.S. troops fought Confederates for control of the town and Maryland Heights, the high ground across the river. Almost 1,500 feet above the water, the heights offered a significant military advantage with its commanding view of the river and the surrounding area.

On April 18, 1861, less than twenty-four hours after Virginia seceded from the United States, U.S. troops set fire to the armory to keep some fifteen thousand weapons stored there out of Confederate hands. Confederate soldiers were able to extinguish the blaze before the buildings were completely destroyed, however, salvaging much of the machinery used for firearms production and shipping it south. Months later, when the Confederate troops were driven out of Harpers Ferry by

A Personal Call to Arms

Dangerfield Newby was forty-eight years old when he became part of John Brown's raiding party. He was born a slave in 1815, in Fauquier County, Virginia, the son of a white slaveholder. His father freed him, but his wife, Harriet, and their children remained enslaved in Virginia. Newby was the first of the raiders to die at Harpers Ferry. This letter, dated August 16, 1859, was found in his pocket. After the letter was found, Harriet Newby was sold to a Louisiana slave dealer.

Dear Husband—It is said Master is in want of money. If so, I know not what time he may sell me, and then all my bright hopes of the future are blasted, for there has been one bright hope to cheer me in all my troubles, that is to be with you. If I thought I should never see you this earth would have no charms for me. Come this fall without fail money or no money. Do all you can for me, which I have no doubt you will. The children are all well. The baby cannot walk yet. You must write soon and say when you think you can come—Your affectionate wife, Harriet Newby advancing U.S. forces, the site was burned again and the railroad bridge was destroyed. The town changed hands eight times between 1861 and 1865. In mid-September 1862, Confederates under the command of Thomas J. "Stonewall" Jackson surrounded the town capturing the U.S. garrison of some 12,500 troops. The U.S. Army took control again, however, in 1863 after their victory at the Battle of Antietam. U.S. soldiers pushed the Confederates back south, and gave President Lincoln the victory he needed to announce his intention to issue the Emancipation Proclamation.

For Harpers Ferry's black population, this constant shifting back and forth from U.S. to Confederate control was especially distressing. Both sides used forced black labor to build and rebuild fortifications, bridges, and other resources needed in the struggle. Some African Americans were even taken south by withdrawing Confederate forces. Finally, in 1863, U.S. forces gained sufficient control of the western region of Virginia to enable the area to break away. It became the thirty-fifth state, West Virginia, on June 20. By that time Lincoln had issued the Emancipation Proclamation, which freed all blacks held by masters disloyal to the United States as of January 1, 1863, and allowed the recruitment of black troops. African Americans from Harpers Ferry joined with more than two hundred West Virginia blacks to offer their service to the U.S. military. They were assigned to the 45th Regiment, U.S. Colored Troops from Pennsylvania. This regiment stood guard at Arlington Heights, defending Washington D.C. It was the only black unit to march in the procession at President Lincoln's second inauguration.

Meanwhile, Harpers Ferry became a major center of refuge for slaves escaping from Virginia and farther south. Thousands of refuges, called contraband, poured into the small town, swelling its black population dramatically and drawing northern reformers who came south to minister to the needs of freedmen during and after the war. Baptist missionaries from New England procured several vacant armory buildings on Camp Hill overlooking the town, where in 1867 they established Storer College, a school open to male and female students of all races. In 1881, Frederick Douglass, then a

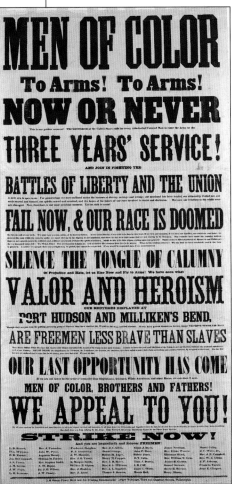

An 1863 broadside calls on black men to join the Union forces in the fight against the Confederacy and asks, "Are Freemen less brave than slaves"? Throughout the South, thousands of slaves fled from their masters to join the Union forces.

White abolitionist Robert Gould Shaw leads the black soldiers of the 54th Massachusetts Regiment in an attack against Confederate forces at Fort Wagner, South Carolina. When the Emancipation Proclamation freed slaves in states disloyal to the Union, more black troops were formed, and men from Harpers Ferry were among those who joined the U.S. military.

trustee of the college, addressed the students, delivering a moving and dramatic lecture dedicated to the memory of John Brown.

For African Americans, John Brown and Harpers Ferry itself remained a symbol of their struggle for freedom. For the students and faculty of Storer College, their location in Harpers Ferry emphasized a special connection to the campaign against slavery, and many set about highlighting that connection in a variety of ways. In 1903 the college began to raise funds to purchase a building referred to as John Brown's Fort. This one-story brick building initially constructed in 1848 for use as a fire station and guardhouse was the structure in which Brown and his men had taken shelter and made their defense in the final hours of the raid. Miraculously, the building survived the devastation that Harpers Ferry endured during the Civil War.

In the 1890s, John Brown's Fort was dismantled and transported to Chicago, where it was displayed at the World's Columbian Exposition. Apparently, the building was not a very popular exhibit, and African Americans argued for its return to Harpers Ferry. Storer students and college administrators joined in the effort, and on the fiftieth anniversary of John Brown's raid the fort was moved to the college. It was erected on Camp Hill, where, during the Civil War, both Confederate and U.S. armies had paraded their troops at one time or another.

John Brown's Fort was returned to Harpers Ferry in the midst of the continuing struggle for African American freedom. Just a few years before, on that ground, the campaign had gained new momentum. In the late summer of 1906, black leaders gathered in Harpers Ferry in the second meeting of a protest organization founded just a year before in Niagara Falls, Canada. The organization became known as the Niagara Movement. Among the more than one hundred distinguished attendees were the great black scholar and philosopher W. E. B. DuBois; the lawyer Richard T. Greener, the first black graduate of Harvard University and former U.S. consul to Russia; and the Civil War veteran Lewis Douglass, son of Frederick Douglass.

At the meeting, the leaders passed resolutions demanding the full voting rights promised in the Fifteenth Amendment to the Constitution, passed during the years after the Civil War, but often denied by violence or cleverly constructed state regulations. They also called for an end to racial discrimination in public accommodations, the enforcement of African American civil rights, and legal protection from violence for black people. Setting their demands in the historic context of the place, they marched at dawn in a candlelight procession, barefoot over the ground made sacred by the actions of John Brown. Their march concluded at the engine house where he had made his stand. There, they sang "The Battle Hymn of the Republic." From this core group, whites and blacks committed to civil rights established the National Association for the Advancement of Colored People three years later on the birthday of Abraham Lincoln.

In 1944 the 2,300-acre site that covers areas of West Virginia, Maryland, and Virginia, just sixty-five miles northeast of Washington, D.C., was designated Harpers Ferry National Historic Park and became a part of the National Park System. Under the stewardship of the park service, there has been a substantial restoration of the old town of Harpers Ferry. In 1960 the park service acquired John Brown's Fort and eight years later moved it from Camp Hill back to the lower town. The structure was not returned to its nineteenth-century

In 1968, John Brown's Fort was moved to its present location, about 150 feet east of its original site. The brick building, originally covered with slate and featuring copper gutters, was the only armory building to survive the Civil War.

location, however, because that site was covered with a railroad embankment in 1894. The present structure is just 150 feet east of the site it occupied when John Brown and his men sought cover there more than 150 years ago.

John Brown's story is central to the history of Harpers Ferry, but the village also tells the story of African America in the critical middle decades of the nineteenth century. The African American history of the village does not end with the Civil War. In October 1867, the Home Mission Society of the Free Baptist Church founded Storer Normal School, which later became Storer College. For the African American graduates of Storer College, education was a route toward intellectual and spiritual transformation. Harpers Ferry was in many ways a typical nineteenth-century working-class town. John Brown's raid changed the place, making it a critical landmark of African American history and hollowed ground for African Americans.

An 1870 lithograph celebrates passage of the Fifteenth Amendment, which granted black men the right to vote. In the bottom right, black and white representatives work together in the legislature; in the panel next to it, black men fill out ballots and cast their votes.

RELATED SITES

The monument to John Brown's black followers in Oberlin, Ohio.

PORT HUDSON

756 West Plains–Port Hudson
 Road
Zachary, LA 70791
888-677-3400
*www.cr.nps.gov/nr/travel/
 louisiana/por.htm*
NHL

For forty-eight days, starting on May 23, 1863, 30,000 U.S. troops battled 6,800 Confederates at Port Hudson, where the mouth of the Red River joins the Mississippi River in Louisiana. Almost five miles of fortified trenches protected the Confederate forces against the advancing U.S. troops, making a frontal assault on Port Hudson almost suicidal. It was the bloodiest fighting in the entire Civil War, and the longest siege in American military history. Among the initial wave of U.S. troops attacking the Confederate fortifications were two African American regiments, the 1st and 3rd Louisiana Native Guards. They paid a heavy price—155 wounded, 116 missing, and 37 killed— fighting for the United States and the respect of white America for themselves and their race.

FORT PILLOW STATE PARK

3122 Park Road
Henning, TN 38041
731-738-5581
*www.state.tn.us/environment/
 parks/parks/FortPillow/*

During the Civil War, southern commanders took few black prisoners, and executed many of those they did take. At Fort Pillow, Tennessee, in the spring of 1864, Confederate forces commanded by General Nathan Bedford Forrest slaughtered hundreds of captured U.S. troops, about half of whom were African American. The fort was manned by 295 white troops of the 13th Tennessee Cavalry and 265 African Americans from the 11th U.S. Colored Troops. Reportedly, Forrest was angered by the fort's refusal to surrender and infuriated by the taunts of the garrison's black soldiers. The Confederates, with more than twice as many men, overran the garrison and then conducted a bloody massacre. Although some soldiers were reluctant to indulge in the carnage, testimony before an 1864 Congressional committee investigating the events at Fort Pillow, revealed that Forrest "ordered [the captured U.S. troops] shot down like dogs." His men complied, clubbing the wounded to death, burning some alive, and nailing others to walls. African American soldiers were singled out for special punishment and were killed disproportionately. About one third of the white U.S. troops were killed while 64 percent of the black soldiers lost their lives.

Northern newspapers carried outraged headlines of the "Fort Pillow Massacre." The *New York Tribune* referred to Forrest—who had been a slave trader before the war and was one of the organizers of the Ku Klux Klan after the war—as "Butcher Forrest." Less than a week after the massacre, 1,200 black troops in Memphis fell on their knees to take an oath of revenge. "Remember Fort Pillow" became their rallying cry.

A MONUMENT TO THE BLACK FOLLOWERS OF JOHN BROWN

Martin Luther King Jr. Park
East Vine Street
Oberlin, OH 44074

Originally erected in 1865 in Westwood Cemetery in Oberlin, Ohio, by Oberlin students and their supporters, this monument honors the three Oberlin blacks who followed John Brown in the 1859 raid on Harpers Ferry. In 1971, the monument was moved to Martin Luther King Jr. Park on the corner of Park and East Vine streets. The inscription reads: These colored citizens of Oberlin, the heroic associates of the immortal John Brown, gave their lives for the slave. Et nunc servitudo etiam mortua est, laus deo. S. Green died at Charleston, Va., Dec. 16, 1859, age 23 years. J.S. Copeland died at Charleston, Va., Dec. 16, 1859, age 25 years. L.S. Leary died at Harper's Ferry, Va., Oct. 20, 1859, age 24 years.

Cedar Hill, Frederick Douglass National Historic Site

Washington, D.C.

Home of the Black Sage of Nineteenth-Century America

Frederick Douglass (above) purchased this home in Southeast Washington, D.C., after he had gained international fame as an antislavery crusader and, after the Civil War, as a spokesman for African American rights. From his home, he prepared speeches and essays in support of a variety of other reform causes as well, including women's rights, temperance, and the end of capital punishment.

Cedar Hill, as Frederick Douglass called it, was a beautiful, unpretentious white-frame, fourteen-room country cottage set in the Anacostia Hills across the Anacostia River from Washington, D.C. From the front porch of this handsome two-and-one-half story Victorian home, the sweeping view of Washington, which included the U.S. Capitol, was stunning. This was a fine and fitting home for Douglass, the former slave whose writings and international lecture tours on behalf of the abolition of slavery and his support of the U.S. cause during the Civil War made him one of the world's best-known black Americans.

The house was originally built in 1859 on a nine-and-one-half acre lot by the Union Land Association, a real estate development company. John W. Van Hook, a partner in the firm, lived in the home for almost fifteen years, until 1877, when it became the property of the Freedman's Savings and Trust Company. During the 1870s, when soaring real estate prices pushed the average cost of property from two thousand to three thousand dollars by decade's end, Douglass purchased the home from the Trust Company in 1878 for the handsome sum of $6,700. He and his family moved in immediately, and over the next few years enlarged the home from fourteen to twenty-one rooms. He installed a china closet, added many trees and outbuildings, and purchased five and three-quarters additional acres.

The purchase of this home was a milestone in Douglass's life, the outward sign of his curious personification of the American self-made man. With strong hands, sharp mind, gifted tongue, and ravenous intellect, he worked, studied, and talked his way up from bondage to this level of Victorian gentility. Born a slave on the Eastern Shore of Maryland in 1818, he was originally given the name Frederick Augustus Washington Bailey. Unmistakably bright as a young boy, Frederick was the son of the slave Harriet Bailey. He was never certain of his father's identity, but his own light skin color and the stories he heard from other slaves convinced him that his father was white. As a young boy, he was separated from his mother, who worked on a plantation twelve miles away. She could make only brief and infrequent visits, walking the distance at night after working a full day. Mother and son were together for the last time in early 1825.

The next year his master sent young Frederick to work for a family in Baltimore. There, though it was illegal, his new master's wife taught him to read. He fell in love with learning and books. By the time he was thirteen years old, Frederick bought his first book, *The Columbian Orator,* a collection of great speeches and a manual on oration. Shortly after that, he joined Bethel African Methodist Episcopal Church, but within the year he was forced to leave Baltimore. He was sent to work on a plantation in St. Michael, Maryland. There, Frederick encountered Edward Covey, "the slave breaker" under whom he suffered many brutal beatings. Finally, refusing to passively suffer the lash, the teenager confronted his tormentor. The two struggled and Frederick emerged the winner. It was the last time that Covey attempted to beat his charge. As Douglass later recalled in his autobiography, *The Life and Times of Frederick Douglass*, "I was a man now."

In 1836, he was returned to Baltimore after attempting to escape from bondage in St. Michael. Now in his late teens, Frederick took advantage of every opportunity open to a slave in an urban setting with a substantial free black population. He learned the caulking trade, waterproofing boats as an apprentice, and joined a black debating society, indulging his continuing hunger for knowledge. Twenty-year-old Douglass met and fell in love with a free woman, Anna Murray, with whom he

Cedar Hill, Frederick Douglass National Historic Site

1411 West Street SE
Washington, DC 20020
202-426-5961
www.nps.gov/frdo/index.htm
NRIS 66000033
NPS

DATE BUILT
1859

SIGNIFICANCE
Cedar Hill served as the home of Frederick Douglas from 1878 until his death in 1895.

would share most of his life. In September 1838, with her help and that of a black sailor who gave Douglass his identity papers for the venture, Frederick escaped from the South and slavery forever. Less than two weeks later, he and Anna were married in New York City, and soon after the couple moved to New Bedford, Massachusetts. It was in this new free life, that Frederick Bailey began to call himself Frederick Douglass. Nathan Johnson, Douglass's friend and host in New Bedford selected the name Douglass for him. Douglass had called himself Johnson for a short time before that.

It was in his new home, in March 1839, that as a freeman Douglass first spoke publicly about his life in slavery. At a meeting in the African Methodist Episcopal Zion Church in New Bedford, Douglass rose to denounce the American Colonization Society plan to settle American blacks in West Africa. He told his story of slavery, arguing that African Americans were Americans and should not be sent away from their homeland, but must be freed in it. His remarks were reported in an issue of the fiery abolitionist Boston newspaper, the *Liberator,* and the abolitionist community took note of this former slave. Prominent white abolitionists asked Douglass to tell his story at antislavery meetings, and he soon became a favorite, for he could talk about slavery with the passion of one who had lived the experience.

William Lloyd Garrison, whose strong condemnation of slaveholders and whose advocacy of civil rights for African Americans made him the most notoriously radical white abolitionist leader of that time, was also the publisher of the *Liberator.* He was so impressed with Douglass that he hired him as a traveling speaker for the Massachusetts Antislavery Society for a three-month trial period. The relationship was long lasting. Abolition became Douglass's central cause, and he became pivotal to the national and international abolitionist movements. During the next few years Douglass lectured exhaustively throughout New England and the North, and in Great Britain, presenting the message of abolition. He soon became antislavery's most effective exhibit in the argument for human freedom.

His first autobiography, *The Narrative of Frederick Douglass,* published in 1845, sold five thousand copies in its first four months. Shortly after its publication, Douglass traveled to England and Scotland promoting its sales and lecturing on behalf of abolition. It was while he was in Britain that British abolitionist friends and colleagues realized that with his new international notoriety, this fugitive slave was in considerable danger of capture and re-enslavement. They bought Douglass's freedom despite the fact that, as some argued, purchasing a slave's freedom seemed to legitimate a slaveholder's right to human property. Still, in this case, the obvious danger that Douglass faced as a fugitive outweighed principle, and papers filed in Baltimore in 1846 designated Frederick Douglass legally free.

Much of this public recognition resulted from his effectiveness as an abolitionist speaker and his more than thirty years as a newspaper editor. Starting with a newspaper, the *North Star,* that he began publishing in Rochester, New York, in 1847, editorial writing filled the major part of Douglass's professional life. The English word, spoken and written, was his weapon against slavery, and he employed it with considerable power. Some white abolitionists criticized him for establishing a newspaper that would be in direct competition with Garrison's

In 144 pages, Frederick Douglass described his life as a slave and his escape from the South in his first auto-biography, published in 1845. Before the book appeared, Douglass's eloquent, analytical speeches calling for an end to slavery—as well as his concealment of some facts in order to avoid being captured—had caused some critics to wonder if such an impressive speaker could really have been a slave.

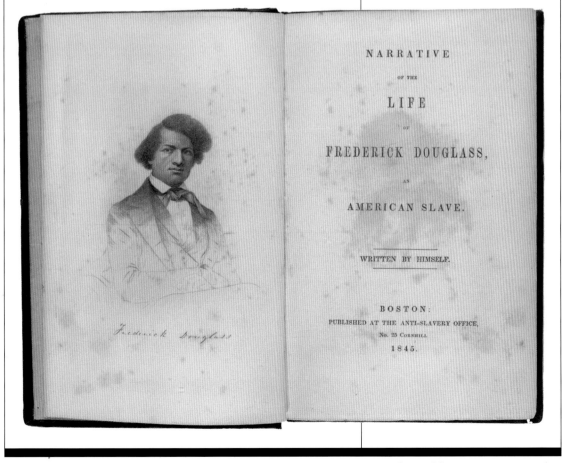

NARRATIVE

OF THE

LIFE

OF

FREDERICK DOUGLASS,

AN

AMERICAN SLAVE.

WRITTEN BY HIMSELF.

BOSTON:
PUBLISHED AT THE ANTI-SLAVERY OFFICE,
No. 25 CORNHILL
1845.

Liberator. Indeed, Douglass's growing reputation and his increasing independence from Garrison's commitment to nonpolitical, nonviolent abolition caused tensions within the antislavery movement.

By the late 1840s, Douglass was changing, moving toward an abolitionist stand that included the use of party politics and a new interpretation of the U.S. Constitution that rejected Garrison's view that it protected slavery. Although slaveholders might misinterpret and misuse the Constitution to support slavery, Douglass believed it was an antislavery document that guaranteed the right of human freedom. By 1850 Douglass had met with the radical abolitionist John Brown and was impressed with Brown's commitment to antislavery action that might include the use of violence. Douglass publicly endorsed the right of a fugitive slave to use violence if necessary in defense of self and family. After Congress passed the Fugitive Slave Law of 1850, which stripped those accused of being fugitive slaves of all rights to trial or even to speak in their own defense, Douglass joined many abolitionists who were stepping over the line of nonviolence. At an October meeting at Boston's Faneuil Hall, abolitionists vowed to stand with fugitives regardless of the new law. As the *Liberator* reported, Douglass warned that should "this law be put into operation . . . the streets of Boston . . . would be running with blood."

Before the 1850s ended, Douglass was convinced that slavery would only be abolished through violent means. He welcomed a war against the slaveholding South and even discussed plans for a raid on Harpers Ferry, Virginia, with John Brown. Douglass did not join Brown and his party, however, because he saw their plan to encourage a general slave rebellion in western Virginia as too dangerous. Such action, he believed, would ultimately be met by the power of U.S. military, and would result in the slaughter of those who rebelled. Even

Frederick Douglass (to the left of the table) attends an antislavery convention in Cazenovia, New York, in 1845. Douglass traveled throughout New England and New York State in the early 1840s and gave hundreds of speeches. Even in the North, however, abolition was a controversial topic, and Douglass and his fellow speakers often faced hecklers and insults, and had rotten vegetables thrown at them.

so, after the raid failed he was sought as an accomplice and forced to flee the country. For six months, Douglass lived in England until the death of his youngest child, Annie, then ten years old, brought him back to the United States in 1860.

This was an election year, and the Republicans nominated Abraham Lincoln for the Presidency. Douglass had favored the Republican John C. Fremont in his unsuccessful run for the Presidency in 1856, and he was relieved to see Lincoln capture the White House four years later. A month after Lincoln's election, South Carolina announced that it would withdraw from the nation, and in February 1861 six other southern states seceded from the United States to form the Confederate States of America.

Douglass welcomed the news of southern secession. He saw it as an opening for the federal government to move against slavery. Since the mid-1850s free blacks had anticipated a war between the "Slave Power," as they called the South, and the forces of freedom. In the last half of the decade they formed military units in northern cities and trained for battle. Boston's Massasoit Guards, New York's Attucks Guards, Cincinnati's Attucks Blues, and similar units announced their readiness to serve in a holy war against slavery "with a bible in one hand and a gun in the other." The abolition of slavery was impossible, they knew, so long as slaveholders could exercise their considerable power over national politics. It was southern secession that made the ending of human bondage practical.

In his third and last autobiography, *The Life and Times of Frederick Douglass*, penned during the 1880s in the seclusion of his Cedar Hill study, Douglass told the story of these early crucial years of the Civil War. Black leaders immediately demanded that African American troops be enlisted to put down what Douglass termed "the slaveholders' rebellion." Although Lincoln and the U.S. War Department initially refused to accept black soldiers, the sheer horror of the human loss moved the Lincoln administration to reconsider its stand against black enlistment. In the summer of 1862 Congress authorized the President to accept African Americans for military service and several black units in Kansas and New Orleans were officially enlisted.

After Lincoln issued the Emancipation Proclamation in January 1863, tens of thousands more blacks joined the U.S. cause. Douglass traveled to the North recruiting black troops, and two of his sons, Lewis and Charles, were among the first to enlist. Recruiting black men into military service was not an easy task given the War Department's treatment of black soldiers. African American soldiers received less pay than whites at comparable ranks, and they were generally expected to serve under white commissioned officers, as very few blacks were commissioned as officers. Additionally, in the spring of 1863, the Confederacy announced that it would treat captured black soldiers and their white officers as criminals and that black prisoners of war would be killed or enslaved. Douglass stopped recruiting in protest of the U.S. government's unfair treatment of black soldiers. Finally in June 1864, Congress equalized the pay, equipment, and medical service available to American soldiers regardless of their race.

When Lincoln ran for a second term in 1864, he asked Douglass to advise him on the campaign and on methods that might speed and secure emancipation for the larger numbers of slaves still held in the Confederacy. Douglass also traveled and spoke in support of the war effort, calling it a holy crusade for human freedom and a second American Revolution. By the time victory came in the spring of 1865, Douglass and millions of other African Americans and progressive white Americans expected that the end of slavery would bring an American rebirth of liberal ideals. Lincoln's assassination and the ascendancy of Vice President Andrew Johnson to the presidency, however, dampened their hopes. Initial impressions of Johnson were not encouraging.

In 1866, Douglass, as a part of an African American delegation, met with Johnson at the White House. The new President was less than accommodating to the distinguished group of black leaders. He expressed support for the restrictive black codes used by

Douglass's sons Lewis (left) and Charles both served in the 54th Regiment from Massachusetts, after their father recruited them for the army. Lewis became the regiment's first sergeant major and participated in the bloody, failed assault on Fort Wagner, South Carolina—from which he was one of the few to return unharmed.

the new post-war southern governments. These codes were intended to maintain control over former slaves and were deemed necessary for the welfare of the majority of southern people. However, as one of the delegation pointed out, in South Carolina—where provisions written into the state constitution, called black codes, were most racially restrictive—the majority of people were black. Johnson refused to engage in debate, and dismissed the delegate's argument without comment. Douglass had only contempt for this former Democrat from Tennessee—the Democratic Party was the traditional party of southern interests—who filled out the remainder of Lincoln's presidential term. Johnson had promised to punish the former Confederates, those who Douglass called "the guiltiest of traitors." Instead, the president issued wholesale pardons to those who just months before had been the enemies of the United States, and sided with the former enemy in restricting the rights of blacks who had successfully defended the nation.

Yet despite the resistance of the Johnson administration, the early years of Reconstruction showed considerable promise. The Thirteenth Amendment, passed in 1865, prohibited slavery. The Fourteenth Amendment, passed in 1866 and ratified in 1868, nullified the Supreme Court's 1857 *Dred Scott* decision by banning the use of race as a bar to citizenship. And the Fifteenth Amendment, passed in 1869 and ratified in 1870, prohibited the use of race to deny men the right to vote. During these years, Douglass worked with the radical Republican plan to aid the former slaves' transition to freedom, to protect their new freedom from southern whites determined to resurrect bondage, and to reconstruct the South around the principle of African American citizenship rights. He encouraged black voting and supported blacks running for political office, and in the Presidential election of 1868 he successfully campaigned for the Republican candidate, Ulysses S. Grant.

In 1872, after a suspicious fire destroyed their home in Rochester, New York, Frederick and Anna Douglass moved to Washington D.C. Initially they settled in a row house on Capitol Hill, just north of where the Library of Congress now stands. During his first two years in Washington, Douglass published the *New National Era,* a newspaper dedicated to uplifting former slaves during Reconstruction. Then, in 1874, he was named president of the Freedmen's Savings and Trust Company. Soon after, economic tragedy struck.

Established in 1865 to serve the needs of newly freed blacks in the post-emancipation South, the savings and trust company, commonly called the Freedmen's Bank, had wavered almost from its inception. Speculative loans and risky investments eroded its financial health. In 1873, the year before Douglass took office, banks nationwide were racked by a severe economic panic. The Freedmen's Bank was especially hard hit. The appointment of an internationally notable black leader to its presidency was a last-minute effort to save the institution. The strategy failed.

Within a few months of Douglass's appointment, the bank went under, leaving destitute hundreds of poor African Americans who had placed the few dollars they had in the bank's care. Douglass also suffered serious financial losses. To make matters worse, some blamed him for the calamity. The black reformer and politician John Mercer Langston charged that Douglass was responsible because his presence in the bank's leadership had led black people to trust an institution that ultimately stripped them of their savings.

The economic downturn that challenged the nation in the early 1870s struck the Douglass household in other ways as well. Douglass's adult children appealed to their father for financial assistance he could ill afford to provide, and in the fall of 1874, *New National Era* faltered when promised financial backing did not materialize. Lecture tours brought in some money, but Douglass took on so much traveling that his family feared it would endanger his health. Then, in 1877, the U.S. Senate confirmed his appointment by President Rutherford B. Hayes as U.S. marshal for the District of Columbia. Among other duties, the position involved ceremonial responsibilities such as leading the presidential inaugural procession through the rotunda of the Capitol. It was a proud moment not only for Douglass and his family, but for all African Americans.

Congratulations poured in from around the country. Old friends from Rochester and Boston and admirers from New York and Pennsylvania all but overwhelmed him with letters and telegrams. Harriet Jacobs, a former slave who had become well known for her widely read autobiography, wrote from Cambridge, Massachusetts,

"There is not a man living that I should so rejoice to see hold this position at the Capitol of the Nation." There was also a very practical consequence of the appointment—finally, his finances were stable. In that year, Douglass purchased Cedar Hill, his final home, a white house situated on a hill fifty feet above the Anacostia section of Washington, D.C., one of the few integrated neighborhoods in the city at that time. Here, Douglass spent the last seventeen years of his life, as actively committed to the cause of human freedom as ever.

In the last of his three autobiographies, Douglass fondly remembered his family life at Cedar Hill. The three Douglass sons, Lewis, Charles, and Frederick Jr., lived in Anacostia not too far from their parent's new home, and were active in the community. Charles served on the county board of trustees and was active in local education. He provided the land for a local school, and from 1871 to 1874 he was a member of the local school board. With family close by, Cedar Hill became a gathering place for three generations of Douglass's. There, many "family battles," as Douglass affectionately termed them, were played out on the croquet lawn, and grandchildren roamed the grounds during family picnics and parties.

The house, always tidy and clean, reflected Anna's passion for order as well as Frederick's passion for collecting. He collected not only books, many of which were autographed by their authors or those who gave them as gifts, but also souvenirs from his travels in Europe. In Germany, Douglass had purchased a finely crafted violin at a cost of one thousand dollars. He later presented the instrument to his grandson Joseph Henry Douglass. Douglass had tutored Joeseph Henry in violin as a child, and he became the first black American touring concert violinist and the first to record his music. Douglass also collected walking canes. One particularly prized cane had belonged to Abraham Lincoln and was

With an eye for a well-made object, Douglass purchased this violin in Germany. A label inside the instrument indicates that it is a copy of a Stradivarius, the Italian violin considered to be the finest ever made.

given to Douglass as a gift by Mary Todd Lincoln after the assassination of her husband. The mantel of his study was covered with busts of friends and luminaries and pictures of friends and associates, including one of John Brown, decorated the walls.

During the late 1870s and early 1880s Douglass treasured the visits of his grandchildren and the opportunity to be a family man. There were also visits from long-time friends and political allies, such as former slave, Underground Railroad conductor, and U.S. Army scout Harriet Tubman and leaders of the woman suffrage movement, including Elizabeth Cady Stanton and Susan B. Anthony. By all accounts Cedar Hill was a busy place. Yet, Douglass also valued those moments when he retired to the solitude of his study where he wrote speeches and articles on American race relations, the rise of the Jim Crow system of legalized racial segregation, and women's rights. His services were in great demand during these years, however, and his writing was often interrupted, as in 1881 when President James Garfield appointed him recorder of deeds for the District of Columbia, responsible for maintaining the land records for Washington.

Then in the summer of 1882, after a long bout with rheumatism, Anna Murray Douglass, his wife of forty-four years, died. Her death hit her children hard and staggered her husband. She had been a major point of stability in all their lives. For Douglass, she had not only been his partner for almost all his adult life, she had also been his connection to his life before freedom, before his rise to international acclaim. For a time, Douglass left Washington, and sought sanctuary in New England to escape the sorrow of the place that had been Anna's last home.

He returned to Cedar Hill in early 1884, and, to the horror of some of his friends and to members of his family, the sixty-six-year-old Douglass, that same year, married Helen Pitts, the forty-six-year-old secretary at the office of the District Recorder of Deeds. Remarrying barely eighteen months after Anna's death was scandalous for some, but the fact that Helen Pitts was white, and a woman with whom Douglass had worked while he was still married, was too much for many. In her book *My Mother as I Recall Her,* published in 1900, Rosetta, his oldest daughter, wrote it was "a bad time for

Anna Murrray Douglass: Reformer in Her Own Right

In 1813, Anna Murray became the first person in her family to be born free. Barely one month before her birth, her parents were freed, giving her that status as well. She lived near Denton, in eastern Maryland, until she was seventeen, when she moved to Baltimore to work as a maid. She was active in what at the time was called "racial uplift," becoming a member of the East Baltimore Improvement Society, an African American mutual aid society. At twenty-five she met Frederick Augustus Washington Bailey, a slave five years her junior who was living in Baltimore with his owner and working as a laborer. She fell in love with him, provided him the money he needed to escape, and later joined him in New York City, where they married. He changed his name and she became Anna Murray Douglass.

The life of Anna Douglass is often overlooked, obscured by the shadow of her husband. Yet, she was an active reformer in her own right. While the family lived in Massachusetts, Anna worked with the Female Abolitionist Society to mount the annual Boston Anti-Slavery Fairs, which raised money crucial to financing antislavery work. Her friends and associates, such as Wendell Phillips and William Lloyd Garrison, included some of the most important abolitionists in Boston. When her husband made a unilateral decision to move the family to Rochester, New York, she was not at all happy to leave her work in Massachusetts. Still, she was able to pick up her work in their new home and filled her time with reform activities and running her household.

She not only raised five children and conducted all the household affairs, but also worked as a shoe binder to help support the family while her husband, Frederick, was

Frederick Douglass was devoted to his wife Anna. In My Mother as I Recall Her, *Rosetta Douglass wrote that the story of her respected father and his "hopes and aspirations and longing desire for freedom . . . was a story made possible through the unswerving loyalty of Anna Murray."*

busy making an international reputation as an antislavery speaker, author, and newspaper editor. Throughout their marriage of forty-four years, Frederick's speaking duties took him away from the family for extended periods. During the 1840s, when he spent almost two years lecturing in England, Anna supervised family affairs alone. Their daughter Rosetta Douglass wrote in her 1900 book, *My Mother as I Recall Her* of her mother's willingness to manage the house, to take pride in the knowledge that "when he [Frederick] stood up before an audience that his linen was immaculate and that she had made it so." "Father was mother's honored guest," Rosetta explained. "He was from home so often that his homecomings were events that she thought worthy of extra notice. Everything was done to add to his comfort."

us," and many blacks as well as whites were highly critical of this interracial marriage. Yet, visitors to Cedar Hill found the couple deeply devoted to each other. Reverend Francis J. Grimké, pastor of Washington's Fifteenth Street Presbyterian Church and member of a well-known abolitionist family, visited Cedar Hill often and in a letter written after Douglass's death, he reported spending "many pleasant days with Mr. and Mrs. Douglass at their beautiful home at Cedar Hill."

As the furor settled, and despite the continued disapproval of some of the Douglass children, Cedar Hill once again became a happy family gathering place. Requests for Douglass's presence and lectures at political and social gatherings resumed, and opportunities for political involvement in local organizations and public activities again filled his life. Soon, Cedar Hill also hosted a variety of Washington's elites, literary figures, and old friends from the abolitionist movement. Advice from the Black Sage of Anacostia, as Douglas came to be known, was in great demand. While Helen's father, a wealthy farmer from New York State and former abolitionist, continued to disapprove of her marriage, other

Douglass and his second wife, Helen Pitts Douglass, pose at Niagara Falls, probably in the summer of 1884. In responding to the controversy surrounding his marriage to a white woman, Douglass claimed that his first marriage had honored his mother's race and his second one would honor his father's. The light-skinned Douglass never knew his father, but he believed him to be a white man.

members of her family became regular visitors at Cedar Hill. Her mother actually moved into the home shortly after Helen and Frederick married, sharing Cedar Hill with the couple and their dog, a mastiff, their devoted and constant companion.

For a decade the couple lived an active and happy life in this home in Anacostia, which was then a growing suburb of Washington. They left periodically, traveling together in Europe and Africa in 1886 and 1887 and then, a year after their return, Douglass was appointed minister to Haiti. The late 1880s and early 1890s, the years of his ministry, were critical years for the only independent black republic in the Western Hemisphere. It was a time of political unrest, as one after another, Haitian rulers were forced from office or killed. It was also a time when U.S. imperialists were casting their eyes toward the Caribbean. Through these years, Cedar Hill remained the Douglass's home base, and they tried to return for at least part of the year even in the spring of 1891, when Helen was taken seriously ill in Port-au-Prince. They were at Cedar Hill in the early winter of 1895.

In late February of that winter, Douglass took a carriage from his home into the city to attend an international rally on behalf of women's rights. Susan B. Anthony, Anna Shaw, and other widely known leaders of the movement greeted him and escorted him to the platform, treating him with the respect due one who had supported the cause for decades. He left the rally early and returned to Cedar Hill to prepare for the evening. He and Helen had plans to attend a church gathering in Anacostia. After supper, while they waited for the carriage, Douglass joked about a speaker he had heard earlier that day. He was playful and energetic and then he fell to the floor. On the evening of February 20, 1895, Frederick Douglass, then seventy-seven years old, died of a heart attack.

Shocked friends and admirers visited Cedar Hill to pay their respects. Public funeral services were held at Metropolitan A.M.E. Church in downtown Washington. Private services open only to family and a few close friends were conducted in the North Room of the home, next to Douglass's study. From this point on Cedar Hill took on a sacred character for Helen. She memorialized the home and all her husband's personal effects, his chair, his desk, his croquet grounds. She envisioned Cedar

A white-haired Frederick Douglass works in his book-lined study at Cedar Hill shortly before his death. He remained busy until the end of his life, drafting speeches and articles and fighting for such causes as an anti-lynching law. When a young black man asked him for advice before starting out in the world, Douglass is said to have replied, "Agitate! Agitate! Agitate!"

Hill, as was later reported in the *Fellowship Herald,* a local newspaper, a "Mt. Vernon for the colored race."

Douglass had left Cedar Hill to Helen in his will, but because he had not had the document witnessed by three people, as required by D.C. law, his children, all of whom had been born to Anna, contested Helen's claim to the property. Undeterred, she set about buying the home from her stepchildren in order to create a memorial to their father. In the years after Douglass's death she borrowed and, with the assistance of African American organizations such as the National Federation of Colored Women's Clubs, raised the funds to preserve the home and grounds as a national shrine. Although her relationship with her stepmother remained strained, Rosetta Douglass also took part in the fundraising effort. As a result of their efforts, in 1900, Congress chartered the Frederick Douglass Memorial and Historical Association.

Helen was never able to pay off the mortgage on Cedar Hill, but others carried on the effort after she died in 1903. Booker T. Washington, the anti-lynching crusader Ida Wells Barnett, and many other black leaders of the early twentieth century joined in the effort to retire the debt on Cedar Hill and thus preserve its memorial status. Finally, in 1921–22 the Frederick Douglass Memorial and Historical Association and the National Federation of Colored Women's Clubs raised the funds necessary to secure and restore the property. They administered the site until 1962, when the federal government took over its administration and, after a second restoration, Cedar Hill reopened as a National Park Service property in 1972.

Today it stands as a magnificent example of a nineteenth-century Victorian home. Ninety percent of the furnishings are original, including the books and pictures in Douglass's study, the comfortable period furniture, and his impressive art collection, which included a portrait of John Brown. His personal possessions are on display, and the home is decorated with reminders of his activist career and of his fellow reformers. Even the set of weights Douglass used to maintain his physical condition remain as if waiting for his regular workout. A cameo of his old friend and abolitionist co-worker Maria Weston Chapman in the parlor no doubt reminded him of the woman who for years managed the offices of the *Liberator*. In the study, his intellectual work space, hang pictures of Gerrit Smith, an abolitionist friend and a major financial backer of the movement; William Lloyd Garrison, mentor, friend, and sometime rival; and Joseph Cinque, African leader of the slave revolt aboard the slave ship *Amistad*. The walls of books in several languages include Alexander Dumas's *The Three Musketeers*, one of Douglass's favorites, and a copy of his first autobiography, *The Narrative of the Life of Frederick Douglass*.

Cedar Hill is the symbol of a man who believed in the American dream as set out in the Declaration of Independence:

> We hold these Truths to be self-evident, that all Men are created equal, that they are endowed by their Creator with certain unalienable Rights, that among these are Life, Liberty and the Pursuit of Happiness — That to secure these Rights, Governments are instituted among Men, deriving their just Powers from the Consent of the Governed.

Frederick Douglass carried on much of his crusade for that dream of liberty and equality from his home at Cedar Hill. It was a family center, a place of planning and intellectual contemplation, and a place of political struggle. As Douglass told an audience in Canandaigua, New York, in 1857 and constantly reminded all Americans, "if there is no struggle, there is no progress." Cedar Hill remains a memorial to its best-known owner, a historic site dedicated to human progress.

HARRIET TUBMAN HOUSE

180 South Street
Auburn, NY 13201
315-252-2081
www.nyhistory.com/
  harriettubman
NHL

Even after she purchased this comfortable home in Auburn, New York, Harriet Tubman continued to travel to the South to help slaves escape and to offer her services to the Union Army. Although illiterate, she was a natural, disciplined leader who felt comfortable navigating the terrain of the East Coast.

Harriet Ross was born a slave in 1819 or 1820, in Dorchester County, Maryland, not far from the birthplace of Frederick Douglass. She was twenty-five years old when she married John Tubman, a free black man, and thirty when she escaped from slavery. Not content with freedom simply for herself she made numerous trips into the South to rescue members of her family and many others from slavery, at least three hundred in all. She became the legendary Moses of her people. In 1857, she brought her parents from St. Catharines, in Ontario, Canada, to live in her home in Auburn, New York. William H. Seward, then a U.S. senator from New York, sold her the house for a modest sum.

During the Civil War, Tubman worked with the U.S. military as a spy, scout, and nurse. She also led soldiers in a military campaign in South Carolina. After John Tubman died in 1867, she later married a soldier, Nelson Davis, whom she met in South Carolina during the war. Their wedding was held in Auburn in 1869, and they lived in the brick house on South Street, which now serves as the home of the resident manager of the Harriet Tubman historic site. Davis died in 1888, but Tubman continued to live in the home, taking in and caring for African Americans in need. In 1896, she was able to raise the money to purchase the twenty-five acres of land on which that house stands. Tubman received a pension of twenty dollars a month for her service during the Civil War, which enabled her to move into a two-and-a-half story clapboard structure on her new property and to support her work with the area's poor black community. In 1903 she donated her home to the African Methodist Episcopal Zion Church for the continuation of her work with the poor. The home became the Harriet Tubman Home for the Aged operated by the church. Harriet Tubman died in 1913 at age ninety-three.

The home continued to operate as a home for the elderly until 1928 when it was closed. In 1953 it was restored with funds raised by the A.M.E. Zion Church, and in 1975 it was designated as a National Historic Landmark.

THE NATHAN AND MARY JOHNSON PROPERTIES

17–19 and 21 Seventh Street
New Bedford, MA 02740
www.cr.nps.gov/nr/travel/
  underground/ma6.htm

Douglass's first home after his escape from slavery in 1838 was located on Seventh Street in New Bedford, Massachusetts. Douglass and his family lived in the home for one year, from 1838 to 1839, and it is the only remaining one of the three homes that Douglass occupied during his stay in the city. The house was one of a number of buildings owned by Nathan and Mary Johnson, free black abolitionists who owned a block of properties including the neighboring Quaker meeting house. The Johnsons were active in the local Underground Railroad, assisting a number of fugitive slaves, including Frederick Douglass. New Bedford was noted for sheltering fugitives, who numbered in the hundreds during the years that Douglass lived there. The Johnsons provided safe houses for many of them.

Nicodemus National Historic Site

Nicodemus, Kans.

In Search of a Promise Land

Land promoter Benjamin Singleton (above) was known as the "Moses of the Colored Exodus" for his efforts to convince southern blacks to move to Kansas. There, blacks could farm their own land, rather than work as share-croppers, and Singleton hoped they would form self-sustaining communities independent of whites.

Twelve miles east of Hill City, Kansas, just off U.S. Highway 24 is the town of Nicodemus. With a resident population of twenty-five, this place is the very definition of sleepy, except for a brief moment in mid-summer, the last weekend in July, when it celebrates homecoming. Then hundreds of people, mainly African Americans, gather in the town to reunite with old friends and family and to commemorate the coming of freedom. Homecoming was first celebrated in Nicodemus on August 1, 1881, in observance of the abolition of slavery in Cuba the year before, and to commemorate American freedom after the Civil War. The event has endured for more than a century and evolved into a kind of family reunion, community remembrance, and freedom celebration. The 123rd annual celebration in 2001 brought at least six hundred former residents and their descendants to enjoy parades, fashion shows, and plenty of food and drink. They came from all over the nation to remember those who established this black town that sheltered its people at a time when America denied civil rights to African Americans. They came to celebrate this place, the only western town established by black people in the post–Civil War period still in existence.

The town of Nicodemus was the result of the dreams of former slaves in the aftermath of the Civil War. Despite their hopes, emancipation seemed to bring little more than a limited freedom. Like most sharecroppers in the post-war South, Solomon Lewis and his family found themselves going further and further into debt each year, even as they produced a larger and larger crop. White landowners handled the finances and juggled the books so that sharecroppers remained in debt. Lewis found himself bound to the land by mounting

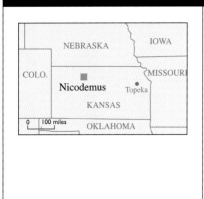

indebtedness almost as securely as pre-war slavery had bound him to a master. There seemed no other choice for the Lewis family, and for hundreds of other former slaves, who found that by the 1870s freedom was not working for them as they had hoped. Some fifty thousand left their southern homes by 1879. They became "exodusters," the term used to describe African Americans who left the South after the Civil War bound for Kansas, Missouri, Indiana, and Illinois in search of the freedom they could not find in the Reconstruction South. Thousands more were turned back by southern whites patrolling the rivers and roads, seeking to prevent the loss of valuable black agricultural laborers.

The spring of 1865 was at once the best and worst of times for African Americans. On April 9, at the Appomattox Court House, Confederate forces under General Robert E. Lee surrendered to General Ulysses S. Grant. Within a few days the Civil War came to an end. Although the U.S. government had not begun the war as an antislavery crusade, President Lincoln's Emancipation Proclamation of 1863 had made it so. Despite its limited application, it sent a strong message of freedom, inviting slaves behind Confederate lines to free themselves by escaping to the U.S. Army. Thousands did, and gradually the Civil War that Lincoln had originally announced was to save the United States, became, for a substantial number of loyal white Americans, a holy war against

Residents of Nicodemus mill about the streets around 1885, at a time when the town was prospering. Commercial enterprises had opened, such as the general merchandise store in the background; civic groups were organizing; and black politicians were winning local offices. By 1886, several hotels in town even welcomed visitors.

slavery. It had always been that for black Americans. The Emancipation Proclamation, the U.S. victory, and ultimately the passage of the Thirteenth Amendment to the Constitution, which abolished slavery forever, brought the freedom for which four million former slaves had prayed.

Blacks participated in the southern state conventions that drew up new constitutions under which the South would be reconstructed. They voted and served in the new southern governments at all levels, from local to the highest state offices. But, the years following the Civil War were not all hopeful. Within days of the Confederacy's surrender, a Confederate supporter assassinated Lincoln, and Andrew Johnson assumed the presidency. From his very first message to the nation, it was clear that this was a man of deep racial prejudice, who, unlike Lincoln, seemed to have gained little respect for African Americans, despite their contributions to winning the war. Even after progressive Republicans gained the legislative upper hand in the U.S. Congress and seemed willing to accept blacks as political allies in the South, all was not well.

There was much obvious racial progress, but the forces of southern conservatism struggled to reinstate racial controls similar to those of the pre–Civil War era—not slavery, but close to it. Congressional efforts to provide the freedmen with land upon which to build economic independence failed. Without access to land, former slaves remained at the economic mercy of their former masters. A landless southern black population all but ensured the continuation of white supremacy.

Almost immediately, former officers of the Confederacy organized the Ku Klux Klan and several other political terrorist groups committed to maintaining racial control. Through quasi-legal and blatantly illegal means, these groups removed African Americans from southern politics. The federal government did not protect its southern black citizens, and soon former slaves faced their new freedom with no resources except their labor and with a legal system stacked against them.

By the 1870s, hope that the American South could be a place of opportunity for former slaves was fading, and some blacks sought to leave the region in search of a brighter future elsewhere. Their choices were few. White laborers, especially, had made it clear that southern blacks were not welcome in the towns and cities of

Nicodemus National Historic Site

304 Washington Avenue
Bogue, KS 67625-3015
785-839-4233
www.nps.gov/nico/
NRIS 76000820
NHL, NPS

DATE FOUNDED
1877

SIGNIFICANCE
Nicodemus is an example of the African American communities formed in the post–Civil War era as a result of the Exoduster movement. It is one of the most successful and long-lasting of the African American colonies of the period.

the North. In December 1875 African American men and women from several southern states held a convention in New Orleans to consider the possibility of migrating to Liberia in Western Africa or to some western territory in the United States. Interest in colonizing Liberia was substantial, not only among southern blacks but among many in the North as well. In 1878, one colonization group in Pennsylvania reported getting inquiries from some fifty thousand African Americans from several states. Yet, most blacks after the Civil War were no more anxious to leave the country than they had been before the war. They saw themselves as Americans and they held out hope for better times to come, especially now that slavery had been destroyed. Only a small number actually migrated to West Africa during these years. Many more migrated to other regions in the United States.

Kansas was an appealing destination for many African Americans. The state had much unoccupied land and it had been long associated with the Underground Railroad and the fiery abolitionist John Brown. Many blacks celebrated Kansas as an abolitionist territory that had battled proslavery forces from Missouri and finally entered the Union as a free state. Emphasizing this history, black supporters of migration to Kansas and a few white allies printed handbills and flyers promoting a new settlement called Nicodemus. The settlement was named in honor of a legendary slave, an African prince who, it was said, was the first slave in the United States to purchase his own freedom. This Kansas settlement was presented as a place for African Americans to establish a new life and experience a new birth of freedom.

By the mid-1870s many southern blacks were taken with "Kansas Fever." Rumors of free land, free transportation, and free supplies further warmed the passion for migration. In Tennessee, blacks met in the spring of 1875 to consider the possibilities of a mass exodus westward. The meeting attendees appointed a board of representatives who would visit regions in the West to evaluate the possibilities and investigate circulating rumors. In the summer of 1875 one member of the board, N. A. Napier visited Kansas. He reported that the talk of free land and transportation was much exaggerated and that a family needed at least two thousand dollars to relocate to Kansas. His estimate included the cost of tools, two good mules, two plows, and about five hundred dollars for transportation and other expenses. Other investigators argued that the migration could be made for far less money and one even suggested an amount one-tenth of what Napier estimated. These lower figures excited great interest.

Benjamin "Pap" Singleton encouraged this interest with large rallies and small church gatherings. Singleton was a tireless worker in the cause of African American westward colonization, called the Exoduster movement. A former slave from Tennessee, Singleton escaped to Canada and then returned to the United States to live in Detroit before the Civil War. He was in his fifties at the time of the war, too old to serve in the U.S. military, but he returned to Tennessee after the war to work for the welfare of black people. He had been a carpenter in slavery, and during Reconstruction he used his skill in the grim business of constructing coffins for African Americans killed by white terrorists. This experience convinced him that a black exodus from the South was a wise strategy. In the wake of growing interest in migration to Kansas, he became an important promoter and guide, helping to found African American communities and leading black settlers to their new homes.

As early as 1873 he visited Kansas and settled some three hundred African Americans in "Singleton's Colony," in Cherokee County in the southeastern corner of the state. He then returned to the South to continue recruiting settlers. Whites as well as blacks joined in the recruiting effort, pooling resources to cut the cost of migration. One black agent for Singleton, George Brown, was able to negotiate the transportation of an individual from Nashville to Kansas City for the remarkably reasonable sum of ten dollars. In a letter to the governor of Kansas during the summer of 1876, Singleton estimated that three thousand blacks might migrate to Kansas that fall. Although his

An announcement of the founding of the town of Nicodemus served as a call to blacks to move West and join the new community. The author of the notice claims "it is the finest country we ever saw" with "rich, black" soil. In fact, the Kansas prairie was a harsh environment, subject to temperature extremes, floods, and dust storms.

To the Colored Citizens of the United States.

3527

NICODEMUS, GRAHAM CO., KAN., July 2d, 1877.

We, the Nicodemus Town Company of Graham County, Kan., are now in possession of our lands and the Town Site of Nicodemus, which is beautifully located on the N. W. quarter of Section 1, Town 8, Range 21, in Graham Co., Kansas, in the great Solomon Valley, 240 miles west of Topeka, and we are proud to say it is the finest country we ever saw. The soil is of a rich, black, sandy loam. The country is rather rolling, and looks most pleasing to the human eye. The south fork of the Solomon river flows through Graham County, nearly directly east and west and has an abundance of excellent water, while there are numerous springs of living water abounding throughout the Valley. There is an abundance of fine Magnesian stone for building purposes, which is much easier handled than the rough sand or hard stone. There is also some timber; plenty for fire use, while we have no fear but what we will find plenty of coal.

Now is your time to secure your home on Government Land in the Great Solomon Valley of Western Kansas.

Remember, we have secured the service of W. R. Hill, a man of energy and ability, to locate our Colony.

Not quite 90 days ago we secured our charter for locating the town site of Nicodemus. We then became an organized body, with only three dollars in the treasury and twelve members, but under the careful management of our officers, we have now nearly 300 good and reliable members, with several members permanently located on their claims—with plenty of provisions for the colony—while we are daily receiving letters from all parts of the country from parties desiring to locate in the great Solomon Valley of Western Kansas.

For Maps, Circulars, and Passenger rates, address our General Manager, W. R. HILL, North Topeka, Kansas, until August 1st, 1877, then at Hill City, Graham Co., via Trego.

The name of our post-office will be Nicodemus, and Mr. Z. T. Fletcher will be our "Nasby."

REV. S. P. ROUNDTREE, Sec'y.

estimate was high, within a year, two black communities were established in Kansas, the first of which was the prairie settlement of Nicodemus. Set in Graham County along the Solomon River, it was the first western town planned by and for African Americans.

In 1880, Singleton was called to testify before a Senate Select Committee investigating the "Negro exodus from the southern states." The committee questioned his motivation and that of his black followers asking, "What was the cause of your going out, and in the first place how did you happen to go there, or to send these people there?" His answer was straightforward,

> My people, for the want of land—we needed land for our children—and their disadvantages— that caused my heart to grieve and sorrow; pity for my race, sir, that was coming down, instead of going up, that caused me to go to work for them. . . . I thought Southern Kansas was conge- nial to our nature, sir; and I formed a colony there, and bought about a thousand acres of ground—the colony did—my people.

African Americans who came to Nicodemus in the late 1870s were recruited by the Nicodemus Town Company. Reverend W. H. Smith, a black minister, was the company's president and W. R. Hill, a white land developer, served as its treasurer. They visited African American congregations in Kentucky boosting Nicodemus as a western Eden, a land of great promise, where hard-working people would be rewarded for their efforts. The original settlers of Nicodemus, about three hundred in all, came in five separate groups from Lexington, Kentucky, arriving on September 17, 1877. Travel to the community was not easy, and although rail transportation had reached the neighboring town of Ellis, the first settlers had to walk the last fifty miles to Nicodemus.

Four "exodusters" pose in front of a home in Nicodemus, Kansas. Early residents of Nicodemus faced harsh living conditions, but eventually formed a thriving town.

Once there, they found life harsh in the extreme. The dry land, with top soil so thin that it could barely support agriculture, made farming difficult and unreliable. The weather was often dreadful, with frequent droughts and incessant dust storms. The severe and relentless cold of winter was relieved only by a brief spring before the scorching heat of summer, which was also tornado season. These conditions combined to make Kansas a hellish place for these earliest residents. They dug homes in the earth because there was little wood or other building material available and faced a thirty-mile walk to reach the nearest supply point.

A settler's first view of Nicodemus was a daunting sight. It was, as one settler described it years later, in 1937, in the *Topeka Daily Capital,* "just a plain prairie country—no houses, no wells, no shelter of any kind, and winter setting in." To many of these settlers, such as young Williana Hickman, the Kansas reality stood in terrible contrast to the "Promised Land" for which they had hoped. She recalled her first impressions in the *Topeka Daily Capital,* "When we got in sight of Nicodemus the men shouted, `There is Nicodemus!' Being very sick, I hailed this news with gladness. I looked with all the eyes I had." "Where is Nicodemus?" she demanded. "I don't see it. My husband pointed out various smokes coming out of the ground and said, `That is Nicodemus.' The families lived in dugouts. . . . The scenery was not at all inviting, and I began to cry."

For these people, migrating as they had from the green fields of Kentucky or Tennessee, where most had lived in wooden cabins, the desolation of the Kansas landscape did not live up to their romantic expectations of self-sufficient living on the frontier. Promotional literature had billed Kansas as a "promised land" where people could live free on their own land, but most found it not so. Many, about one hundred, returned to Kentucky or went on farther west. Williana and Daniel Hickman were among those who chose to stay. They lived in dugouts "like prairie dogs," as they described it, among the grasses of the plains. With only a thin, winding line of trees along the Solomon River providing relief from the bitter winds, these early settlers found the first winter a brutal experience. Some left in the spring, but other settlers came the next year. In the spring of 1878 more families and additional women arrived at the largely male settlement, bringing Nicodemus's population to seven hundred. By 1880, however, because many families moved on west or turned back east, it had dropped again to less than three hundred.

Nicodemus slowly became a functioning town, with businesses established to serve the needs of its residents. A land office and a hotel soon joined the livery stable, general store, and post office. By 1881, there were some thirty-five residential and commercial structures in Nicodemus, and within a few years the town boasted a baseball team, a literary debating society, mutual aid societies, and fraternal lodges. The local ice-cream parlor was a favorite gathering spot for young people, and by the end of the decade, the community's children attended classes in a four-room schoolhouse. In 1886, A. G. Tallman opened the town's first newspaper, the *Western Cyclone,* and in just over a year H. K. Lightfoot established a competing publication, the *Enterprise.* In the same year, a white man, A. L. McPherson, provided the community with its first bank. Nicodemus was rapidly becoming an important commercial center for the entire county.

As Nicodemus grew in economic significance, its residents also became more politically active. In 1879, they petitioned the county commissioner for township status. County officials granted the petition, and in that year Nicodemus held its first township elections. A biracial slate of candidates consisting of five white men and three blacks, "the Equal Rights Ticket," won the election. Dreams of African Americans holding political power showed signs of coming true when blacks were elected justice of the peace, clerk of the township, and overseer of county roads. These were the first of many local offices that black men held during this period. At a time when African Americans were losing their political influence throughout the South and terrorist groups such as the Klan were assassinating black people who dared to participate in southern politics, blacks in Nicodemus held positions as county attorney and county commissioner, as well as a number of other elected and appointed county and state offices.

Edward McCabe, a real estate agent who came to Nicodemus from Chicago, was one of the most notable black politicians in Kansas. In 1880 he represented the state as delegate-at-large at the Chicago convention of the Republican Party. Two years later, he gained office as Kansas state auditor, becoming the highest elected black official in nineteenth-century Kansas and the first African American outside of the South to win a statewide election. McCabe served as Cook County clerk in the early 1870s. After leaving office in Kansas he moved to Oklahoma as part of the black migration to that territory. There, he continued in politics and helped to found the all-black town of Langston. In an 1883 review of black political progress in the post–Civil War era, the editor of the *New York Globe* selected McCabe as one of a number of young "self-made [black] men, who make their impressions upon our times by sheer force of character." Nicodemus was an attractive place for men such as these.

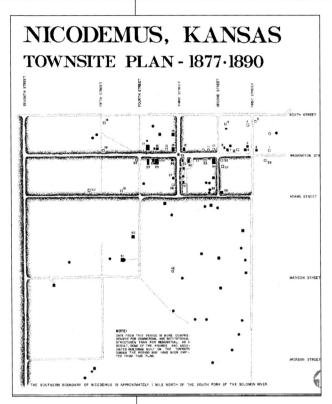

NICODEMUS, KANSAS
TOWNSITE PLAN - 1877·1890

The town plan for Nicodemus reveals a neat grid of streets and blocks, with streets named for Presidents. By 1886, Nicodemus had a bank, four general stores, three grocery stores, four hotels, and various other businesses.

The 1880s were heady years for the young community, especially contrasted with the declining prospects for blacks in the South. During these years, Mississippi hammered out its laws of racial injustice. The Mississippi Plan, as these measures were collectively known, became law in 1890. They established the legal framework of racial segregation that served as a model for the southern Jim Crow system. In public transportation and public accommodations, in employment, and in legal standing generally, African Americans confronted segregation and racial prejudice, the hallmarks of southern social, political, and economic life. Although not generally enforced by law, a similar situation existed in the North. Yet, for a time, Kansas seemed an oasis of racial opportunity with Nicodemus as its center. Much of this would, however, prove to be an illusion.

Reckless land promoters and railroad agents exaggerated the qualities of soil and climate in this promised land of the plains. They aimed to populate the West, at inflated land prices, to create markets for railroad services. Speculators came to invest in the blossoming community under the impression that the coming of the railroad would lead to a land boom. They were wrong. Despite the determined lobbying of town boosters, in 1888, the Union Pacific bypassed Nicodemus, laying its tracks six miles to the south through open prairie. Many other towns bypassed by railroads withered and died, and this was one of the earliest factors that led to Nicodemus's decline.

Over the next several decades residents continued their efforts to build the town, but many businesses moved to the other side of the Solomon River, to a Union Pacific Railroad camp that later became the town of Bogue. Ultimately the struggling community of Nicodemus languished, but the decline was slow. The town actually reached its population peak in 1910 with a reported 595 black residents. The population subsequently dropped sharply, and by 1950 only sixteen people remained. Almost all its businesses had failed, and in 1953 the town post office closed. After seventy-six years the town was all but gone, its people scattered across the nation.

The town's yearly homecoming celebration is an important part of the effort to keep the memory of this remarkable community alive. Descendants of the original black settlers come from around the country to take part in the Annual Nicodemus Emancipation Celebration. During the last weekend of July, they pay tribute to their heritage and renew their spiritual bonds with the history of this community, the only remaining black town west of the Mississippi. There is music, food, parades, and a general festival. From July 31 to August 2, 1998, the community celebrated their 120th annual homecoming, which included its dedication as a National Park site, a buffalo soldier cavalry exhibition, a wagon ride tour, a western fashion show, food, dance, and a variety of music from jazz and gospel to rap and rock and roll.

Boy Scouts from Atlanta participate in the Nicodemus homecoming, when descendants of the town's settlers gather in Kansas to honor their ancestors' achievements and struggles. The yearly celebration evolved from the early town's Emancipation Day, which celebrated the freeing of slaves in the West Indies.

Five Historic Buildings in Nicodemus

In 1973, a study conducted by the Afro-American Institute for Historic Preservation and Community Development was provided to the U.S. Interior Department. This study brought Nicodemus to public attention after almost a generation of neglect. In 1976, the U.S. secretary of the interior designated Nicodemus as a National Historic Site. Twenty years later, the U.S. Congress officially recognized the historic importance of the town and included the Nicodemus National Historic Site in the National Park system. Currently, the Park Service is working with the people of Nicodemus to interpret the town's history and preserve its five remaining historic buildings.

The African Methodist Episcopal Church is one of two church buildings still standing in Nicodemus. Black churches thrived after the Civil War, and founding a church was one of the first tasks of Western settlers.

The First Baptist Church, a one-story building, is constructed of native limestone covered with stucco. It was built in 1908 to replace a building of similar construction, which in turn had replaced a church made of sod. Even this sod structure was an improvement over the original church, which was dug out of the prairie soil. The church was first established in 1877 and still functions, although the congregation now meets in a brick building just north of the original site. Another church, the African Methodist Episcopal Church, was established in 1885. Its building, completed in about 1907, is constructed of native limestone blocks salvaged from the second building of the First Baptist Church. The church remained active until the 1940s. In 1998, the building became part of the National Park Service and is undergoing structural rehabilitation.

Two remaining secular buildings are also constructed of limestone, which was more readily available than wood in the grassy plains. The Fletcher-Switzer House, formerly the St. Francis Hotel, is one of the original buildings from the nineteenth-century town. This one-and-one-half-story limestone structure was built in 1878. Its original owner, Zachariah T. Fletcher—who lived in the building with his family—operated it as a stagecoach station and hotel. The building also housed the town's first post office. Its exterior walls are now covered with stucco and it is currently a private residence. The Nicodemus Township Hall was built in 1939. A single story with high ceilings and a stage, this assembly hall served as meeting space for the town government in its earliest days. The building is still used for community meetings.

Established in 1879, the Nicodemus School met in a sod building until 1887, when the town built a wooden four-room school building. After it burned down in 1918, a new Nicodemus School District No. 1 building, replaced the old wooden structure. The new school was a one-and-one-half story square-frame building with a wood shingle roof and a raised porch marking the main entrance. The school closed in 1955 for lack of students. The building is now the property of the American Legion, which bought it in 1983 to use for meetings.

LINCOLNVILLE HISTORIC DISTRICT

Bounded by Cedar, Riberia,
Cerro and Washington
Streets and DeSoto Place
St. Augustine, FL 32084
904-829-1711
*www.cr.nps.gov/nr/travel/
civilrights/f1.htm*
NPS

About the same time that
Nicodemus was established
in Kansas, a group of former
slaves in northern Florida
leased a tract of land from the
city of St. Augustine, Florida,
to build a community. The
settlement was named
Lincolnville in honor of the
fallen President, the person
credited by most African
Americans at the time with
abolishing slavery. Now, they
were determined to assert
themselves as free people. In
Lincolnville, their own independent community, blacks
attempted to do just that.
During the Reconstruction
era, African Americans exer-
cised political leadership
within the Republican Party.
Blacks held important local
offices in St. Augustine,
including city council member, town marshal, and street
commissioner. Black business
leaders were central to the
city's economy, and black
civic associations played a
major role in St. Augustine's
social life. In the twentieth
century, however, the southern Jim Crow system
removed African Americans
from positions of influence
and segregated city facilities.
During the 1960s Lincolnville

*Established in 1866, Lincolnville is filled with a wide variety of both houses
and churches from the nineteenth and early twentieth centuries. What was
originally an independent community later became the black subdivision of
segregated St. Augustine.*

residents worked with the
Southern Christian Leadership Conference (SCLC) and
Martin Luther King Jr. to end
segregation in St. Augustine.

OKMULGEE DOWNTOWN HISTORIC DISTRICT

Bounded by 4th Street, Frisco
Avenue, Eighth Street and
Okmulgee Avenue
Okmulgee, OK 74447
918-758-1015
www.tourokmulgee.com

In 1838 the U.S. government
forced thousands of Native
American Creeks from their
land in Alabama and Georgia.
These Indians founded
Okmulgee, from the Creek
meaning "boiling water." The
town became the Creek
national capital. Among those

who migrated to this community during the 1830s were
more than a thousand people
of mixed Indian and African
American descent, former
slaves and free blacks who
had lived within the Indian
settlements in the South prior
to migrating. After the Civil
War, other blacks migrated to
the community, which
became a settlement of
Creeks and Creek Freedmen,
as the former slaves were
known. In 1898 each Creek
Freedman was granted 160
acres of land and, as a group,
they became important members of the community. They
built some of the earliest
buildings in the town. In
1928 they constructed the
Masonic Lodge, which
remains one of the town's significant historic structures.

Sweet Auburn Historic District

Atlanta, Ga.

A Haven in a Hostile World

Martin Luther King Jr. (above), who lived on Auburn Avenue as a child, grew up with the social activism of a black community that fostered self-sufficiency and dignity. In his last book, Where Do We Go from Here: Chaos or Community?, *King wrote: "The Negro will only be truly free when he reaches down to the inner depths of his own being and signs with the pen and ink of assertive selfhood his own emancipation proclamation."*

In Atlanta, the intersection of Peachtree Street and Auburn Avenue was, for most of the past century, the confrontational juncture at which the elegant white business district met the proud and protective commercial center of Atlanta's black elite. John Wesley Dobbs, civic leader and noted political orator, was inspired to name the black district Sweet Auburn after reading the opening line of the poem "The Deserted Village" by the Irish poet Oliver Goldsmith: "Sweet Auburn, loveliest village of the plains." Dobbs thought it a fitting description of this solidly professional and middle-class section of Atlanta's black community. For him and for many other blacks, it was the symbol of progressive Atlanta. As such, the meeting of Peachtree Street and Auburn Avenue was the intersection of the slaveholding old South and the progressive new South.

On December 8, 1976, the federal government recognized the historic significance of the Sweet Auburn District of Atlanta by designating it a National Historic Landmark area. By that time it had also become legendary as the birthplace and home of Martin Luther King Jr.; Maynard Jackson Jr., Atlanta's first black mayor who served from 1974 to 1982; NAACP leader Walter White; and countless other regional and national civil rights leaders. But Sweet Auburn was more than a home for notable black leaders. By the early decades of the twentieth century, it was the center of African American life in Atlanta and the mainspring of the city's black culture. "To walk the Avenue on any summer evening," Dobbs recalled in a 1935 article in the *Atlanta Daily* "was to experience the vitality of black life in the city." It was the spiritual soul of black Atlanta and a place that nurtured black dreamers.

For the generation of blacks living in Atlanta in the first decades the twentieth century, Sweet Auburn became an almost mythical place of possibilities and, as such, was a symbol of black success for African Americans across the country. But it had not always been that way. This area of Atlanta was originally part of the city's Fourth Ward, north of the Georgia Railroad. In 1853 a major thoroughfare named Wheat Street, after prominent Atlanta merchant Augustus M. Wheat, was cut through the area. The new street followed an old trail that had connected a local Indian village to its burial grounds near present-day Lawrenceville, Georgia. The trail also linked the village to an area used for powwows, a place local Indians called peach tree.

As the area filled with non-Indians, the Native Americans were displaced, and on the eve of the Civil War, white Americans of various ethnic backgrounds settled next to free African Americans. One of the earliest black residents of the area was Mary Combs, a member of Atlanta's free black community during the years before the Civil War. By the spring of 1856 she had saved enough money to purchase land there, at a time when

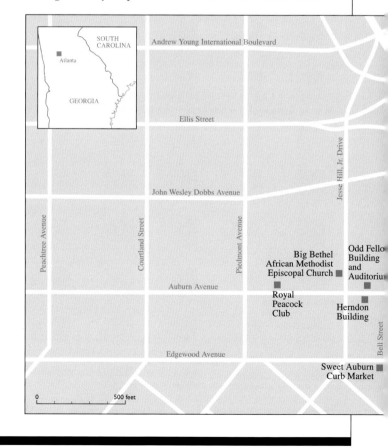

the city was growing dramatically and becoming a major southern railroad center. A combination of sharp business dealings and luck brought Combs a 100-percent profit on her land. She sold it in 1862 for five hundred dollars, a sum she used to buy her husband out of slavery. Already Sweet Auburn had become the stuff of dreams for at least one black family.

The Civil War dramatically changed the course of Atlanta's growth. After U.S. forces under General William T. Sherman burned 40 percent of the city to the ground, the land that today marks the intersection of Peachtree and Wheat streets was almost worthless. At war's end in 1865, Atlanta and much of the South was politically and economically devastated. Over the next century, however, the spot where Peachtree met Wheat became home to a rising black middle class. A 1953 *Fortune* magazine article called Wheat Street the "richest Negro street in America." Doubtless, it was the black intellectual and business capital of Atlanta and of the twentieth-century South.

By 1890, Atlanta had undergone a rebuilding and an economic rebirth. It was recovering from the destruc-

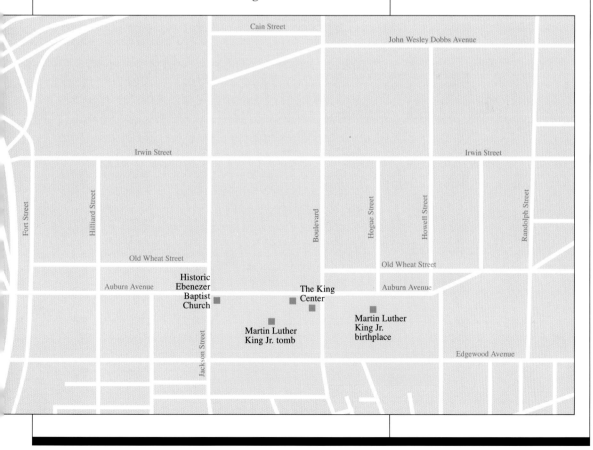

Sweet Auburn Historic District

Auburn Avenue
Atlanta, GA 30312
404-222-6688
www.cr.nps.gov/nr/travel/atlanta/
  aub.htm
NRIS 76000631
NHL

SIGNIFICANCE
Sweet Auburn Historic District was the site of one of America's most important twentieth-century black communities. It is also the birthplace and one-time home of Martin Luther King Jr.

tion brought by the Civil War. The Peachtree and Wheat streets area was home to a small black community just east of and adjacent to the upscale shops and residences of many of the city's affluent whites. In 1891, black Atlantans constructed the stone building at the corner of Wheat and Calhoun (now Piedmont) streets to house the congregation of the Big Bethel African Methodist Episcopal Church. The church was established at the end of the Civil War, in 1865, but with the new building it expanded its services as a religious and social center. Several small businesses and an orphanage were among the earliest community institutions. The area was becoming a desirable place to live and work, and, in the spring of 1893, white residents convinced the city council to change Wheat Street's name to what they considered the more stylish sounding Auburn Avenue. Within a decade, at least ten black-owned businesses opened, and the homes and offices of black professionals dotted the area. As the area was becoming a thriving, racially integrated community, there were troubling changes taking place in the city.

As the nineteenth century drew to a close, southern society was undergoing a significant social and demographic transformation. African Americans, most of whose parents or grandparents had been slaves, now found themselves bound to the land almost as tightly by the sharecropping system. Ideally, sharecropping should have worked to the advantage of both landholders, who needed labor, and agricultural workers, who wanted more independence than that of an ordinary hired hand, but who could not afford to buy a farm. At harvest time the crop was split between landowner and sharecropper, with the costs for rent, food, seed, and equipment paid out of the sharecropper's portion. Yet, because sharecroppers where often illiterate and could not depend on legal protection, whites routinely manipulated southern law to ensure maximum advantage to white landholders at the expense of black farm laborers.

All across the South, a system of laws referred to as the Jim Crow system restricted interracial association and segregated every phase of southern life, from public accommodations to educational opportunities to basic citizenship rights. With the rate of lynching at an all-time high—85 were reported in 1890, 113 in 1891, and 161 in 1892—some blacks moved northward, while others seriously considered migrating to Africa or the Caribbean. Most blacks who left the southern countryside in the 1880s and 1890s, however, settled in the southern cities. There, black communities sprang up offering employment, exciting social and cultural centers, and platforms for political organization. They also provided shelter and a degree of protection for a people vulnerable to the racial injustice particularly rampant in that era.

In the hostile environment of the segregated South, blacks established, in their own communities, institutions, businesses, and community-based services that were unavailable to them in the general society. Within these urban black communities of the South, "race leaders" were born, nurtured, and educated. And from these communities emerged the civil rights leaders who broadened opportunities for African Americans and, in the process, changed America. Their determination to fight racial injustice often emerged from the everyday reality of black life, a reality that contradicted American ideals and the stereotype of southern gentility, the popular image of the South in the early twentieth century.

In the 1896 case of *Plessy* v. *Ferguson* the U.S. Supreme Court declared racial segregation constitutional. Consequently, racial separation increased over the next two decades in Atlanta and throughout the South. Regulations restricting black access to public facilities and political influence took hold, and housing opportunities were increasingly limited. In Atlanta, racial segregation had been mandated by law since 1892, but during the first years of the twentieth century blacks and whites continued to share several racially mixed communities in the city. However, the race riot of 1906 changed the patterns of Atlanta's residential and business communities. At the turn of the century, racial tensions were more volatile than they appeared at the surface of Atlanta's polite society. Middle-class blacks, however, worked diligently to disprove negative racial stereotypes. In 1902, six thousand blacks gathered in the city for a meeting of the Negro Young People's Christian Education Congress to demonstrate and celebrate African American accomplishments before the world. These highly educated, Christian middle-class black people hoped to counter the charges of racial inferiority and degeneracy that whites raised to justify legalized racial discrimination. The congress took its cues from the black educator

Blacks often gathered at beauty parlors and barber shops, not only for a haircut but also to pass along news, share gossip, and organize for political action. As in the white community, men and women generally visited separate shops.

In an 1895 speech in Atlanta, Booker T. Washington called for the gradual uplift and self-improvement of blacks rather than immediate equal rights. Many African Americans disagreed with this accommodating stance and Washington's claim, directed to the whites in his audience, that "in all things that are purely social we can be as separate as the fingers, yet one as the hand in all things essential to mutual progress."

Booker T. Washington's strategy of racial accommodation that seemed to accept segregation as an inevitable fact of southern life. In speeches and written resolutions, members assured white southerners that "right thinking Negroes" did not seek "social intrusion." This attitude was not universal among Atlanta's blacks as most white Atlantans knew, but they welcomed the congress to the city as an example of "reasonable" racial thinking.

Black leaders in Atlanta, such as Reverend Henry Hugh Proctor of the First Congregational Church on Houston Street, worked tirelessly for educational progress among African American youth and as boosters of the city in every conceivable way. Reverend Proctor, educated at Yale and a follower and friend of Booker T. Washington, was the all-black church's first black minister. His active ministry and popular sermons brought it great attention and prestige. This black institution, visited by presidents and former presidents, became the seat of African American efforts in the city to prove the worth of black society. It held to the most rigid standards of middle-class society and demanded that its members display only the most proper education and upbringing at all times. The church valued intellect over emotion. Unlike most black churches, emotional outbursts during religious services were not tolerated at First Congregational, and the folklore among long-time church members was that a minister could be fired if "his noun and verb did not agree."

Through the black churches and other institutions, the city's black middle-class and professionals kept up a steady campaign against gambling, drinking, or vice of any kind among African Americans. Still, race relations grew steadily worse as local white newspapers—reflecting the racial fears and assumptions of the time—warned of African American crime and vice and sensationalized the slightest incident that seemed to support their charges. The influx of blacks from rural Georgia into the city was a source of constant concern. Within a few short years Atlanta's major newspapers, the *Constitution* and the *Atlanta Journal,* worried openly about what they saw as poorly motivated workers migrating to the city who were threatening its tranquility and productivity. "The willingness of the southern [N]egro to work is fast dying out," declared a reporter for the *Constitution* in early 1905. There were rumors about the evil character displayed by some of these blacks, rumors that fed traditional racial stereotypes depicting blacks as lazy, ignorant, violent, and emotionally and sexually excessive.

Race relations in Atlanta, as elsewhere, were also aggravated by southern politicians who encouraged racial prejudice for their own political gain. Hoke Smith's 1906 run for governor of Georgia was marked by the then-typical southern political practice of using racial prejudice to gain power. He claimed that African American efforts to vote signaled black attempts to rise above their racial station in southern society and constituted a danger to southern white womanhood. This illogical charge, and speculations in local newspapers about similar concerns, inflamed racist feelings and set off a level of violence in Atlanta not seen since the Civil War.

All day on Saturday, September 22, 1906, newsboys hawked their wares with cries calculated to sell. "Extra, Extra, Third Assault on White Woman by Negro Brute!" "Extra, Extra, Bold Negro Kisses White Girl's Hand!" "Extra, Extra, Bright Mulatto Insults White Girls!" A local newspaper, the *Georgian* reported eleven attacks on white women by blacks. No matter that these alleged assaults were never verified and most probably never occurred, the news reports continued. Another local paper, the *Evening News*—after reporting that a black man broke into the home of an eighteen-year-old white woman—asked the white men of Atlanta, "What will you do to stop these outrages against the women? Shall these black devils be permitted to assault and almost kill our women, and go unpunished?"

The answer came that day and continued for four days and nights as roving white gangs attacked African Americans in the downtown area and in black neighborhoods. Before the riot was over, more than ten thousand whites, from all levels of Atlanta society, had taken part. Significantly, the mob made few distinctions in its attacks. "Right thinking," church-going, well-educated, economically secure blacks were not safe. In fact, the mob particularly targeted black businesses. When it became clear that city authorities would not help, many blacks armed themselves, defending their families and their property. Police officers often took the side of the white mob, increasing the level of violence. At one point, gun battles raged in the streets. Twenty-five blacks were killed, none

Huit pages : CINQ centimes

Le Petit Parisien

SUPPLÉMENT LITTÉRAIRE ILLUSTRÉ

DIRECTION: 18, rue d'Enghien (10e). PARIS

MASSACRE DE NÈGRES DANS LES RUES D'ATLANTA

A French newspaper supplement put "The Massacre of Negroes in the Streets of Atlanta" on its front page. White men beat blacks and burn their businesses in this graphic depiction of the 1906 riot, in which white politicians fueled fears of a black crime wave—and which garnered international attention for the city.

of whom was suspected of a crime. Two hundred more blacks were wounded, hundreds were arrested, and more than one thousand were forced to flee the city. One white police officer was also killed.

It took martial law and negotiations between white authorities and local black leaders to end the violence. The rumors of black crimes that had precipitated the riot turned out to be greatly exaggerated, nonetheless these rumors accelerated segregation in the city. African American merchants formerly located on the Peachtree Street among white businesses, relocated eastward along Auburn Avenue, a racially "safer" area of the city. By 1909 most of Auburn Avenue's white residents had moved to other parts of the city, leaving blacks as the majority in the area, which was fast becoming a new black business district. Sweet Auburn was taking form, encouraged by the terrible reality of racial violence and a 1913 law that officially segregated housing and public accommodations in the city. When those who had fled the riot returned to the city, many of them settled in Sweet Auburn, a place of relative safety.

By 1920 the racial divide was clear. There were a few white-owned businesses along Auburn Avenue from Peachtree Street eastward to Pryor Street, but beyond that businesses were primarily black-owned. Although Georgia's State Supreme Court later struck down the 1913 law, residential segregation increased, policed by white supremacist groups. Three white businesses—Antonio Graves's real estate office, Elmer Hatchett's tailor shop, and James Holloway's jewelry store—operated in the borderlands just west of Courtland Street. Beyond them, came the solidly black section that led into the heart of Sweet Auburn. In 1930, robed and hooded members of the Ku Klux Klan marched through the area to intimidate any, even professional, blacks, who might dare attempt to integrate other parts of the city.

As Sweet Auburn became exclusively African American, its businesses and institutions became a supportive network that served the people. Not all of the

Sweet Auburn community was affluent. One section, known as "Darktown"—much of which was destroyed by fire in 1917—was home to a poor working class. Darktown was never completely separated from the rest of Sweet Auburn. Racial segregation was a fact of life in Atlanta that most black people dared not challenge, but its effects were not all negative. Segregation promoted a degree of integration among different classes of blacks. In cities such as Atlanta—where the black population was large enough to sustain major black-owned institutions—it was not unusual for working-class blacks to share the same neighborhood or even block with black doctors, lawyers, bankers, and newspaper editors. Class was a major force in black social and political associations, but the limitations on blacks enforced by racial segregation ensured a degree of community cooperation, especially in politics.

There were community responsibilities that accompanied privileged status in Sweet Auburn. The well-educated and the economically comfortable were expected to contribute time and resources to those in the community with less. Black businesses served multiple functions. Grocery stores often loaned money and allowed generous credit for food. Barbershops were often places where people sought workers among the barbershops' clientele and political organization and debate. Churches provided for the poor and the ill, educated the children, and hosted political organizations.

Although Auburn Avenue was simply a mixed residential and commercial district with businesses of varying sizes, types, and degrees of solvency, Atlanta's blacks saw Auburn Avenue as a special place. In their minds, Sweet Auburn took on the character of its most desirable areas. Older residents called it a "street of pride." In interviews, one remembered it like a "grand lady." Another recalled, "in her prime she was the talk of the town—young, vivacious, and beautiful. Everyone loved her, respected her, and wooed her." Local residents took pride in this rapidly developing neighborhood of Atlanta's black middle class. Many accepted John Wesley Dobbs's description of Auburn Avenue that surpassed the 1953 *Fortune* magazine claim. He called it the richest Negro street not in America, but in the world.

Sweet Auburn was a complete, largely self-sufficient community. Black-owned hotels, small shops, and

From Slave to Business Leader

Alonzo Herndon was born in 1858 on a plantation in Walton County, Georgia, the son of his master. After working as a farmhand for his father and former master, he moved to the town of Senoia, Georgia, near Atlanta, where he learned the barbering trade. Herndon was offered a lucrative position at Atlanta's Dougherty Hutchins's barbershop, the most prosperous black-owned barbershop in the city. His skill and engaging manner won him the favor of the shop's wealthy white clientele, and in less than a year he became a partner.

In 1902 Herndon opened an elegant barbershop at 66 Peachtree Street, around the corner from Auburn Avenue. Behind the solid mahogany doors and beveled glass, the crystal chandeliers hanging from the ceilings were reflected in the gilt-framed mirrors in this spacious salon with twenty-five chairs and eighteen baths. The shop drew white patrons and spectators from Atlanta and from as far away as Richmond, Virginia, and Mobile, Alabama.

At the beginning of the twentieth century, Alonzo Herndon, former slave, was a rich man, and he expanded his business interests, buying hundreds of residential and business properties. In 1905 Herndon became a major investor in the Atlanta Benevolent and Protective Association, a community based insurance company founded by black ministers. He supervised its reorganization, renamed it the Atlanta Life Insurance Company, and became its president. In 1920, the company moved its headquarters to 148 Auburn Avenue, becoming one of the most prominent businesses in Sweet Auburn. The company expanded into six other southern states and became the second largest black-owned insurance company in the nation, second only to the giant North Carolina Mutual in Durham. Herndon headed the company for twenty-two years. His son, Norris, succeeded him as president of the Atlanta Life Insurance Company after his death in 1927.

The large professional staff of the Atlanta Life Insurance Company poses for an office portrait in 1922.

churches shared the area with much larger and wealthier operations. Long-time residents remember the Gate City Drug Store, which was much more than a pharmacy. Its soda fountain was popular with local residents and visitors alike as a place to engage in congenial political and social conversation. When Booker T. Washington came to town to attend the Atlanta Exposition, an 1895 international trade fair, he stopped by the Gate City Drug Store to meet friends and to discuss his educational, economic, and political strategy.

A soda at Gate City or a meal in one of the many local restaurants on Auburn Avenue might bring one into contact with some of the most important and influential African American business and political leaders in the nation. Alonzo Herndon, a former slave from Walton County, Georgia, operated a string of barbershops in the city and by 1900 became the largest black landowner in Atlanta. In 1905 he founded the Atlanta Life Insurance Company. The business grew to become the second largest black insurance company in the United States, with forty-two branch offices by 1910. Businessman and politician Henry A. Rucker was the proprietor of the Rucker Building, Atlanta's first black-owned office building. It was constructed at 156 Auburn Avenue in 1904 and, in 1927, the building was remodeled adding a Beaux Arts style facade. This opulent architectural style, characterized by grandiose, greatly detailed symmetrical columns was often used in bank buildings, courthouses, and railroad stations. On August 5, 1928, when twenty-six-year-old William Alexander Scott II founded the *Atlanta Daily World,* the first black-owned daily newspaper in the country, he located its offices on Auburn Avenue.

The district was also home to a number of well-established and important African American churches, such as the Ebenezer Baptist Church, Martin Luther King Jr.'s home church. Like most black churches, those in Sweet Auburn often served multiple purposes beyond their purely religious functions and drew a wide range of community members. Wheat Street Baptist Church housed a YMCA for blacks in its basement. Big Bethel African Methodist Episcopal Church was headquarters for the Standard Life Insurance Company.

Churches in Sweet Auburn also offered a venue for professional entertainers. Henry McNeal Turner, a bishop

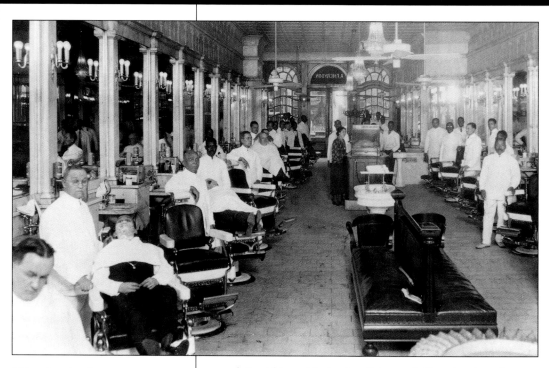

African American businessman Alonzo Herndon operated this elegant barbershop—called the Herndon Tonsorial Palace—in downtown segregated Atlanta, where the customers were white and the barbers were black. Black-owned barbershops with black customers were relegated to Sweet Auburn.

of the African Methodist Episcopal Church who advocated the emigration of American blacks to West Africa, offered his People's Tabernacle as a community music hall. Entertainers also performed in various local theaters. The Royal Theater opened in the Odd Fellows Auditorium in 1914 and hosted blues singers Bessie Smith and "Ma" Rainey and many other African American entertainers. The Royal Peacock, which opened in 1938 and later became the Top Hat Club ballroom, entertained black Atlanta, drawing the likes of Nat "King" Cole, Cab Calloway, and, by the 1950s and 1960s, B. B. King, the Four Tops, the Tams, and Atlanta's own Gladys Knight. Some have called this area Atlanta's Harlem, although Sweet Auburn predated the New York City black community and center for African American entertainment by a generation or more.

Like Harlem, Sweet Auburn was a strong community that helped educate and develop major figures in African American society. Some of twentieth-century America's most important advocates for racial justice came out of its nurturing environment. One such advocate was Michael King Jr., who was born the son and the grandson of Baptist preachers. When Michael was five years old, his father, Michael King Sr., was inspired during a visit to the Wittenburg, Germany, birthplace of Protestantism to change his first and middle name and those of his son to Martin Luther, the name of the leader of the Protestant Reformation. The young Martin Luther King Jr. grew up on Auburn Avenue in a two-story frame home built in 1894. The home was built in the Queen Anne style, which typically includes elaborate chimneys, corner turrets, and bay windows. It has tall, slender windows, a front-facing gable wing, and a sweeping wraparound porch. Just two blocks from this home is Ebenezer Baptist Church, where young King's fraternal grandfather and father served as ministers.

Ebenezer Baptist Church is located at the corner of Auburn and Jackson streets and served the black community from its beginnings in 1914. The massive two-story brick building was built in the Gothic Revival style, with a characteristic arched porch, pointed-arch windows and two square towers that rise on either side of the entrance. Martin Luther King Jr.'s maternal grand-father, Reverend Alfred Daniel Williams presided over the completion of the church's construction in 1922, and its subsequent transformation from a small, relatively insignificant church to one of the most prominent in Atlanta. Reverend Williams was one of Atlanta's most important activists, joining with black historian and political activist W. E. B. DuBois of Atlanta University and Bishop Henry McNeal Turner in the struggle for civil rights in the city.

In 1929, they established Booker T. Washington High School, Atlanta's first institution for black secondary education. The school became the pride of the community, offering educational programs for honor students and establishing the Music Festival and Dramatic Association that sponsored popular entertainment locally and elsewhere in the state. Following the practical educational philosophy of the black educator after whom it was named, the school taught manual skills as well as academic subjects. Students could take courses in manual training, automobile mechanics, household management, home nursing and child care, in addition to a standard secondary academic curriculum.

Reverend Williams was also a leader in a boycott of the *Georgian*. This local white newspaper in the William Randolph Hearst national newspaper chain used racist rhetoric to criticize African American activists, referring to them as "dirty and ignorant" troublemakers. The boycott was so successful that it contributed to the newspaper's eventual failure, evidence of the potential of black influence even in this highly segregated southern city. In his efforts to promote and to serve the needs of Atlanta's black community in general and Sweet Auburn specifically, Reverend Williams worked with such men as Benjamin Jefferson Davis, editor of the *Atlanta Independent*. Davis's black newspaper publicized the accomplishments of the Sweet Auburn community to counter the racist stereotypes promoted by whites.

Davis was a key promoter of and fundraiser for the Odd Fellows Building, completed in 1912 at 228–250 Auburn Avenue, which provided space for many businesses in the community. The building's entrance, framed by twin terracotta and stone African heads, stood as a point of racial pride. The construction of an adjacent grand auditorium that housed offices, stores, and meeting space accentuated the prosperous appearance of the area. This large hall, in addition to hosting entertainers, became a facility for national conventions and the meetings of civil rights organizations and political protest groups, activities in which Reverend Williams and his son-in-law, Martin Luther King Sr., were important leaders.

Martin Luther King Sr., called "Daddy King," married into the Williams family and took over Ebenezer Baptist Church after Reverend Williams died in 1931. He also became the president of Atlanta's branch of the major civil rights organization the National Association for the Advancement of Colored People (NAACP) in the 1930s. Following in the footsteps of his father-in-law, Daddy King was active in voting rights and education issues. He was one of the charter members of Atlanta

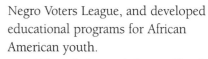

Negro Voters League, and developed educational programs for African American youth.

Although Sweet Auburn offered some sanctuary from the harsh racial realities of the city, Atlanta in the early twentieth century could be a humiliating place even for middle-class black people. Daddy King, a determined man who confronted racism wherever he found it, was intent on having his son Martin understand the value of maintaining

The birthplace of Martin Luther King Jr. still stands at 501 Auburn Avenue. He lived in this spacious home with his immediate family as well as his grandmother and an aunt. However, he and his brother sometimes had to sleep in the hall when his parents opened their home to visitors who could not get a hotel room because of segregation.

personal dignity. Once when father and son were confronted by a white Atlanta police officer, who, in keeping with southern custom at the time, referred to the senior King as "boy," Daddy King responded directly. Pointing to young Martin, he explained to the policeman, "That's a boy, I'm a man."

Incidents such as this formed young Martin's recollections of his father and testify to Daddy King's courage in the face of increasing racial intimidation. At a time when Atlanta blacks could not find a place downtown to sit and have a meal or even a cup of coffee, when segregated public restrooms and water fountains were constant reminders of the society's racial hierarchy, and when regional etiquette demanded that blacks step off the sidewalk to allow a white person to pass and required that they never make direct eye contact with southern whites, Sweet Auburn was a haven. It protected most of its residents from these humiliations, most of the time. It provided a base from which the black community could launch its attacks on injustice. The security offered by Sweet Auburn helped Daddy King, and other blacks, to stand up to the racist society outside.

Martin Luther King Jr. got a solid education at Booker T. Washington High School and then attended Morehouse College, also in Atlanta. There, he came under the influence of the theologian Benjamin E. Mays, who was then president of the college. Theology courses at Morehouse convinced King that religion, especially liberal Christian thought, could bring great change in the world. After graduating from Morehouse, King attended Cozer Theological Seminary in Pennsylvania, and in 1951 he began a doctoral program at Boston University, which he completed in 1955. In the late summer of 1954 he became the pastor of Dexter Avenue Baptist Church in Montgomery, Alabama. It was here that he came to international attention as leader of the Montgomery bus boycott, one of the most important direct action campaigns of the modern civil rights movement. In 1960, Martin Luther King Jr. joined his father as co-pastor of Ebenezer Baptist Church. Despite his on-going leadership of the national civil rights movement, which

Martin Luther King Jr. prepares to board the first desegregated bus in Montgomery in 1956, after a yearlong boycott. During this time, he honed his protest strategy by mobilizing black churches and advocating nonviolence.

kept him from the pulpit much of the time, he served in that position until his death in 1968. He is buried down the street from the church.

For King and others who grew up in the early twentieth century, black communities such as Sweet Auburn hold a significant and a warm place in their memories. Like New York City's Harlem, Chicago's Southside, and Washington's Shaw district, Sweet Auburn was a place of comfort and security in an otherwise hostile American society. Most of these communities took form, in part, as a response to racial restrictions that few would want to recreate. Yet these were places where black people felt at home in ways that many have not been able to duplicate in even the most affluent and physically comfortable integrated communities of the late twentieth and early twenty-first centuries. During the most active phase of his civil rights work, Martin Luther King Jr. often explained his vision of the "beloved community," the nurturing environment of brotherhood he wished to see constructed in the nation as a whole. This vision came from his religious beliefs and was almost certainly fostered by his experience growing up in the supportive and protective community of Sweet Auburn.

In 1976, Sweet Auburn was designated a National Historic District, but that designation did not save the area from the problems afflicting most of the nation's inner-city neighborhoods. Poverty and crime threatened to destroy many of its middle-class community traditions. As residential integration in Atlanta and expanding civil rights enabled middle- and upper-class blacks to seek better, safer, and more comfortable living areas outside the center city, Sweet Auburn became disproportionately underclass. The neighborhood fell victim to urban blight with many of its buildings abandoned and its tax-paying population severely decreased.

Still, many struggled to rebuild the area, and in 1992 the National Trust for Historic Preservation identified it as one of America's Eleven Most Endangered Historic Places. The Historic District Development Corporation, formed in 1990 as a community-based revitalization effort, set its sights on revitalizing the area. The corporation acquired vacant or decaying structures, rehabilitated and then sold them at affordable prices to low- and moderate-income households. Since its inception, the organization has partnered with local financial institutions to build and rehabilitate more than 110 single-family homes and more than 50 affordable rental housing units. Currently it is working with the National Park Service and the National Trust for Historic Preservation to broaden its restoration efforts. Eventually they hope to include the commercial areas of the district as well. Working together, these organizations hope to restore the Sweet Auburn Historic District to the economically diverse and interdependent community that it once was.

Ebenezer Baptist Church remains a spiritual home to many Atlanta residents. Martin Luther King Jr., whose grandfather had been pastor at the church, became co-pastor with his father in 1960.

The Sweet Auburn Historic District is part of the Martin Luther King Jr. Historic District, located along Auburn Avenue, roughly between Courtland Street and I-75/85 in downtown Atlanta. In addition to the Ebenezer Baptist Church and Martin Luther King Jr.'s birthplace, the district is also home to the Martin Luther King, Jr. Center for Nonviolent Social Change. The center includes King's burial place in the center of a reflecting pool. Fire Station No. 6, also in the district, was built in 1894, and it played an important role in the Sweet Auburn community and in the desegregation of the Atlanta Fire Department. The Peace Plaza at 450 Auburn Avenue is a restful and beautifully landscaped area featuring the Peace Rose Garden, waterfalls, and the "Behold" monument, which honors the "historic principles that guided the life and works of Dr. Martin Luther King Jr." The National Park Service is restoring the houses on the block from 472 to 535 Auburn Avenue, which includes Martin Luther King Jr.'s birthplace, to their 1930s facades.

Sweet Auburn is significant as a place where, despite the handicap and horrors of racial injustice, African American commerce, education, and arts blossomed in the early twentieth century. The neighborhood nurtured some of the most influential leaders of the modern civil rights movement, including Martin Luther King Jr. It is also an example of the supportive strength of the African American family and community that thrived within its boundaries.

BLACK METROPOLIS-BRONZEVILLE DISTRICT

Bordered by Thirty-first Street, State Street, Pershing Road, and King Drive
Chicago, IL 60616
312-744-3200
www.ci.chi.il.us/Landmarks/B/ BlackMet.html

During the First World War, factories in Chicago and other northern cities cried out for laborers. Blacks eager to escape the racial segregation and violence of the South migrated to the North, especially to Chicago, in search of better jobs and better, more secure lives. After 1910 more than fifty thousand African Americans per decade settled in Chicago, more than doubling the city's African American population, which topped 100,000 by 1920. Most of these migrants settled in an area of the city dubbed "Metropolis" by its residents. This was a diverse neighborhood, like the Sweet Auburn area of Atlanta. It was a city within the larger city, a black community of mixed incomes and educational levels. Domestic workers and manual laborers shared the neighborhood with bankers, doctors, teachers, and entrepreneurs. Andrew "Rube" Foster, the founder of the Negro National Baseball League, and Ida B. Wells, the nationally known civil rights activist, journalist, and organizer of the NAACP, lived in the area, as did Bessie Coleman, the first African American female

pilot, and Louis Armstrong, the legendary trumpet player and bandleader.

Today, nine sites constitute the Black Metropolis-Bronzeville District of Chicago. They include the *Chicago Defender* Building, home of the influential African American newspaper from 1920 to 1960, and the Wabash Avenue YMCA that housed many newly arrived migrants, provided them with job training, and was general community center for political and social organization. In 1915 the Association for the Study of Negro Life and History, one of the first and most important organizations in the nation devoted to recording and interpreting African American history, was organized in this building by Carter G. Woodson, the father of black historical study. At 315 East Thirty-fifth Street stands the building that once housed

the Sunset Café. Built in 1921 its walls reverberated with the music of jazz greats from Earl "Father" Hines and Louis Armstrong to Jimmy Dorsey, Benny Goodman, and Gene Krupa. The district includes a memorial to the 8th Regiment, an African American WWI soldier, armed and in combat uniform standing atop a granite pedestal with inset bronze panels. The 8th Regiment Armory at 3533 South Giles Avenue, the first armory in the United States built for an African American military regiment, was constructed in 1914. The Victory Monument at Thirty-fifth Street and King Drive was constructed in 1926 in honor of the 8th Regiment's service in France during World War I. Just as Harlem was becoming the most well-known northern black community in the East, Metropolis was the black capital of the Midwest.

Starting in 1917, Unity Hall housed the People's Movement Club, a political organization founded by Oscar Stanton DePriest, the first northern African American elected to the U.S. House of Representatives. Originally constructed in 1887 as a Jewish social club, the building is a rare example of nineteenth-century clubhouse architecture.

The Apollo Theater

New York, N.Y.

Harlem's Stage of Dreams

In 1947, the Apollo was a fashionable destination for both blacks and whites, who line up here for a show in their hats and ties. One of the theater's most popular events was amateur night, which began in 1934. That year, Ella Fitzgerald (above) made her debut as a singer, wearing hand-me-downs instead of the evening gowns she would later wear.

Although 125th Street was in the heart of predominantly black Harlem, in the early 1930s it was known as a white street. All the stores and restaurants were owned by whites, and African Americans generally were not welcome. Some store owners on the street might sell to blacks, but they would not hire them. During the Great Depression of the 1930s, when black unemployment soared to twice or three times that of whites, this kind of discrimination, especially in Harlem, became increasingly intolerable. In the summer of 1934 blacks organized the "Jobs for Negroes" campaign. They boycotted and picketed stores with restrictive racial hiring policies, advising African Americans, "Don't buy where you can't work." The campaign against Blumstein's Department Store went on for six weeks before store officials agreed to hire blacks as sales clerks. Although some other white stores followed Blumstein's lead, Harlem's Chamber of Commerce, an all-white body in the 1930s, continued to discourage black businesses from leasing stores in the area, and movie houses seated blacks in the balcony only. Although there were pockets of progress, before World War II, it remained true, as almost every black New Yorker understood, that 125th Street was racially segregated, even if it did not display signs announcing the fact.

During the nineteenth century, Harlem, in northern Manhattan, was a poor white neighborhood. Harlem grew rapidly during the real estate

boom that began in the 1870s. Real estate speculators hoping to attract affluent residents to the area built a mix of single-family row houses, luxury apartment houses, and new commercial properties to serve the growing community that they anticipated. Religious, educational, and cultural institutions moved into the area, making it even more desirable. The western portions of Harlem developed slightly later than East Harlem because transportation improvements did not bring the subway to the area until the late 1890s. Although the New York and Harlem Railroad had operated from lower Manhattan to Harlem beginning in 1837, service was poor and unreliable and the trip was long. The impetus for new residential development in this area came with the arrival of three lines of elevated rail service which, by 1881, ran as far north as 129th Street, and by 1886 extended farther north.

After the subway connected the neighborhood to the rest of the city, western Harlem became fashionable and prosperous. It had some of the most luxurious apartment buildings in the city, many with elevators, a new innovation of the period. In 1904 the Lenox Avenue subway opened at 145th Street, making this section of Harlem more accessible to downtown. The addition of a number of modest multi-family housing units drew a working-class population, including recent immigrants from Great Britain and Germany. By then overspeculation in real estate was starting to take its toll. There was little vacant land left in Harlem. The area's population grew, but not enough to fill the new buildings, resulting in extensive vacancies. Landlords desperate to recover their investments cut rents and the real estate market in Harlem collapsed.

In 1904, Philip Payton, an African American businessman, founded the Afro-American Realty Company in hopes of developing part of Harlem as a black community. His timing was excellent, for the neighborhood's real estate problems gave him an opening that might not otherwise have been available to blacks. He was able to obtain five-year leases on white-owned property that he rented to blacks at prices above the area's generally deflated rents. For the city's middle-class African Americans this was a rare opportunity to live in one of New York City's better neighborhoods and, despite having to pay rents higher than those available to white people, many came to take advantage of it. In a 1914 report, the Urban League, a black civil rights organization, called Harlem "a community in which Negroes as a whole are . . . better housed than in any other part of the country."

During World War I, the labor demands of war industries changed the character of many northern cities, as tens of thousands of African Americans migrated north from the South, where they had traditionally lived, in search of work. Harlem's black population grew dramatically as this "Great Migration" of African Americans from the South brought waves of blacks to New York City. Although Harlem rents rose after the war, it remained one of the few places open to black settlement, and families doubled up, sharing living space and splitting the rent. Manhattan's black population grew from about 25,000 in 1890, to 90,000 in 1910, and to 150,000 by 1930. Most lived in Harlem, the most internationally celebrated black community of the twentieth century.

The 1920s brought not only increasing numbers of blacks to Harlem, it also brought a cultural renaissance with an explosion of African American literature, art, music, and theater. This was the Harlem within which the Apollo Theater emerged. It was located just across the street from Blumstein's. At the Apollo, a change in racial policy early in the 1930s set an example for the entire area. The Apollo replaced Hurtig and Seamon's Burlesque Theater built in 1914, which had featured striptease and vaudeville acts for whites-only audiences for more than a decade. Businessman Sidney Cohen purchased the old theater in 1928, changing its name to the Apollo, a name taken from a smaller theater located just a few doors away. Early on, Cohen featured black entertainers. In 1932, piano great Duke Ellington and his band appeared at the Apollo to make the profound musical statement, "It Don't Mean a Thing (If It Ain't Got That Swing)." Then, in January of 1934, the Apollo changed its policy of serving only whites and became the first theater on 125th street to offer entertainment for African American audiences. As a result, its popularity and audience numbers mushroomed.

Rental agent Philip Payton attracted middle-class blacks to Harlem with his advertisements of apartments with such amenities as "steam heat and hot water supply." The rents were more than whites would have paid, but African Americans were eager for decent housing in a good neighborhood.

Apartments To Let

OFFICE OF

PHILIP A. PAYTON, Jr.

44 & 46 West 99th Street.

4 & 5 Rooms and Bath, Steam Heat and Hot Water Supply, Open plumbing. Rents $23 to $27 per month.

49 West 99th Street.

Rooms and Bath, Hot Water Supply, Open plumbing. Rents $19 to $22 per month.

236 West 134th Street, Bet. 7th & 8th Aves.

6 Rooms and Bath, Steam Heat and Hot Water Supply, Open plumbing, Tiled halls and Bath. Rents $27 to $30 per month.

6-8-10-12-14 West 136th Street.

5 Rooms and Bath, Hot Water Supply. Rents $21 to $23 per month.

285 & 287 West 147th Street.

4 Rooms Apartments. Rents $17 to $18 per month.

PRIVATE HOUSES FOR RENT.

169 West 63rd Street.

3 Story and Basement, 10 Rooms and Bath. Rent $1000 per year.

35 West 99th Street.

3 Story and Cellar, 14 Rooms and Bath. Suitable for business purpose, size 25 x 100. Rent $1200 per year.

102 East 103rd Street, Cor. of Park Ave.

3 Story and Basement, 12 Rooms and Bath. Rent $720 per year.

134 East 124th Street.

3 Story and Basement, 10 Rooms and Bath. Rent $780 per year.

APPLY TO

PHILIP A. PAYTON, Jr., Agent

67 West 134th Street.

Telephone 917-918 Harlem.

The theater, built in 1913 to accommodate an audience of 1,700, was one of the few in New York City with two balconies. Before 1933, there were a café and a cabaret in the basement, a commercial store and main theater used for burlesque shows on the ground level, a restaurant on the second floor, and a loft containing offices and meeting rooms. The tiered seating in the main theater was set on a curve to allow for unobstructed views of the stage. The curved balconies, brass handrails, ornamented walls, and elaborate moldings carved in the shapes of flower garlands and ropes made the theater's interior both impressive and memorable. The lobby and box office areas were equally ornate. This was one of the most distinctive burlesque houses in the city, and perhaps the nation.

Situated in the midst of Harlem, the Apollo had a ready and enthusiastic clientele. Although these urban blacks were poor working people, they had some disposable income. Musical entertainment was an important diversion from the toil of manual labor, and Harlem was a major entertainment capital. Early jazz musicians such

In the 1930s, Harlem was hard-hit by the Great Depression. Men could not find work, and buildings became more crowded with tenants as southern farm families moved to northern cities, hoping for work.

as pianists Fats Waller and Willie "The Lion" Smith, were regulars at the Lafayette Theater on 132nd Street and 7th Avenue. The Lafayette was probably the first New York theater to integrate, admitting black patrons as early as 1912. Fletcher Henderson, who led the most commercially successful of the African American jazz bands of the 1920s, and jazz drummer Chick Webb also played there. Jazz dancer Florence Mills delighted black audiences during the 1920s, as did tap dance sensation Bill "Bojangles" Robinson, who was known to his fans as the "Mayor of Harlem" because his skilled and stylish dance seemed to represent the spirit of the community.

These musical diversions became even more psychologically important after the stock market crash of 1929 and the onset of the Great Depression of the 1930s than they had been in the 1920s. At a time when American tastes in entertainment were almost as segregated as the society itself, the Apollo's—featuring jazz, African American performers, and catering to a black audience—brought a spirit-lifting distraction that Harlem needed. Almost immediately, it became the most popular musical theater for African American patrons. Its first show in 1934, "Jazz a la Carte," featuring saxophone player Benny Carter's big band, was a hit.

Under the direction of band leader Frank Schiffman, the Apollo stage became home to the greatest performers of the time. Singers, comics, big bands, and dance shows featuring chorus lines with elaborate costumes and lavish and imaginative stage sets were the Apollo's trademark presentations. It soon eclipsed the Lafayette and the other black theaters in the city. The Apollo moved theater entertainment to a new level in terms of the quality of performances and entertainers, sharing the spotlight with Harlem's dance clubs and ballrooms such as Small's Paradise and the Savoy Ballroom. By the mid-1930s, the Apollo became New York City's premier showcase for black talent.

In 1934 Cohen began an experimental amateur night at the theater. It proved to be the Apollo's most successful act. Its popularity grew still more after film actor and producer Ralph Cooper began hosting the show. Amateur night became a regular program that drew performers from all over the city. Competition was stiff, and the notoriously demanding audiences chose the winners by the level of their applause. "If you can make

The Apollo Theater

253 West 125th Street
New York, NY 10035
212-531-5300
www.apollotheater.com
NRIS 83004059

DATE BUILT
1914

SIGNIFICANCE
The Apollo Theater is a major cultural center and entertainment venue in Harlem, New York, one of the most important African American communities of the twentieth century. It remains one of the best-known theaters for African American entertainment in the world.

Josephine Baker: An Amercian Exile, An International Star

In 1906 Josephine Freda MacDonald was born in St. Louis, Missouri. She grew up to be Josephine Baker, international entertainer, singer, dancer, Broadway actress, and movie star.

In 1921, as a fifteen-year-old, she danced in the chorus line of the black musical *Shuffle Along,* which burst onto the stage in New York City at the onset of that incredible time of artistic, musical, and intellectual creativity known as the Harlem Renaissance. While still a teenager, she toured with the veteran dancer and blues singer Bessie Smith. Smith was at the height of her career when Baker briefly joined her act in the early 1920s. Unlike Smith, whose rough and crude manner offended some, Baker's exotic beauty and talent drew a broad audience to Harlem's most popular nightclubs to see her dance and hear her sing.

Josephine Baker would not tour in the South, where she was expected to travel on segregated transportation, to eat in segregated restaurants—when food was available at all—to find sleeping accommodations in Jim Crow hotels, and to perform for segregated audiences. When she was allowed to perform in white establishments, it was to all-white audiences with very definite assumptions about how a black performer should conduct herself on stage. She objected to performing in a racially stereotyped style—to sing what she called "mammy songs."

In 1925 she went to Paris, where she was know as "Le Sauvage" (the savage) and sometimes played on racial stereotypes. In Europe she was a sensation and never suffered the abuse faced by even the most popular black stars in the United States. Baker was never completely comfortable when she returned to the United States on her few American tours. When World War II broke out in Europe, Baker used her fame to support the allied effort. She entertained American troops stationed in North Africa, worked with the Red Cross in Belgium, and joined the resistance movement in France. After the war, the French government awarded her the Legion of Honor.

Baker was a staunch advocate of integration and racial equality. She adopted twelve children of various races from around the world. She called them her Rainbow Tribe. During the 1950s and early 1960s Baker was a strong supporter of the American civil rights movement. She refused to perform for segregated audiences and forced the integration of several Las Vegas nightclubs. In 1963, she flew to the United States from Paris specifically to take part in the March on Washington. Josephine Baker died in 1975 in Paris, after a performance and a large party in her honor. She died the way she had told a reporter fifty years before she wished to die, "breathless, spent, at the end of a dance." At a time when race limited opportunities for most black artists and musicians, Josephine Baker carved out a remarkable career on both sides of the Atlantic.

As a dancer, Josephine Baker captivated audiences in the United states as well as in Europe. As a civil rights activist, she fought for integrated theaters, refusing to go on stage until blacks were allowed to sit with whites.

it at the Apollo," went the popular wisdom in Harlem, "you can make it anywhere." Young Ella Fitzgerald was facing a difficult challenge when she entered the Apollo's amateur night show in November 1934. Fitzgerald was a teenager struggling to survive on the streets of Harlem. She had musical talent, but it was raw and undisciplined, much like the appearance of this rough, unkempt young woman. She was living a precarious life, seemingly without much of a future, but all that was about to change with her debut at the Apollo Theater.

Fitzgerald went to the theater for the Monday auditions intending to perform as a dancer, but her competition was the Edwards Sisters, one of the hottest dance teams in the city. Moreover, the duo was noted for their attractive costumes—sequined dresses and professional dancing pumps. Fitzgerald had arrived at the theater wearing cast-off clothing and men's boots. On the spot, she decided to audition for the contest as a singer. This was, no doubt, a life-changing decision.

She survived the audition, winning the ten dollar cash prize and an invitation to return later that week to appear on stage. She made her debut at the Apollo on Wednesday, November 21, 1934, singing two songs, "The Object of My Affection" and "Judy." The show began at 11:00 PM and ended at midnight. Before Fitzgerald took the stage, she joined the other contestants assembled in the tense atmosphere of the Green Room beneath the stage. Contestants knew that if they did not please the audience they would be booed off the stage before their performances were complete.

It was house policy that contestants be accompanied by whatever band was currently playing at the theater. This gave the amateurs the opportunity to perform with the finest bands in the country, but often this only added to the pressure. Nervous performers found themselves on stage with the likes of Duke Ellington, Jimmie Lunceford, Louis Armstrong, Lionel Hampton, or other legendary band leaders. On the evening of Ella Fitzgerald's debut, the Benny Carter Orchestra provided the accompaniment, which added to the stress of the moment for a young woman with little stage experience. According to the host Ralph Cooper, initially, Fitzgerald was "jumpy and unnerved." Her voice cracked as she started her first song and the audience immediately reacted with booing and jeering. Cooper stopped her in mid-performance

A 1936 handbill advertises Duke Ellington's appearance at the Apollo. A bandleader, pianist, and prolific composer, Ellington was an innovator who borrowed rhythms from European, African, and American music. He was one of the originators of big-band jazz and always popular with audiences.

and urged her to start again. She regained her composure and this time she was marvelous. At the end of the show, she was called back to the stage and it was clear from the audience's enthusiastic reaction that she had won the contest.

Even as the Apollo's reputation drew top black stars and an increasing number of white patrons, Harlem continued to reflect the racial restrictions of American society, and the economically depressed circumstances of New York City during these years. Life in this much-romanticized black community was difficult. Poverty, unemployment, and illness weighed heavily on its African American residents. The unemployment rate, as high as 30 percent across the nation during the depression, was over 50 percent in Harlem. Yet, only 9 percent of Harlem's families received government relief jobs. Rents were generally higher in Harlem than for comparable housing elsewhere in New York City, and racial restrictions severely limited blacks' access to housing in other parts of the city. The pneumonia and typhoid rates in Harlem were double the rates in Manhattan as a whole. Five Harlemites suffered from tuberculosis for every one white New Yorker with the illness, and black mothers and black babies died at childbirth at a rate twice that in the city at large. This health crisis was further complicated by the fact that at Harlem General Hospital, the community's only public health facility, a mere 273 beds and 50 bassinets served the community's 200,000 residents.

These conditions exacerbated existing conflicts with city authorities, making for a volatile situation. Tensions between the people of Harlem and the New York City police, always high, boiled over in March 1935 when rumors spread that policemen had beaten a young black boy to death after he was arrested for shoplifting a pocketknife. In reality, the police did beat a seventeen-year-old, but he was not dead. No matter, ten thousand Harlemites swept down the main thoroughfare of Lenox Avenue attacking white-owned businesses and battling police. By the following day three blacks were dead, more than thirty were injured, and more than a hundred were jailed. New York newspapers warned the city's white citizens against visiting Harlem. The papers falsely charged that black anger over the deplorable conditions they faced in the community and the prejudice they met at the hands of city officials and some white business owners resulted in their general hatred of white people.

This was the context within which the Apollo had broken the color line on 125th Street and was seeking to establish itself as the venue for black music, and making that music available to a white, as well as a black, audience. Whites were reluctant at first to come to the theater, but the Apollo brought its music and its amateur night to a wider public during the 1930s on New York City's WMAC radio. The Apollo Amateur House, as the broadcast was called, was a great success attracting a mass following among blacks and whites. Eventually, it became one of the most popular radio programs in the country, airing regularly on twenty-one stations. The music from the Apollo was music that white radio stations usually did not play, and music with which most older white people were not familiar. The Apollo Amateur Night broadcast made the theater immensely popular and brought larger and larger crowds. Although there were many places in Harlem that whites would not visit during the 1930s and 1940s, they came to the Apollo. Its popularity helped other Harlem clubs and nightspots to draw large audiences from outside the community,

Billy Ward's Dominoes perform to a full house at the Apollo in 1952. The theater booked acts that catered to a black audience, but white patrons from other New York neighborhoods often traveled to Harlem for a show.

showcasing black entertainers and launching the careers of many black stars.

In addition to Ella Fitzgerald, singers Pearl Bailey and Sarah Vaughan also won amateur night contests in the early years. In 1937 the Count Basie Band took the Apollo stage for the first time with singer Billie Holiday. During the swing era of the1940s, Apollo audiences thrilled to the mellow tones of singer Nat "King" Cole, the rhythms of saxophonist and bandleader Louis Jordan, and the unparalleled entertainment of young singer and dancer Sammy Davis Jr. While other black clubs and theaters fell on hard times during the 1950s when the swing era began to fade, the Apollo remained popular, becoming home to rhythm and blues, gospel, and the new sounds of rock and roll. Black comedians such as Jackie "Moms" Mabley, Redd Foxx, and Pigmeat Markham became regulars, and in 1958 a young singer, Dianne (later Dionne) Warwick, won the amateur contest singing gospel songs.

Through the 1960s, the Apollo remained New York City's musical mecca. It attracted top white performers such as Bob Hope, Joan Crawford, and Betty Grable to its audiences to be entertained by black stars, the likes of Smokey Robinson, the Four Tops, the Jackson Five, Jackie Wilson, and a child prodigy known as "Little Stevie Wonder." One of the greatest performances ever witnessed at the theater is preserved on a 1963 album by James Brown, the Godfather of Soul, entitled "Live at the Apollo."

During the 1960s the success of the Motown sound brought black music to a wide audience, and racial barriers in the entertainment world were gradually breaking down. By the late 1960s and beyond, premier white clubs and theaters were courting the top black entertainers, and the Apollo was facing greater competition for both performers and audiences. Such headliners as Michael Jackson, Gladys Knight, and Aretha Franklin now commanded enormous fees and were capable of drawing tens of thousands to the huge venues of major stadiums and arenas. The Apollo could not compete on this scale. By the mid-1970s, having difficulty attracting the big names in black entertainment and with audiences dwindling, the historic theater was suffering substantial financial hardship. Finally, in 1977, the Apollo declared bankruptcy and closed its doors.

Its distinctive history and its long tradition of service to the community of Harlem moved many for whom the Apollo was an icon of African American achievement to come to the aid of the struggling theater. In 1981 the Inner City Theater Group, a group of investors lead by former Manhattan borough president Percy Sutton, acquired the Apollo for $225. Two years later, Congress placed the theater on the National Register of Historic Places. The State of New York helped to underwrite its mortgage, and in 1988 the theater underwent a $20 million facelift. It became a home for cable television programming and amateur night was restored. Still the Apollo struggled to stay afloat, losing an estimated two million dollars a year.

Andy Kirk conducts his band, the Clouds of Joy, as their composer and arranger, Mary Lou Williams, plays the piano in 1937.

Then, in 1991, the Inner City Theater Group gave the Apollo as a gift to Harlem. The community established the Apollo Theater Foundation, a nonprofit group led by New York congressman Charles Rangel. The foundation took control in 1992, and the Apollo became a symbol of the effort to restore and revitalize 125th Street. By the mid-1990s the big names were back. Luther Vandross, B. B. King, and many of today's top singing stars now grace the stage. The theater has recently instituted a "kids night show" that attracts some of the most extraordinarily talented children in the nation, including the remarkable stand-up comic Marc John Jeffries, who won the Apollo talent contest at age five.

Clearly the Apollo Theater is undergoing a revival. In addition to audiences attracted to its musical shows, it is also a major tourist destination. Its new popularity recalls the 1920s Harlem Renaissance, when the neighborhood was known internationally as the most fashionable African American community in the world.

EAGLE SALOON AND ODD FELLOWS MASONIC BALLROOM

401–403 South Rampart
    Street
New Orleans, LA 70112

The Eagle Saloon was a favorite drinking and gathering place for local jazz and blues musicians, who came here to relax between shows at the Odd Fellows Hall and Masonic Hall next door. The popular Frankie Dusen's Eagle Band took its name to honor the saloon. With the third floor Odd Fellows Masonic Ballroom above, the Eagle Saloon was part of a jazz complex that drew some of the best musicians in the New Orleans area. From 1900 until 1906, Buddy Bolden and his hot trumpet were among the regulars, as were Papa John Joseph, Willie Foster, and Bob Lyons, who all became legendary jazz figures in the first two decades of the twentieth century. Another club, the Little Gem Saloon, was located at the corner of South Rampart Street and Poydras Street. During the early twentieth century it was an important site for jazz and blues until Prohibition restricted its operation. Part of the Little Gem's claim to fame was that it was just a few doors from the Zulu Social Aid and Pleasure Club's Jazz Funeral. The Jazz Funeral mourned the death, but also celebrated the life of the departed through music, dance, and a funeral parade that blended ancient African and more

recent African American music and cultural traditions of syncopated rhythms and improvisation. A parading jazz band of horns and drums, led by an elegantly dressed grand marshal waving a handkerchief and carrying an elaborately bejeweled umbrella, moved through the streets attracting hundreds of onlookers, some of whom joined in the rhythmic march. Sometimes lasting four hours or more, the parade, marked by pauses to accommodate dancing and singing and the prayers in remembrance of the dead, was widely known and tremendously popular.

NEW ORLEANS JAZZ NATIONAL HISTORIC PARK

419 Rue Decatur
New Orleans, LA 70130
504-589-4806
www.nps.gov/jazz/
NPS

New Orleans is often considered the birthplace of jazz. The city's unique cultural setting, which blended Latin, Anglo, and African heritage, formed a hothouse for work songs of the rural South, gospel music, and blues. These musical styles fused and gave way to ragtime and Dixieland in the 1890s and early decades of the twentieth century. In an effort to preserve and interpret the city's musical heritage, the U.S. Congress established the New Orleans Jazz National Historical Park in 1991. The 400 block of South Rampart Street, a historic district nes-

tled in the heart of one of New Orleans's black communities, is an important part of that effort. The historic structures found on this block offer a look back to the time when such jazz greats as pianist Jelly Roll Morton and trumpeters Louis Armstrong and Buddy Bolden were regular figures in the neighborhood. Their music became the foundation of the New Orleans jazz that was nurtured in the saloons, theaters, and ballrooms along the 400 block of South Rampart Street.

THE IROQUOIS THEATER

413–415 South Rampart
    Street
New Orleans, LA 70112

The Iroquois Theater seated two hundred when it opened in 1912 and was the home of black vaudeville. The jazz pianist Jelly Roll Morton claimed to have been greatly influenced by the music of singer-pianist Butler "String Bean" May who performed at the theater regularly. The popular Bruce Jazz Stock Company and other well-known groups of the day provided the jazz and blues that accompanied the shows. Jazz drummers such as Eddie "Rabbit" Robinson, so called because of his fast hands, and blues guitarist Lonnie Johnson who performed with these groups went on to make great names for themselves in the rapidly expanding world of jazz. A young Louis Armstrong gave his first known public performance here, winning the Iroquois Theater talent contest. Today the Iroquois stands as one of the only intact small theaters from the early-twentieth-century jazz era in New Orleans.

KARNOFSKY'S STORE/MORRIS MUSIC RECORD SHOP

427–431 South Rampart
Street
New Orleans, LA 70112

In 1908, Louis Karnofsky, a New Orleans junk dealer, hired eight-year-old Louis Armstrong to assist him in his business. Karnofsky knew the Armstrongs well and helped them through some tough financial times. When he opened a secondhand store in 1913, Karnofsky continued to employ young Louis. Karnofsky gave him an advance on his wages so that he could purchase his first cornet from a nearby pawnshop. Later Louis Karnofsky's son, Morris Karnofsky, turned the store into a jazz record store, the first to cater to the New Orleans black community.

BEALE STREET HISTORIC DISTRICT

Second to Fourth Streets
Memphis, TN 38103
901-526-0110
www.bealestreet.com

Located in Memphis between Second and Fourth streets, the Beale Street Historic District is one of the most significant sites for blues and jazz in the country. In the early twentieth century, the

The lights of Beale Street today advertise a variety of music and entertainment, including the blues at B. B. King's Blues Club.

area boasted an exciting musical nightlife and was home to such pre-eminent blues musicians as William Christopher and W. C. Handy. The music played here inspired the African American sound of urban blues that become popular after World War I and evolved into what by the mid-twentieth century was beginning to be called rock and roll.

FLETCHER HENDERSON HOUSE

1016 Andrew Street
Cuthbert, GA 39840

Built in 1888 this single-story house with a welcoming front porch was the boyhood home of Fletcher Henderson Jr. and his brother, Horace. Sons of Professor Fletcher Hamilton Henderson, a prominent educator in the community, the brothers were both important jazz musicians and composers. Fletcher Henderson Jr. made his reputation writing and playing jazz with his

own band in New York City, inspiring such jazz greats as Count Basie, Louis Armstrong, and clarinetist and bandleader Benny Goodman. During the mid-1930s, he provided arrangements for Benny Goodman's band. Horace Henderson arranged music for the Glenn Miller Orchestra in 1938, and played with jazz singer Lena Horne during the mid-1940s. Horace also played with Fletcher's band during the 1940s and continued into the 1970s playing with small modern jazz groups.

THE SCOTT JOPLIN HOUSE

2658 Delmar Boulevard
St. Louis, MO 63103
*www.mostateparks.com/
scottjoplin.htm*

Scott Joplin was a pioneer of the musical form know as ragtime. With its unique rhythmic structure, ragtime captured the musical imagination of America and much of the world during the early twentieth century, and Joplin wrote and arranged many of the most popular tunes. Between 1900 and 1903, three of his most productive years, Joplin resided at an apartment on Delmar Boulevard in St. Louis. While living there he wrote "The Entertainer," a tune popularized fifty years later in the 1973 Paul Newman movie, *The Sting.* Joplin also wrote "Peacherine Rag" and "The Little Black Baby" while living at this address.

USS *Arizona* Memorial

Honolulu, Hawaii

Race and War in Paradise

On board a warship in Pearl Harbor (above), Admiral Chester Nimitz pins the Navy Cross on Doris Miller "for distinguished devotion to duty, extraordinary courage and disregard for his own personal safety" during the Japanese attacks months earlier.

In the Hawaiian waters of Pearl Harbor, astride the sunken hull of a 184-foot-long battleship, the USS *Arizona* Memorial stands in honor of all those who suffered in the Japanese military attack that drew the United States into the Second World War. Early Sunday morning, December 7, 1941, a Japanese force of six aircraft carriers, thirty-three warships, and other auxiliary craft lay 230 miles off the northern coast of the main Hawaiian island of Oahu. At 6:00 AM the carriers launched 354 warplanes in the first of multiple attack waves on the U.S. naval base at Pearl Harbor. For almost two hours, from 7:55 to 9:45 AM, Japanese planes bombed, torpedoed, and strafed the harbor, sinking or severely damaging eighteen American ships, including three destroyers and eight battleships. Japanese dive-bombers also attacked adjacent Hickham Airforce Base destroying aircraft still on the ground. Wheeler Airfield and Schofield Army Barracks in central Oahu were also targets, as were Bellows Airfield and Kaneohe Naval Air Station on the windward side of the island. Before the raid was over, the U.S. sea and air forces in Hawaii were severely crippled, and thousands of military and civilian personnel were killed or wounded.

The Japanese losses were comparatively light, only twenty-nine planes and five midget submarines. One Japanese submarine was captured when it ran aground off the coast of Bellows Airfield, its captain taken prisoner by U.S. forces. Although the attack on Pearl Harbor was a success for Japan's military, it served to unite a previously divided American people, bringing the United States into the war in Europe as well as the Pacific. Black historian, writer, and civil rights activist W. E. B. DuBois expressed the feelings of many African Americans who, like white Americans, feared an Allied defeat. "If Hitler wins," he wrote in a newspaper article in 1941, "every single right we now possess, for which we have struggled here in America for more than three centuries, will be instantaneously wiped away." Black Americans knew a civil rights struggle was necessary to move the United States toward racial justice, but as DuBois argued, "If the Allies win, we shall at least have the right to continue fighting for a share of democracy for ourselves."

Commissioned in 1916, the USS *Arizona* was one of the 130 vessels of the U.S. Pacific Fleet, and one of seven battleships docked along "Battleship Row" on the southeast shore of the harbor's Ford Island. At approximately 8:10 AM a 1,760-pound armor-piercing bomb hit the *Arizona* and slammed through her deck, igniting her forward ammunition magazine, a storage area containing explosives. The vessel exploded and sank, trapping its 1,177 crew.

During the confusion of the attack, men and women distinguished themselves with acts of humanity and heroism. One such hero was Mess Attendant Second Class Doris Miller, an African American from Willow Grove, near Waco, Texas, who was serving aboard the USS *West Virginia*. Miller was aboard the ship attending to his regular duties, serving breakfast and cleaning up afterward, when an enormous explosion caught the entire crew by surprise. The ship's captain was gravely wounded, and some of the crew, including Miller, carried him to the relative safety of the deck's fortified anti-aircraft emplacement. On the deck was a chaotic and terrifying scene. Men lay wounded, dead, or dying, and the overwhelming fire and smoke made it all seem surreal.

In the midst of this turmoil, Miller came upon a gunner dead at his battle station. He had never fired an anti-aircraft gun before, as the navy only instructed whites in the use of such a weapon. "I had watched the others with these guns," he later reported to the press. Despite his lack of training, Miller manned the gun and opened fire on the attacking

The USS Arizona *burned and sank in less than nine minutes after being hit by a Japanese bomb. Half of the 2,390 people killed that day were on the* Arizona.

USS *Arizona*
Memorial

1 Arizona Memorial Place
Honolulu, HI 96818
808-422-0561
www.nps.gov/usar/
NRIS 66000944
NPS

DATE DEDICATED
1962

SIGNIFICANCE
A memorial to those who lost
their lives on December 7, 1941,
in the Japanese attack on U.S.
military forces at Pearl Harbor.
Despite racial restrictions,
African Americans played critical
combat roles in defense of the
American forces.

Japanese planes. Due to the confusion on deck during
the attack, it is not clear how many enemy planes Miller
brought down. He later told a navy friend that he
believed he had destroyed three or four planes, but
some witnesses put the number at as many as six of the
twenty-nine Japanese planes shot down by American
gunners. "It wasn't hard." he recalled. "I just pulled the
trigger and she worked fine."

Doris Miller—addressed as Dorie by most of his
shipmates, who thought it more fitting for such a power-
fully built man—was well known in the military community at Pearl Harbor before the raid. A fine athlete, he
had been a fullback on his high school football team
and was the USS *West Virginia* heavyweight boxing
champion. He survived the attack on Pearl Harbor and
became a hero to his shipmates, many of whom had
witnessed his action, but early naval reports mentioned
him only as a "Negro cook" who assisted the ship's
captain. Months passed before the secretary of the navy
officially recognized Miller with a letter and, finally, the
President of the United States, Franklin D. Roosevelt,
sent a letter of commendation.

On May 7, 1942, Admiral Chester Nimitz presented
Miller with the Navy Cross, making him the first African
American in U.S. history to receive such an honor and
the first American hero of World War II. In the citation
for the award, Miller was credited with protecting and
assisting his wounded captain in the face of enemy fire.
It did not mention the number of enemy aircraft he shot
down, acknowledging only that he "later manned and
operated a machine gun directed at enemy Japanese
attacking aircraft until ordered to leave the bridge."
Many, including some congressmen, believed that Miller
should have received the Congressional Medal of Honor
for his action. However, due to the prevailing racial prejudice of the time, bills introduced in Congress to bestow
the honor invariably got "lost" in committee.

Doris Miller was not the only black hero on that
day. Mess Attendant Third Class William Jeremiah
Powell of North Carolina manned an abandoned gun
aboard the USS *Curtiss* and shot down a Japanese fighter
bomber. The plane crashed into the deck of the ship
killing Powell, one of at least two messmen to die in that
action aboard the *Curtiss*. Apparently other black messmen also took on combat duties during the heat of the

battle, but their stories are only starting to emerge, mainly from the memories of eyewitnesses.

Miller survived the attack, but was killed in action two years later aboard another ship, the *Liscome Bay*. The bravery of African Americans such as Miller and Powell makes Pearl Harbor not only a national landmark, but also a landmark of African American history. Although not officially recognized by the military as a significant site for African American history, it was a place celebrated in the pages of the wartime black press for the distinguished actions of black troops. African American heroism under fire was a conundrum to some in the U.S. Navy, as it underscored the racial injustice of the service. African Americans had served the nation at sea since the Revolutionary War. Yet, in 1941, the navy was the least racially progressive of the national military services.

After the attack on Pearl Harbor, the navy continued to turn down scores of blacks who volunteered for service. In a single day it rejected three hundred black volunteers in New York City. Of those it enlisted, the rules were clear: blacks could only serve as cooks, waiters, and personal attendants to the officer personnel. Black women were denied any opportunity to serve in the navy or the marines. Despite the protests of civil rights organizations and the African American press, the limited number of black men who were accepted could hope for little advancement in the navy. In its official records, the navy declared, "The policy of not enlisting men of the colored race for any branch of the naval service but

"above and beyond the call of duty"

DORIE MILLER
Received the Navy Cross at Pearl Harbor, May 27, 1942

A promotional poster printed by the U.S. government in 1943 features a portrait of Doris Miller, wearing his Navy Cross, as a man who went "above and beyond the call of duty" in the attack on Pearl Harbor. At the outset of the war, relatively few blacks participated in the armed forces, discouraged by racism and the chance to perform only menial jobs. By 1945, however, nearly 1 million black men and women served in the military, primarily in the army, followed by the navy.

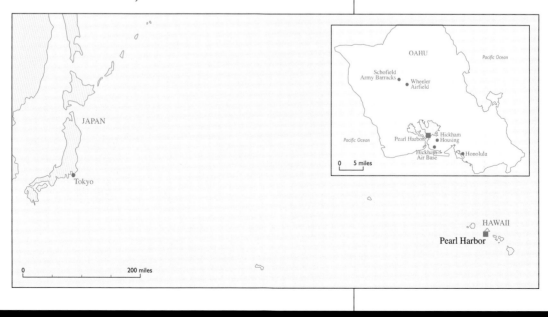

the messman branch was adopted to meet the best interests of general ship efficiency."

The navy contended that this restriction benefited not only the service, but also "served as well the best interests of [Negroes] themselves." The policy also protected the racial sensitivities of white sailors, especially those from the South. Apparently this reasoning was strictly adhered to. Of the more than four thousand black seamen at the opening of the war, there were no officers and few at the advanced noncommissioned ranks. In the 1940s, the navy reflected, more than other branches of the service, race relations during this period in the American South.

This prejudice found in mainland America came face-to-face with quite a different racial tradition in the Hawaiian Islands. The rapid growth of the military and civilian worker population in the islands in the wake of the attack on Pearl Harbor was the catalyst for racial struggle and change in mid-twentieth-century Hawaii. Before the war, there had been a small African American presence in the islands for more than a hundred years. When the king of Hawaii, Kamehameha conquered Oahu in 1796, Black Jack, called Keaka'ele'ele locally, was already living in the islands. Most of the earliest blacks, such as Anthony Allen, a former slave from New

Doris Miller mans an anti-aircraft gun and brings down a Japanese bomber in this government-sponsored cartoon promoting the war effort and exhorting Americans to "Remember!!" the day of the Pearl Harbor attack.

York State, came in the late eighteenth century and early nineteenth century as sailors and stayed to become landowners and traders. By mid-nineteenth century some, such as William Johnson, Spencer Rhodes, and Charles Nicholson, ran barbershops, tailor shops and other small businesses. Allen's son became a cowboy on a cattle ranch on the Big Island of Hawaii in the 1820s. Betsy Stockton, a servant to white missionaries from New England, founded a school on the island of Maui.

By the late nineteenth century, blacks were participating in Hawaiian politics and even holding office. Attorney T. McCants Stuart served in the royal cabinet of King Kamehameha IV. With the assistance of U.S. Marines, a group of Hawaiian-based American sugar planters staged a coup, overthrowing the government of Queen Lili'uokalani in 1893. The new government they established supported Hawaii's annexation to the United States, which became official in 1898. In the early twentieth century, African Americans continued to play a role in Island politics. William Crockett became a senator in the territorial government and his son became a county official on Maui. By 1920 a black woman, Eva Jones Smith, was hosting her own radio show, the first woman in the islands to do so.

As most blacks married into the island community and faded into the local population, there was no distinctive African American community. Racial categories in Hawaii were often confusing by mainland standards; thus, official Hawaiian census figures are ambiguous on this point. For example, census data for the islands in the early twentieth century often listed those who might be counted black on the mainland as Puerto Rican. As Puerto Ricans were often classified as Caucasians by Hawaiian census officials, some residents of African descent were officially listed as Caucasian. Significantly, Hawaii's elite whites—who often married into prominent Hawaiian families—generally took pride in the racial blending of island people. Patterns of intermarriage also ensured that African Americans often became an indistinguishable part of the local population. Under these circumstances, the 1940 census, listing only 255 blacks in Hawaii, probably underestimated the numbers of islanders of African descent.

Clearly, Hawaii was different from the mainland in terms of its racial traditions and assumptions. In the

March 1939 issue of *Asia* magazine, an article entitled "Hawaii Has No Race Problem," set forth this idyllic vision: "Today the races of Hawaii live together as one people, owning one common allegiance to their American nationality. Racial origin means nothing to the individual in his status as an American. Among the racial groups there is mutual understanding and friendly sympathy." Although this article greatly exaggerated the situation, Hawaii's relative racial harmony was disrupted by the presence of the U.S. military. Tensions between the local population and the U.S. military, which was a presence on the island since the early twentieth century, often centered around issues of race and color.

At the beginning of the 1940s, Honolulu's local population had not forgotten the vivid example of racial injustice, widely known as the Massie Case, that occurred a decade earlier. In the fall of 1931, Thalia Massie, wife of a navy lieutenant, Thomas Massie, claimed to have been beaten and raped by a group of local Hawaiians. Despite inconsistencies that raised serious suspicions about her story, the police arrested five local men.

The local press fanned the flames of racial intolerance. Withholding Massie's name, the Honolulu *Star-Bulletin,* referred to her only as "a white woman of refinement and culture." Soon mainland papers picked up the story and many of their readers reacted, imagining an island-wide plot by Hawaiian men to trap and assault white women. "The situation in Hawaii is deplorable," declared one letter that appeared in the San Francisco *Examiner.* Offering no shred of evidence, the writer claimed, "Outside the cities and small towns the roads go through jungles and in these remote places bands of dangerous natives lie in wait for white women driving by."

The response from some of the top ranking naval officers in Hawaii was equally racist, and even more bellicose. One navy admiral was infuriated, as he told a local reporter from the Honolulu *Star-Bulletin* at the thought of "Half-breed hoodlums" violating a white woman, the wife of a navy officer, "raised in a cultured American home." "Our first inclination," he told the reporter, "is to seize the brutes and string them up on trees." *Time* magazine joined in the racist stereotyping, claiming that "five brown-skinned young bucks," had assaulted Thelma Massie because the "lust of mixed breeds for white women."

In this racially charged atmosphere, the accused were brought to trial and found not guilty by a jury of five whites and seven local people of color. The navy admiral in Honolulu telegraphed Washington, declaring that he would triple the strength of the shore patrol, "to protect the homes of naval personnel while they are away on maneuvers." The press continued its furious reporting. "To the outside world Hawaii thus says: 'Bring white women here if you wish. We need tourists.'" One writer remarked sarcastically to the New York *Evening Post,* "'But if our people rape them, we won't punish the rapists.'" When it became clear that some of the white jurors had voted for acquittal, the *Capital Journal* in Salem, Oregon, reasoned that whites in Hawaii had mixed with Hawaiians and "gone native and lost their racial pride."

Enraged by the acquittal, Thomas Massie, assisted by two friends and his mother-in-law, kidnapped and killed Joseph Kahahawai, one of the Hawaiian men who had been charged in the case. His mother-in-law, Grace Hubbard Bell Fortescue—the niece of the inventor Alexander Graham Bell—who had come from the mainland to be with her daughter, was discovered by police driving the car in which Kahahawai's body was found. Lieutenant Massie, Fortescue, and two navy enlisted men who worked for Massie were arrested by Hawaiian police and brought to trial for murder. Internationally known trial lawyer Clarence Darrow, then seventy-five years old, came to Honolulu to defend the trio in what was to be his last case. He caused a sensation by referring to the murder as "an honor slaying."

Again, race surfaced as an important factor in the case. Mainland newspapers focused on the story as a kind of soap opera, wondering rhetorically if Honolulu was a safe place for white women. The trial became a social spectacle drawing many of Hawaii's white elite and triggering nonstop reporting in local newspapers. One navy official wondered aloud if white jurors would, "bow to the dictates of the orientals." His answer was not long in coming. Lieutenant Massie admitted his role in the murder, although he said he could not remember actually shooting the victim. Despite Darrow's dramatic and emotional closing argument, which presented Lieutenant Massie as insane at the time of the killing, the jury convicted his clients of manslaughter.

Navy lieutenant Thomas Massie and his wife, Thalia, were at the center of a racial crisis in Honolulu when she claimed to have been raped by a group of Hawaiian men. When the defendants were acquitted at trial, sailors rioted in the streets and Admiral George Pettingill telegraphed to Washington headquarters that "Honolulu was not a safe place" for white women.

The mainland press was incensed by the guilty verdict. "The whole island should be put under martial law and perpetrators of outrages against white women should be promptly tried by courts martial and executed," argued an editorial in the San Francisco *Examiner*. The New York *Evening Post* excused Kahahawai's murder on the grounds that it was the accuseds' only recourse, as Hawaii would not protect white women or punish their attackers. In Washington, southern congressmen threatened to suspend the Hawaiian territorial government. Some called for the imposition of martial law. In an attempt to shift the focus away from Hawaiians, one reporter at the *Star-Bulletin* claimed that the accused Hawaiian men were not Hawaiian at all. "There is not a full bred Hawaiian among them."

Mainland Americans were generally mystified by Hawaii's multiracial, multicultural society. A California reporter writing on race in the islands called Hawaii the "most fantastic Potpourris of alien blood that was ever mixed into a hell's broth." It soon became clear that powerful leaders in the U.S. government would not permit the punishment of prominent whites for crimes against people of color, even when the crime was murder. Herbert Hoover, President of the United States, in cooperation with Congress, pressured the Hawaiian territorial governor Gerrit P. Judd to intercede. The governor commuted the sentences of all four accused. The sentences, which would have been ten years to life, were reduced to one hour served in the governor's office.

Although this shameful incident took place a decade before the attack on Pearl Harbor, it remained vivid in local memory. Hawaiians deeply resented the accusations and actions of white Americans, the national government, and especially the military. They saw their behavior as blatant racism and understood that mainland Americans and the national government viewed island people within a biased context. The Massie Case helped to shape the racial climate in Hawaii during the buildup of the U.S. military on the islands in the 1940s. It also promoted empathy between local people and the African American U.S. military population, which grew significantly during this period.

Mainland racial attitudes mixed with, and often complicated, attitudes particular to Hawaiian society. Hawaiians were not free of racial prejudice. Ethnic rivalries and racial stereotyping occurred among Japanese, Chinese, Filipino, Portuguese, and other ethnic and national groups, and sometimes these rivalries led to hostilities. Yet, compared to the racial patterns common in the continental United States, Hawaii was still very progressive. The unique racial climate in Hawaii was not lost on mainland military and civilian workers who flooded into the islands during the war years. It was especially striking to many black servicemen, especially those who, like 75 percent of American blacks, were from the South. In the early 1940s, one young black man wrote to his girlfriend then living in the South: "Honey, its just as much difference between over here and there as it is between night and day." Others vowed never to return to the South after seeing the relations between the various races in Hawaii. Mainland whites, too, marveled at the unfamiliar patterns of race relations in Hawaii. One nurse new to the islands wrote in a letter to friends at home of Hawaiian society: "They have come as close to solving the race problem as any place in the world," She admitted, "I'm a little mystified by it as yet."

Although some mainland whites found Hawaiian race relations refreshing, interesting, or even strange, but not offensive, others, especially white southerners, were offended indeed. "Down here they have let down the standards," complained one woman in a letter to her family on the mainland. She worried what impact this comparative racial equality would have on her children. In letters to friends and relatives back home, some white southerners expressed their concern about the future of blacks who experienced Hawaiian racial conditions and then returned to the South. "Over here," one southerner wrote, "[African Americans are] on the equal with every-one. . . . They're in paradise and no fooling." Another sailor was brutally direct in his reaction. "Boy the niggers are sure in their glory over here." He predicted that white southerners would not long stand for the situation, even this far from home. "They are going to overstep their bounds a little too far one of these days and these boys from the South are going to have a little necktie party," he wrote, insinuating that southerners would bring the brutal practice of lynching to the islands.

If Hawaii was a place that offered the possibility of greatly improved opportunities for some African

The Tuskegee Airmen in Combat

The first group of black aviators to graduate from the Tuskegee flight school served in the 99th Fighter Squadron in North Africa. They were later joined by the 100th, 301st, and 302nd African American fighter squadrons to form the 332nd fighter group, which served in Italy. They flew under the command of Colonel Benjamin O. Davis Jr. who earned his wings in Tuskegee's first graduating class and who was the first African American in the twentieth century to graduate from West Point. Under his command, the highly motivated 332nd flew successful missions over Sicily, the Mediterranean, and North Africa. They escorted bombers flawlessly, never losing a single plane to enemy fighters. Grateful bomber crews nicknamed them "Red-Tail Angels" after the red tail-markings on their aircraft. German Luftwaffe pilots respectfully called them "Black Bird Men." Their record was impressive, completing 15,500 missions, downing more than 260 enemy aircraft, sinking an enemy destroyer, and destroying countless enemy installations. Of the 450 Tuskegee Airmen who saw combat abroad, 150 were killed.

Some of the Tuskegee Airmen were bomber pilots, but they generally received less attention than the fighter group. The 477th Bombardment Group composed of Tuskegee Airmen trained for deployment in the Pacific Theater, but Japan surrendered before it saw action. The men of this unit were noted for the battles they fought for freedom at home. In April 1945, one hundred of its black officers staged a nonviolent protest against segregation and general racial discrimination at Freeman Field, in Indiana. This was part of the famed double V campaign—"Victory at Home. Victory Abroad"—encouraged by

The Tuskegee Airmen, some of whom signed their names on the picture, pose with their flight goggles and headgear in front of one of their planes. Before 1940, African Americans were not allowed to fly for the military.

the black press and civil rights leaders. Three years later, partially in response to this and other protests, President Harry Truman issued Executive Order No. 9981 integrating the armed forces.

The exploits of the Tuskegee Airmen became legendary. Their honors included, from the U.S. military, Distinguished Flying Crosses, Legions of Merit, Silver Stars, and Purple Hearts, and from international governments the French Croix de Guerre and the Red Star of Yugoslavia. In 1945 the 332nd Fighter Group was awarded a Distinguished Unit Citation for "outstanding performance and extraordinary heroism." On November 6, 1998, President Bill Clinton honored their memory by signing Public Law 105-355, which established the Tuskegee Airmen National Historic Site at Moton Field in Tuskegee, Alabama. The site is still under construction.

Americans, it was a place of unthinkable calamity for some whites. Southern whites, mainly military men, led a campaign to replicate the mainland racial hierarchy on the islands. As World War II wore on, Hawaii became a federally controlled racial battleground. After the attack on Pearl Harbor, the federal government imposed martial law on the islands. As tens of thousands of African American men and women passed through Hawaii during the war, military law regulated race relations on the islands.

During the First World War, the American military high command had to instruct their European allies in the ways of American race relations. The French allied forces, for example, were instructed to see that the French civilian population respected American racial etiquette. To treat black soldiers as equals or to show them respect would, they were told, offend white American soldiers. This was especially true when French women socialized with black men. Similarly, in the 1940s, some in the official military structure in Hawaii attempted to teach local Hawaiian people traditional mainland racial prejudice. A 1942 U.S. government publication called "Treatment of Negro Soldiers" dictated to locals that black troops must be treated in a way that would not offend or be seen as "contrary to the will of the majority of the citizens of the Nation." In the American South racial segregation was enforced by state and local laws, depriving black people of the right to vote, to serve on juries, or to be respected as full citizens. These laws determined where black people could go to school, eat, ride in public conveyances, work, even which public telephones they could use, and which Bibles they might swear on in a court of law. Although such restrictions were not generally written into law in the northern states, customary segregation was so much a part of the culture that the effect was much the same. Now in Hawaii, military regulation sought to establish race relations on the mainland model.

The U.S. military was racially restricted and base facilities reflected that policy. On-base military housing was segregated, and off-base public facilities in Honolulu were patrolled by military police who enforced the racial restrictions imposed under martial law. No blacks were allowed to enter the luxurious Royal Hawaiian Hotel, to walk on Waikiki Beach, or to attend any but a handful of the city's popular nightclubs and restaurants. Whole sections of Oahu were declared off-limits to African American servicemen. U.S. military police even attempted to enforce rules of racial segregation in the prostitution trade that flourished on Honolulu's Hotel Street.

Meanwhile, white servicemen spread racist stereotypes among local women, telling them that if they had a child by a black man, "the baby would be a monkey." Some black military men found that, in the wake of discriminatory military regulations and racist rumors, some Hawaiian people refused to associate with them. The local Japanese population—under intense pressure and scrutiny from the FBI and military intelligence for possible collusion with Japan—could ill afford to socialize with black servicemen, an act deemed suspicious, even provocative.

When African Americans joined local people for social occasions the effect of racist propaganda was often evident. One story that spread among military personnel about a group of black enlisted men who were invited to a social gathering at the home of a local family demonstrates the absurd influence of the racist rumors. It became clear during the course of the evening that the hosts had fitted special heavily cushioned chairs for the black men. When questioned, the local host explained with some embarrassment that they were just attempting to make sitting more comfortable for their guests as they had been told that African Americans had tails. Clearly, racist propaganda had an effect during these years, as one black serviceman observed in a letter home: "The old settlers here tell me this place was once a paradise for Negroes. Since the war, a Negro finds things very unpleasant here."

The military had anticipated that problems might erupt in the island setting when the disproportionately southern military personnel encountered the dark-skinned local population. Adding African Americans to this mix would further complicate the matter, many believed. There was some debate over whether black military people should be sent to Hawaii at all. Such concerns were, however, overshadowed by the necessities of war. Thus, the military tried to control racial tensions among its service people by reproducing, to the extent it was possible, the racial structure of the mainland. Sometimes, however, the rigid segregationist policies common in the deep South were incompatible with military regulations, customs, and protocol.

The arrival of the "Harlem Hellfighters," as the African American 369th Coast Artillery Regiment was known, severely tested the tensions between military discipline and military racial policy. Originally an elite National Guard unit from New York City, the Hellfighters were brought on active duty as the 369th regiment in 1941. It was one of the few black regiments commanded by black officers. The men of the 369th, mainly New Yorkers whose military base had been situated in the heart of Harlem, were a source of racial pride in the black community, and they knew it. The National Guard unit had established its valor during the First World War, for which it was awarded the war medal, the Croix de Guerre, by the French government. Fifty-five of those men who had fought in France were still serving with the 369th when its almost two thousand men came to Hawaii.

A core group of the unit hailed from the boroughs of New York City. Many had attended the same high schools, the same churches, and some were related to one another. Other men were added to the unit, however. By the time the 369th was assigned to protect Honolulu and Pearl Harbor just a few months after the Japanese attack, the unit was more diverse and included some southern black men. To these men, Hawaii—except for the military character of Pearl Harbor—was an almost totally unknown place. The actions of some white servicemen must have made it seem more familiar.

One major issue that quickly became quite public was the matter of white enlisted men saluting and otherwise observing military courtesies toward black officers. What military regulation demanded, southern custom forbade. Some southern whites hit upon the novel idea of substituting a handshake for a salute, but the black officers of the 369th would have none of it. As he later explained in an interview, Major Edward I. Marshall was direct with one white lieutenant. "Do not shake my hand. I

Lieutenant James Reese Europe served as a jazz bandleader with the 369th Regiment during World War I, when his band went to France as part of this combat unit to perform for the troops—as well as the French public. After the United States entered World War II, this all-black unit was called to Hawaii to protect Pearl Harbor.

don't like you and you don't like me. But I am a major!!! You are a lieutenant!!! Salute me!!!" Military law was clear and it had to be observed. The lieutenant complied. Lieutenant General Delos Emmons, military governor of Hawaii, supported proper military protocol as one means of keeping the lid on interracial conflict in the islands. He pressed his officers to do all in their power to enforce military decorum because it ensured a more respectful relationship among the troops.

During the war, Pearl Harbor remained a vital military center, and Hawaii continued to be racked by the tensions between island and mainland racial customs and assumptions. Despite the military policy of racial segregation and the effort to recreate the mainland racial hierarchy in Hawaii, black troops and civilian workers at Pearl Harbor and in Honolulu found life to be not free from racism but superior to that most had known elsewhere. The men of the 369th constantly challenged public racism wherever they found it and were often supported by local islanders, many of whom identified with the struggle to uphold the rights and dignity of dark-skinned peoples. When the executive secretary of the National Association for the Advancement of Colored People, Walter White, visited Honolulu in the winter of 1944, he found enthusiastic support for establishing a local NAACP branch. By the mid-1940s, the organization was sponsoring protests against discrimination in Hawaii's public accommodations.

Many African Americans who came to Hawaii after the attack on Pearl Harbor remained after the war. Census figures for 1950 indicate an immense percentage increase in the black population on the islands. A population that grew from a few hundred people in 1940 to more than 2,600 a decade later. By then segregation in public accommodations in Hawaii had been abolished. The events of that Sunday in early December 1941, of which black servicemen such as Doris Miller and William Jeremiah Powell were a part, played a central role in these demographic changes and in the political and social life of the islands. In less than two hours on that early morning, events at Pearl Harbor changed the lives of all Hawaiians, all Americans, and most people on the face of the earth.

Today the National Park Service maintains the USS *Arizona* Memorial, which serves as a reminder of that

An African American of the Highest Rank

Benjamin O. Davis Sr. was the first African American to hold the rank of general officer in the U.S. Armed Forces. Born in Washington, D.C., in 1877, he entered the military in 1898 during the Spanish American War. He later served with the Buffalo Soldiers, the highly regarded African American cavalry units, in the Philippines and in Wyoming. Davis was commissioned as a lieutenant in 1901 and rose through the ranks to the level of brigadier general by 1940. During his military career he served in a number of positions both in the United States and abroad, including military attaché to Monrovia, Liberia; professor of military science and tactics at Tuskegee Institute, Alabama, and at Wilberforce University in Ohio; and as an instructor for the Ohio National Guard, stationed at Cleveland. He retired in July 1941, only to be recalled to duty to serve during World War II. He was assigned to the European Theater of Operations as advisor to the U.S. military on issues of race. By the end of the war he was serving as special assistant to the commanding general of the European Theater of Operations, stationed in Paris.

Brigadier General Benjamin Davis surveys his troops in France.

After the war, General Benjamin O. Davis retired for the final time after fifty years of service to his country through two world wars. For his efforts during the Second World War he was awarded the Distinguished Service Medal. The citation reads, "for exceptionally meritorious service to the Government in a duty of great responsibility from June, 1941, to November, 1944, as an Inspector of troop units in the field, and as special War Department consultant on matters pertaining to Negro troops." He also received foreign awards and honors, including the Croix de Guerre with Palm Leaf, which the French government gave to distinguished combat pilots, and the Grade of Commander of the Order of the Star of Africa from Liberia.

The Davis family was one of the most distinguished military families of World War II. General Benjamin O. Davis Sr. was joined on active duty by his son Benjamin O. Davis Jr., who served in the U.S. Air Force, and who also rose to the rank of general officer. Davis Jr. was the fourth African American graduate of the U.S. Military Academy at West Point. During the last year of World War II, he flew sixty combat missions and was awarded the distinguished Flying Cross.

fateful morning. The 184-foot-long structure spans the mid-portion of the sunken battleship. The memorial is divided into three main sections: the entry and assembly rooms, a central area intended for ceremonies and general observation, and the shrine room, where the names of the 1,177 killed on the *Arizona* are engraved on the marble wall. Although the campaign to create a memorial to honor those killed in the attack on Pearl Harbor began as soon as the smoke cleared, it was not until 1949 that the Territory of Hawaii established the Pacific War Memorial Commission. President Dwight D. Eisenhower approved the creation of the memorial in 1958; with a combination of public and private funding, it was completed in 1961 and dedicated in 1962. In the words of its architect, Alfred Preis, who spoke at the dedication, the design of the memorial, whose "structure sags in the center but stands strong and vigorous at the ends, expresses initial defeat and ultimate victory. . . . The overall effect is one of serenity. Overtones of sadness have been omitted to permit the individual to contemplate his own personal responses . . . his innermost feelings."

By the time the USS *Arizona* Memorial was dedicated, racial relations in Hawaii were returning to their former openness. Those African Americans who remained in Hawaii after World War II generally blended into the Hawaiian society much as blacks had done in the eighteenth and nineteenth centuries. By the late twentieth century, blacks remained so widely dispersed in Hawaii that some felt the lack of a cultural center, a neighborhood, or community. Yet, generally, most seemed to feel comfortable. As one long-time black Hawaiian resident told a *Star-Bulletin* reporter in the mid-1990s, "nothing serious ever happened [here] to make me feel like an outsider."

The Japanese attack on Pearl Harbor had momentous consequences for America and for the world. It was also a pivotal occasion for African Americans and for race relations in Hawaii. The world is not likely to soon forget the events at Pearl Harbor commemorated with the USS *Arizona* Memorial. The heroism of African Americans, many of whom gave their lives in the service of their country during that day in 1941, is an important part of the history of Pearl Harbor.

TUSKEGEE AIRMEN NATIONAL HISTORIC SITE

1616 Chappie James Avenue
Tuskegee, AL 36083
334-724-0906
www.nps.gov/tuai/
NPS

The demands of World War II encouraged the U.S. military to heed political pressure from civil rights groups and the black press to open the military to African Americans. In 1941 the federal government established a flight-training program for black pilots. This move marked a significant departure from the Army Air Corp's "whites only" policy, and provided opportunities of which African Americans were quick to take advantage.

In 1939 Congress passed the Civilian Pilot Training Act and military officials selected Tuskegee Institute—the black Alabama college founded by African American educator and activist Booker T. Washington in 1881—as the training center for African American pilots and maintenance personnel. In 1942 the military completed Moton Field, named for Robert Russa Moton, Tuskegee's second college president. It included two aircraft hangers, a control tower, and maintenance and storage buildings. The Tuskegee Experiment, as the program was called, had begun. The program graduated hundreds of pilots, navigators, and bombardiers, backed by ten thousand instructors, mechanics, and

One of two aircraft hangars constructed at Moton Field, on the campus of Tuskegee Institute.

other support staff. In March 1942 five cadets earned their silver wings to become the first Tuskegee Airmen. Over the next four years almost one thousand others would join them, and the Tuskegee Airman proved to be some of America's best combat pilots.

PORT CHICAGO NAVAL MAGAZINE NATIONAL MEMORIAL

Port Chicago Highway North
Danville, CA
925-838-0249
www.nps.gov/poch/
NPS

On July 17, 1944, a crew of military and civilian workers were loading a munitions ship at the U.S. naval facility at Port Chicago, on Mare Island, near San Francisco. Just before 10:20 PM, during the loading operation, five thousand tons of munitions exploded, killing more than 320 men, at least 200 of whom were African American. This was the largest homeland disaster of the Second World War. The incident helped to highlight the vital role that blacks were playing in the war, and the racial inequality they faced in the American military at that time.

The white officers who survived the explosion were allowed thirty days recovery leave, customary after such a horrendous event. The black sailors, however, were granted no leave, not even those who had been hospitalized as a result of the explosion. They were expected to report for duty as soon as they were medically able, loading munitions under the same conditions as before. When some refused, they were initially imprisoned for three days on an overcrowded barge in the stifling heat of summer. The 208 African Americans were given bad conduct discharges and fined three months pay, and, in 1944, another 50 were court marshaled, dishonorably discharged, and sentenced to prison for periods ranging from eight to fifteen years. NAACP lawyer Thurgood Marshall attended the trial and was appalled by its obvious racial injustice. "The court-martial proceedings," he later reported in a speech to the NAACP "were one of the worst frame-ups we have come across."

The incident was a national scandal and prompted an expansion of civil rights protests. The furor encouraged President Harry Truman to integrate the U.S. military in 1948. Although the fifty men were released from prison in January 1946, after the war was over, they were not pardoned. Finally, in 1992 Congress created the Port Chicago Memorial at the site of the explosion, and in 1999, President Bill Clinton granted a pardon to Freddie Meeks, one of the sailors convicted in the Port Chicago incident.

Brown v. Board of Education National Historic Site

Topeka, Kans.

The Supreme Court and Public Education

At the corner of Fifteenth and Monroe streets in southeast Topeka, Kansas, stands the Monroe School, an imposing two-story red brick building. The story of this place begins before the Civil War, when a white abolitionist, John Ritchie, purchased 160 acres in Topeka. After the war, Richie gave the land to newly freed black people migrating to the city from the South. There, African Americans established a settlement, and during the 1870s the city built the Monroe School to serve black children in the community. The first permanent structure to house the school, a four-room brick building, was erected in 1874. It was rebuilt in 1926, designed anew by the prominent Topeka architect Thomas W. Williamson, who designed all the public schools in Topeka in the first half of the twentieth century.

The 1926 building was the newest of Topeka's four segregated black schools. Its original thirteen classrooms served kindergarten through eighth grade students until 1941, when the three upper grades were transferred to the city's integrated junior high schools. The school offered art and music classes, and it had a lunchroom that was opened in the space formerly occupied by the upper grade classes. Across the street there were playgrounds and fields used for softball, baseball, track, and football. Generally, most parents and school officials agreed that in terms of its curriculum, teachers, and its facilities, the Monroe School was equal to most of the white elementary schools in Topeka. The city also offered free bus service to blacks who needed it. Yet, in the mid-twentieth century,

The Monroe School was one of four segregated schools in Topeka. Black children from all over the city were forced to attend one of these schools instead of white schools closer to their own neighborhoods—before the Brown decision made segregated educational facilities illegal.

Monroe became a part of a national struggle over the integration of public education. There were many other schools in many other cities that played prominent roles, but Monroe came to exemplify the national civil rights campaign.

In 1950 at least seventeen states required that public schools be segregated, and in four other states the question of racial segregation was left to the discretion of local authorities. Students who were socialized in racially separated schools were also being readied for life in mid-twentieth-century America. Through law and custom most of the society was racially segregated. Topeka, a city of one hundred thousand people, did not officially segregate its public schools until 1927. By then most of the public facilities in the city were segregated. Six of its seven movie theaters did not admit blacks and the seventh admitted them only to the balcony. Blacks could not swim in the city pools except on one day of the year, and, as one resident recalled, signs in restaurants announced that only whites would be served in their dining rooms. Nonwhites could only buy food to take out of the restaurants, and they had to pick up their meals in bags from the back door. "Colored and Mexicans served in sacks only," these signs read. These policies were, at the time, sanctioned by the nation's highest court.

In 1896 the Supreme Court decision in *Plessy* v. *Ferguson* declared that the U.S. Constitution allowed racially separate public facilities as long as they were equal facilities. The decision was the result of charges brought by the state of Louisiana against Homer Plessy. Plessy, an African American, purchased a first-class ticket on the East Louisiana Railway from New Orleans to Covington, Kentucky, and refused to give up his seat in the whites-only first-class car when ordered by the conductor to take a seat in the "colored" section of the train. He was arrested and brought to trial for violating Louisiana's racial segregation law of 1890. His conviction and the subsequent failure of his appeal to the U.S. Supreme Court encouraged the system of legally enforced segregation that was being constructed throughout the South.

Starting in the 1890s and continuing for the next three generations, southern law demanded the separation of the races in everything from water fountains and public restrooms to picnic areas and public telephone

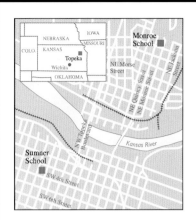

This map shows the distance between Linda Brown's home, near the all-white Sumner School, and the Monroe School, which she attended. Her trip to and from school took her one hour each way.

booths. This system did not always provide separate facilities for African Americans; in many southern towns, for instance, public libraries were not open to blacks at all. And almost never were the public facilities open to blacks equal to those provided for whites. Black public schools were underfunded and generally second class, as was seating for blacks on all forms of public transportation. Blacks could not depend on equal protection from local police, some of whom supported the racial hate groups that terrorized black communities. State and local officials often looked the other way when blacks were assaulted or killed, sometimes in the most public manner. Despite the demands of civil rights organizations and the tireless efforts of Ida B. Wells and other anti-lynching crusaders, Congress refused to make lynching a federal crime, leaving its victims to the unreliable protection of local and state governments. The Supreme Court's "separate but equal" ruling, as *Plessy* v. *Ferguson* came to be known, allowed, even encouraged, racial injustice, and was taken by some white extremists as a sanction to murder.

The belief in white supremacy was nationally held. In the North, racial discrimination was also a common practice, but it generally did not carry the force of law. Northern and midwestern communities segregated

Public water fountains— one for whites and one for "colored"—were just one example of the segregation that was the way of life in the South before the 1954 Brown decision ushered in a new era of civil rights. The doctrine of "separate but equal," upheld earlier by the Supreme Court in the 1896 case of Plessy v. Ferguson, affected all aspects of public life, from transportation to sports to employment.

blacks as a matter of custom and informal understanding. Sometimes facilities were segregated only erratically. Despite Topeka's widespread discriminatory policies, its buses and the waiting rooms at the train and bus stations were integrated, and there was at least some integration in the residential areas of the city. The junior high schools and the high school were also integrated, although school sports teams and most school clubs were not. Blacks were generally steered away from classes in typing, stenography, and some of the advanced sciences on the grounds that they could never find employment in those areas after graduation.

Despite these examples of integration in the city, the face of racial injustice and the assumptions of black inferiority were everywhere. They did not go unchallenged, however. Between 1881 and 1949 civil rights groups brought eleven cases seeking the integration of Topeka schools before the courts. All these attempts failed, but they were part of a broad effort to overturn the court decision in the *Plessy* case. The National Association for the Advancement of Colored People (NAACP) had been fighting in the courts for the desegregation of schools since the 1930s. For most of that time, its legal team was directed by Charles Hamilton Houston, dean of the Law School at Howard University, the nation's most prestigious university for African Americans. Houston died in 1950, leaving one of his former students, Thurgood Marshall—who went on to become a Supreme Court justice—as lead strategist and counsel for the school integration cases. Under Marshall's direction and using the latest psychological research, the NAACP's legal team argued that racial segregation sanctioned by law engendered feelings of inferiority among black students that sapped their motivation and limited their ability to learn.

In the fall of 1950, the local chapter of the NAACP, led by McKinley Burnett, championed the cause once again in Topeka. Burnett, a Kansas native and long-time civil rights activist warned the Topeka Board of Education that if it refused to act, the NAACP would go to court to force school integration. The board was unmoved, however, and the NAACP attorneys opened a case on behalf of a group of thirteen African American parents and their twenty children demanding the desegregation of the city's public schools. Burnett instructed parents to attempt

Monroe School, *Brown* v. *Board of Education* National Historic Site

1515 North East Monroe Street
Topeka, KS 66608
785-354-4273
www.nps.gov/brvb/
NPS

DATE BUILT
1926

SIGNIFICANCE
Parents of Monroe Elementary School students sought to test the premise that separate educational facilities could provide equal educational opportunities when they brought suit against the Topeka Board of Education in a case that became known as *Brown* v. *Board of Education*. In 1957, the Supreme Court ruled that "separate educational facilities are inherently unequal," a landmark decision that inspired much of the 1960s civil rights movement.

Thurgood Marshall: A Strong Voice for Freedom

Thurgood Marshall, the lawyer who directed the long legal campaign that resulted in the ending of legal segregation in America, was born and grew up in Baltimore, Maryland. Marshall's mother, Norma Arica Marshall, was one of the first blacks to graduate from Columbia Teachers College in New York City. His father, William Canfield Marshall, was a railroad porter, the head steward at an exclusive white club, and the first black person to serve on a grand jury in Baltimore in the twentieth century.

Some speculated early on that with this heritage Thurgood Marshall was destined to make a significant contribution to society. He graduated from an all-black high school at age sixteen and attended Lincoln University in Chester County, Pennsylvania, the nation's oldest historically black college. As an undergraduate, Marshall took part in a successful sit-in at a local movie theater. Protesters occupied the theater's "whites-only" seats to bring an end to the practice of segregating black patrons in the balcony. This early experience with civil rights protest was only the beginning of his battle against racial discrimination. He graduated with high honors from Lincoln in 1930, but the University of Maryland School of Law rejected his application because of his race. He then applied to and was accepted at Howard University Law School in Washington, D.C., where he graduated first in his class in 1933.

For three years Marshall worked in a private law practice in Baltimore, and then in 1936 he took a position as staff lawyer for the National Association for the Advancement of Colored People in New York City. From 1939 to 1961, he served as director and chief counsel for the NAACP Legal Defense and Education Fund, for which he helped develop and implement a strategy to fight racial segregation throughout the nation. Working with other civil rights attorneys, Marshall compiled an impressive record in the courtroom. During the 1940s he argued several cases before the Supreme Court, and won almost every one. His legal victories ended the practice of white primaries limiting black participation in the Democratic Party in the South and made illegal the restrictive covenant, used to maintain segregated housing. In 1950 he won unanimous decisions forcing the universities of Oklahoma and Texas to integrate their law schools.

During the late 1930s and the 1940s, Marshall served under the leadership of his Howard University law school mentor, Charles Hamilton Houston, who led the NAACP legal team at the time. When Houston died in 1950 Marshall assumed the role of NAACP senior attorney. In this position he planned and executed the legal strategy in the case of *Brown* v. *Board of Education*. In 1961 President John F. Kennedy appointed Marshall to the United States Second Circuit Court of Appeals, and in June 1967 President Lyndon B. Johnson nominated Marshall to the U.S. Supreme Court. The U.S. Senate confirmed the appointment of Thurgood Marshall, who thus became the first African American to serve on the high court.

During the late 1970s and the 1980s, as the Supreme Court became increasingly conservative, Marshall was a strong dissenting voice of the liberal minority. He spoke out against the Court's hostility to affirmative action and its support of capital punishment. In poor health, Marshall retired from the Court in 1991. In 1993 heart failure took his life. Until the end, Thurgood Marshall remained as he had been for his entire professional life, a strong voice for social justice and civil rights. He is buried in Arlington National Cemetery.

to enroll their children at the public school nearest to their home, regardless of whether the school was for whites only—on the appointed day of fall registration. When school officials refused to register the children, the NAACP filed suit against the city's board of education.

On February 28, 1951, thirteen African American parents filed a complaint in the United States District Court of Kansas under the name *Oliver L. Brown v. Board of Education of Topeka, Shawnee County, Kansas.* Oliver L. Brown, a welder for the Atchison, Topeka, and Santa Fe Railroad and an assistant pastor at a local Methodist church, joined the case on behalf of his young daughter Linda. If alphabetical order had been strictly followed, as it was in most such cases, this case should have been filed under the name *Darlene Brown v. Board of Education of Topeka.* But Oliver L. Brown (no relation to Darlene) was a solid family man, a railroad union member with a stable job, and the only male listed among the plaintiffs. It is likely that these issues weighed heavily in the decision to file the case under his name.

The court rejected the NAACP's argument. The public schools in Topeka, it ruled, were equal institutions and therefore not in violation of the "separate but equal" provision set down in the *Plessy* case. The court did, however, leave the door open to further NAACP action. It seemed to accept the contention that black children, forced to attend racially separate facilities by law, were made to feel inferior and, as a result, were psychologically damaged by the experience. This was the argument that the U.S. Supreme Court ultimately found persuasive in 1954, but there would be much debate and anguish before this decision was reached.

The *Brown v. Board of Education* case was the first of five desegregation cases moving through the courts at roughly the same time. In Delaware two school desegregation cases were combined and filed as *Belton v. Gebhart.* In the District of Columbia the case of *Bolling*

Thurgood Marshall (standing) meets with a client in 1935 (center), who wanted to attend the University of Maryland's law school, but was denied admittance because of his race. Marshall and NAACP lawyer Charles Houston (right) won the case, on the grounds that the state did not offer a "separate but equal" law school for blacks. For almost twenty years afterward, Marshall honed his arguments against segregation until he triumphed in the Brown *case with the claim that the practice itself was unconstitutional.*

v. *Sharpe* involved eleven black students who were denied entrance to all-white schools. In South Carolina the case of *Briggs* v. *Elliott* was filed on behalf of 12 black elementary school students, and 117 African American high school students brought suit in Virginia in the case of *Davis* v. *County School Board of Prince Edward County.* These cases were brought before the court one year after *Brown,* but each was directly affected by the others.

The NAACP lost the initial *Brown* case in the district courts, but it was eventually heard by the U.S. Supreme Court. At that level four cases were combined under the name *Oliver L. Brown et al.* v. *Board of Education of Topeka, Kansas et al.,* leaving *Bolling* v. *Sharpe,* involving the District of Columbia, to be tried separately from those concerning states. On May 17, 1954, Chief Justice Earl Warren announced the court's unanimous opinion that legally enforced segregation was psychologically detrimental to those students set apart as inferiors. The Court declared school segregation in the United States unconstitutional and, with this ruling, reversed its earlier decision in the *Plessy* case.

Although the *Plessy* decision had addressed matters of transportation, and the decision in *Brown* focused on education, both rulings carried broader implications for race relations in the entire society. Both marked a major transition in American law. The *Plessy* decision had paved the way for the system of racial segregation that defined southern society and helped to shape northern racial patterns for most of the twentieth century. Similarly, *Brown* was a crucial step in the increasingly effective civil rights movement of the 1950s and 1960s. As the Court acknowledged, its ruling in *Brown* signaled a major shift in the nation on issues of race. It traced some of the major court rulings on segregation and explained that public education had grown in significance over the twentieth century to become "perhaps the most important function of state and local government." It agreed with the plaintiff's argument that segregating children in public school solely because of their race "generates a feeling of inferiority. . . that may affect their hearts and minds in a way unlikely ever to be undone." Then, speaking for the Court unanimously, Chief Justice Warren explained "We conclude . . . that in the field of public education the doctrine of 'separate but equal' has no place."

Brown exploded like fireworks across an American night sky. Throughout the nation, especially in the black communities and among civil rights advocates, it was hailed as the beginning of the end of racial segregation. Sara Lightfoot, a ten-year-old at the time, later recalled her excitement in her memoir, "Jubilation, optimism, and hope filled my house." Julius Chambers then a boy from rural North Carolina who later became a leading civil rights lawyer, remembered, "We assumed that *Brown* was self-executing. The law had been announced, and people would obey it. Wasn't that how things worked in America, even in the white America?"

The answer to his question was quick in coming and at first seemed to be encouraging. In New York City, the staff at NAACP headquarters was stunned by the decision. One staff member told interviewers, from the *New York Times*, "The only emotion we felt at that moment was awe—everyone felt it." Liberal southerners felt it, too, and even traditional southern segregationists seemed to see the handwriting on the wall. In Alabama, Governor "Big Jim" Folsom, who had not publicly favored integration, seemed to indicate his acquiescence. "When the Supreme speaks," he told the press, "that's the law." In Arkansas, the governor announced that his state would abide by the decision, and in the upper South officials in Delaware, Kentucky, Missouri, Oklahoma, West Virginia, and Washington, D.C., agreed.

The Brown *Supreme Court decision was front-page news. The local Topeka paper anticipated the struggle to come in implementing desegregation when it declared: "Thus many months—perhaps more time will elapse—before the historic ruling actually wipes out the separate schools now in existence in many states."*

In 1947, student protesters in Texas rally around the NAACP banner to call for an end to segregation in education. The NAACP was founded in 1910 with the goal of ending segregation and securing for blacks equal education and the right to vote. It was NAACP lawyers who filed the suits against segregated schools around the country until the practice was declared illegal.

Yet, there was also strong resistance to the idea of integration, especially in the South, where some declared that they would never obey and talked of a second civil war. Shortly after the *Brown* decision became public, a former World War II and Korean veteran, Bryant Bowles, founded the National Association for the Advancement of White People, headquartered in Washington, D.C. He and his group encouraged white parents to resist the integration of their local schools. Opposition soon surfaced in Delaware, in southern Virginia, and in North Carolina. In South Carolina, officials refused to recognize the Supreme Court as the last word on racial policy. Membership in the Ku Klux Klan rose rapidly and white segregationists formed other groups, less violent, perhaps, but equally committed to white supremacy. In Mississippi, the White Citizens Council was established in the town of Indianola just two months after the Supreme Court ruling. This was one of a number of organizations sporting a more polite demeanor than the Ku Klux Klan, but with the same agenda. Civil rights advocates referred to them as the uptown Klan.

To clarify the intended timetable for carrying out the Court's desegregation ruling, the NAACP urged the justices to issue an order to expedite the implementation of school integration. They asked the Court to demand that public school desegregation begin "forthwith," meaning immediately. In his *Brown II* decision announced in 1955, Chief Justice Warren—convinced that resistance to school desegregation was so great that only slow steps toward integration were practical—declared that desegregation should be implemented "with all deliberate speed." For years after, resistance groups took advantage of this ambiguous language to delay and avoid compliance with the original *Brown* decision.

Finally, the Court began to express misgivings about the phrase. In 1964, almost a decade after it had prescribed "all deliberate speed," Justice Hugo LaFayette Black declared in the 1959 decision *Griffin v. County School Board of Prince Edward County (Virginia)*: "There has been entirely too much deliberation and not enough speed in enforcing the constitutional rights which we held in *Brown*." "The time for mere deliberate speed," he proclaimed, "has run out." By that time, the 1960s civil rights movement was changing the face of American race relations. In July of that year, President Lyndon Johnson signed the national Civil Rights Act of 1964 into law, striking down racial segregation in public places, such as theaters, restaurants, and hotels and outlawing discrimination in employment.

In the decades after the landmark Supreme Court decision the name Brown has become synonymous with the civil rights movement. Seven-year-old Linda Brown walked through a railroad switch-yard and across a major commercial thoroughfare then boarded a bus for the ride to the Monroe School, a trip of at least an hour each way. Meanwhile, Sumner School, which her white playmates attended, was only five blocks from Linda's home, at the end of a far less perilous ten-minute walk. This story of Linda's journey to school caught the attention of the media. *Life* magazine published a large picture of Linda and her mother walking through a railroad yard on the way to the Monroe School. And after the decision, many newspapers ran a picture of the young girl and her mother holding a newspaper with the banner headline, "High Court Bans Segregation in Public Schools." The case has become an important symbol, even if an oversimplification of the motivation that led to the desegregation suits in Topeka and elsewhere.

The accounts of Linda's long journey to school are all true, but the determined effort to integrate Topeka's public schools involved more than parental concerns about the length and perils of one child's daily journey

to school. The *Brown* case was the result of decades of planning and court litigation, and involved hundreds of plaintiffs in the five cases that came before the U.S. Supreme Court and many others before them in the long struggle to integrate public education. The fact that the case took the name of the first male plaintiff is partly a measure of mid twentieth-century class and gender conventions. As Stephen E. Adams, superintendent of the *Brown* v. *Board of Education* National Historic Site has written, "Ascribing the case history to one child in Topeka, Kansas is grossly inaccurate." There was surely more at stake than a shorter walk to school. Yet, the *Brown* decision was pivotal. Many Americans date the modern civil rights movement from that 1954 ruling.

Ironically, Linda Brown never attended the Sumner School that was desegregated as a result of the Court's decision. By the time of the ruling in the first *Brown* case, she had already completed grammar school and moved on to Topeka's integrated junior high school. Her younger sister Cheryl was the first Brown to attend the newly integrated Sumner School. Another irony is that Linda faced such a substantial journey to the Monroe School because the Brown family lived in an integrated neighborhood, where many of Linda's playmates were white. Yet, perhaps the greatest irony of all is that the whites-only Sumner School built in 1936 was named for Charles Sumner, the abolitionist lawyer and Civil War–era Massachusetts senator who advocated for the civil rights of southern blacks emerging from slavery after the Civil War. In 1849 he had partnered with the black lawyer Robert Morris in the case of *Roberts* v. *Boston,* arguing in favor of school integration. Sumner's argument became an important precedent for the legal suit filed in the *Brown* case.

The Monroe School continued to serve many students in the black community. A third generation of the Brown family attended the school during the late 1960s, and in 1972 Cheryl Brown Henderson, Linda Brown's younger sister, began her educational career teaching sixth grade at the school. Finally, in 1975, declining enrollments forced the school's closure. The school district began using the building as a warehouse and the grounds as lots to park buses and perform vehicle maintenance. Then in the mid-1980s the building that had housed Monroe Elementary for more than sixty years was put up for sale.

In 1988, Cheryl Brown Henderson and other Topeka residents established the Brown Foundation for Educational Equality, Excellence, and Research as "a living tribute to the attorneys and plaintiffs in the landmark U.S. Supreme Court decision of 1954 *Brown* v. *the Board of Education.*" The organization sponsors scholarships and education on civil rights and race-related issues, and has worked with the National Park Service to preserve the Monroe School and other sites related to civil rights. In 1987 the Sumner School was designated a National Historic Landmark, and in 1991 the Monroe School was also designated. In 1993 the two Topeka sites, the Sumner Elementary School at 330 Western Avenue and the Monroe Elementary School at 1515 Monroe Avenue, were added to the National Park Service system with the official designation of *Brown* v. *Board of Education* National Historic Site.

In 1993, the two Topeka sites, the Sumner Elementary School and the Monroe Elementary School were added to the National Park Service system with the official designation of *Brown* v. *Board of Education National Historic Site.* Today it stands as an important reminder of the long struggle so many dedicated people waged for civil rights in the twentieth century. It is a landmark of the movement for racial justice in America.

DEXTER AVENUE KING MEMORIAL BAPTIST CHURCH

454 Dexter Avenue
Montgomery, AL 36104
334-263-3970
*www.cr.nps.gov/nr/travel/
    civilrights/al7.htm*
NHL, NPS

Built with bricks discarded by city workers constructing Dexter Avenue, the Second Colored Baptist Church was a vital center of Montgomery's black community throughout the first half of the twentieth century. Eventually it changed its name to the Dexter Avenue Baptist Church, and, in 1954, a new young energetic minister became its pastor. It was from this church that Martin Luther King Jr. launched himself, and many in his congregation, into one of the first major campaigns

The Montgomery bus boycott was launched at the red-brick Dexter Avenue Baptist Church, whose congregation was instrumental in the campaign's success.

of the emerging modern civil rights movement. Their protest was directed at a local ordinance that dictated that when the white section at the front of a city bus was full, blacks seated in the front of the "Negro section" at the rear of the bus were to stand and give their seats to white passengers. On December 1, 1955, Rosa Parks, the secretary of the local NAACP branch office, refused to give up her seat to a white man. She was removed from the bus and arrested. The next day, activist and former local NAACP president, E. D. Nixon called a meeting of the African American community in the basement of the Dexter Avenue Church. Reverend King, who had at first been reluctant to participate, quickly became the leader of the protest movement that launched the Montgomery bus boycott.

The struggle lasted more than a year, but it brought about the integration of the city buses and propelled the young minister into the national spotlight of civil rights leadership. In 1974 the church was designated a National Historic Landmark by the National Park Service. Two years later the city of Montgomery listed the church as a historic site, and in 1980 unveiled a historic marker on its grounds.

BIZZELL LIBRARY AT THE UNIVERSITY OF OKLAHOMA

401 West Brooks Street
University of Oklahoma

Norman, OK 73019
405-325-2640
*www.cr.nps.gov/nr/travel/
    civilrights/ok2.htm*
NHL

In 1948, George McLaurin applied to the doctoral program in education at the University of Oklahoma. He was rejected, although he was a retired professor and well qualified. He was also black, and in Oklahoma at the time interracial education was illegal. McLaurin sued for admission, and the U.S. Supreme Court ruled that the state must provide him with an opportunity to acquire a graduate education equal to that of its white citizens. He was admitted to the school, but was segregated from the rest of the students. The only African American student, McLaurin was forced to sit at a desk placed outside the classroom and to eat lunch at a different time from the white students. He was also barred from the general reading room in the Bizzell Library and was provided with a desk labeled "for colored only" on the mezzanine level.

Once again McLaurin filed suit, and in 1950 the U.S. Supreme Court ruled unanimously that McLaurin's segregation prevented him from fully benefiting from graduate instruction and violated his rights under the equal protection clause of the Fourteenth Amendment. This case was one of many that led to the NAACP's victory in the case of *Brown v. Board of Education.*

The F.W. Woolworth Building, Downtown Greensboro Historic District

Greensboro, N.C.

The Start of the Student Sit-in Movement

Standing before a large crowd in Canandaigua, New York, on August 4, 1857, Frederick Douglass addressed the issue of emancipation in the West Indies. Those "who would be free, themselves must strike the blow," he argued. Douglass argued that it was unrealistic to believe that freedom could be won without a struggle. "Those who profess to favor freedom and yet deprecate agitation are men who want crops without plowing the ground. They want rain without thunder and lightning. They want the ocean without the awful roar of its waters. Power concedes nothing without a demand. It never did, and it never will."

It is unlikely that Ezell Blair Jr., Franklin McCain, Joseph McNeil, and David Richmond had read Douglass's speech, but a hundred years later they acted in the spirit of his words. At 4:00 PM on February 1, 1960, these four freshmen from the Greensboro campus of the North Carolina Agricultural and Technical College made a demand, broke the rules, and began a struggle. They did all this simply by entering the downtown store of F.W. Woolworth and Company in Greensboro, North Carolina, seating themselves at the lunch counter, and ordering a cup of coffee.

Starting with a small drygoods store in Utica, New York, which opened in 1879, Frank Woolworth and his brother Charles S. Woolworth, founded F.W. Woolworth Five-and-Ten-Cent Store in 1911. This was the first of what would be many retail establishments to sell general merchandise at discounted prices. "Five and ten cent stores" bought in volume and could therefore generally sell name-brand products at prices below those offered by local merchants. By 1919, when Frank Woolworth died, the Woolworth chain had grown to include more

Clean-cut, neatly dressed students (above) join a sit-down strike at the Woolworth's lunch counter in Greensboro, after four freshman initiated the action. Across the South, students were soon participating in sit-ins at other lunch counters, as well as "read-ins" at libraries, "wade-ins" at pools, and other forms of nonviolent protest.

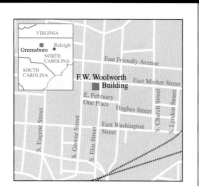

than one thousand stores in the United States and abroad. By then, Woolworth had expanded its offerings to include a wide variety of clothing, some household furnishings, and eventually lunch counters, which served as a gathering place. By the mid-twentieth century, Woolworth's Five-and-Ten-Cents Stores were common fixtures in many American cities.

In 1958, at the request of George Simkins, a local NAACP leader, the Greensboro Woolworth store manager, Clarence "Curly" Harris, had removed the signs desig-nating the counter for "whites only" but everyone understood the racial customs in Greensboro. Yet, these four young men sat down and waited to be served. One of the black workers at the counter explained that they could not be served in that section of the store. The stu-dents responded that they would sit at the counter until served. In the South of 1960, this was a revolutionary act. The mid-twentieth-century South was a dangerous place for blacks who challenged the racial structure. This form of public protest was almost certain to pro-voke violent retaliation. In a later interview, one of the students, Joe McNeil, remembered the astonished and then disapproving looks they received from store patrons and employees. Franklin McCain, who grew up in Washington, D.C., and spent one year attending Greensboro's Dudley High School, later recalled that he had not slept the night before, not afraid, but filled with anxiety at the probable consequences of their actions. He expected to be arrested, beaten, or worse.

Geneva Tisdale, a black waitress working at the Woolworth lunch counter, thought at first that the four did not understand the racial rules of Greensboro. She later explained in an interview with the *Greensboro News and Record* that initially she paid little attention to the students, recalling, "I just thought there was somebody here from someplace else that didn't know they didn't serve blacks, so I kept on doing what I was doing." When it became clear that the students were demanding service as a protest, the store's black employees reacted. They "looked at us with disbelief . . . concerned for our safety," McCain remembered. There was good cause to be concerned. To southern blacks, familiar with the price paid by African Americans who dared ignore the Jim Crow system—the legal structure that enforced racial segregation—this act must have seemed foolhardy.

These four young black men were confronting racial taboos long established and deeply ingrained. They were on their own, challenging not only segregated seating, but, by direct implication, white supremacy itself. They placed themselves in danger without the permission or even the knowledge of their college or their parents. According to McCain, they were fully prepared to be expelled from school, to face parental disapproval, or whatever might happen. In a taped interview years after the event, McNeil called their actions "a down payment on manhood." "The secret of life," he said, "is knowing when to take on something difficult and to take something on that might have enormous risks and implications." Clearly, segregation was something worth taking on.

By breaking the racial rules so blatantly, these protestors risked more than their personal safety. One of the African American store workers lectured them about the consequences of their action for black employees of the store and for other blacks in the city if angry whites sought to punish all blacks for the demonstration. Then store manager Harris approached, attempting to convince them that their protest was unreasonable and unlikely to achieve its purpose. When this tactic proved ineffective, Harris left the store briefly to walk to the nearby police station, where he explained the situation to the local police chief. The chief laid out the choices. He could either have the students arrested, or allow them to sit at the counter, unserved, until they decided to leave. Harris elected to follow the latter course and told his staff to ignore the students.

The four continued to sit at the counter in silent protest until past closing time. They were never served. At one point, McCain told an interviewer from the *News and Record*, an elderly white woman approached the group, put her hand on his shoulder and offered words of encouragement. "Boys, I am just so proud of you," she said. "My only regret is that you did

A section of the lunch counter from the Greensboro Woolworth's is preserved at the Smithsonian. The sit-in lasted six months before African Americans were served at the store.

Sitting for Justice
The Greensboro Sit-in of 1960

F.W. Woolworth Building, Downtown Greensboro Historic District

132 South Elm Street
Greensboro, NC 27401
336-379-0060
*www.cr.nps.gov/nr/travel/
civilrights/nc1.htm*
NRIS 82003458
NPS

DATE BUILT
1930

SIGNIFICANCE
The student sit-in at the Woolworth lunch counter in 1960 confirmed the power of passive resistance, while providing young people with an important way of fighting segregation. Although their effort to integrate the lunch counter might have seemed a limited goal, its real power was in illuminating racial injustice to millions of television viewers and newspaper readers.

not do this 10 or 15 years ago." The sentiment meant a great deal. "I got so much pride and such a good positive feelings from that little old lady," McCain remembered years later. "She'll never know it, but that really made the day for us."

The students left the store about 6:15 PM, unharmed and elated at what they had done, but not everyone at the college was immediately impressed. Many would not believe them and it took some time to convince their fellows that this was not some imaginative joke. Finally, room by room, dormitory residents pledged to join the protest. When the four protesters returned the next day, eleven other students accompanied them. Again they were not served. The local police and Harris's supervisor from the Woolworth company were sure that the protest would be short-lived.

Harris, however, had been keeping abreast of the civil rights movement that was blossoming throughout the South, and understood full well that the protests in his store would not just go away. "It won't blow over, it is for real," he told a *News and Record* interviewer that he had remembered thinking. He was right. When the students returned on the third day, they were accompanied by 150 of their fellow students. The demonstration continued, and at one point it included most of the North Carolina A&T college football team. Before the protest ended at least one thousand people had participated.

Confronting Jim Crow was no easy task. Whites reacted by insulting, harassing, and violently attacking the demonstrators. It was a dangerous, potentially deadly business that demanded patience and determination. As the numbers of protesters increased, growing numbers of angry whites entered the store to heckle and assault the protesters. One employee reported that members of the local Ku Klux Klan had planted a bomb in the store, and as the situation became more dangerous fewer people seemed willing to participate in the protest. One early lesson the students learned was the difficulty of maintaining momentum. "What people won't talk [about], what people don't like to remember is that the success of that movement in Greensboro is probably attributed to no more than eight or 10 people," McCain recalled to a *News and Record* reporter in 1998. "I can say this: when the television cameras stopped rolling and we didn't have eight or 10 reporters left, the folk left. I mean, there were just a very faithful few. McNeil and I can't count the nights and evenings that we literally cried because we couldn't get people to help us staff a picket line."

Yet, there were enough black people who were willing to stay the course that the protest went on for five months. There was help along the way from the black women of Bennett College, also in Greensboro, and from the students' own A&T College, which allowed its buildings to be used for protest strategy sessions. There were also some whites in town willing to lend a hand. Ralph Johns, a white merchant, often encouraged his black customers to challenge the city's racist policies. He talked to the Greensboro Four, as the students came to be known, before their protest and supported any action they might mount, but he knew nothing of the specifics of the Woolworth sit-in until the students passed his store moments before it occurred. Johns's encouragement was more than moral support. He promised bail money to anyone who was arrested in the cause of freedom. McCain and his colleagues were extremely grateful for Johns's help and encouragement.

The students also received assistance from a local newspaper reporter, Jo Spivey, whose stories favoring the sit-in infuriated the Ku Klux Klan. One of the many harassing phone calls she received at her home threatened her preschool-age daughter. Still, she continued to support not only this protest action, but a variety of other protests at the public swimming pool and other facilities in the city. Her writing was aimed at the conscience of the city's progressive people and designed to encourage help from sympathetic white students at the University of North Carolina at Greensboro, Greensboro College, and Guilford College, also in Greensboro. With this kind of publicity, white protesters joined blacks, filling every seat in the store and putting additional pressure on the store to change its racist policies.

All this disruption inevitably resulted in plunging sales and increasingly negative publicity for Woolworth nationwide. Its stores were picketed in the North in support of the Greensboro action and its profits suffered nationally. This was all magnified as the protest quickly spread beyond Greensboro. Within days of the original protest, there were sit-ins in at least fifteen communities across the South, including the nearby cities of Durham and Winston-Salem, North Carolina. In just two months, the sit-in movement had spread to fifty-four cities in nine states. Throughout the South, black college students led the way. Police used tear gas to disperse student protesters in Tallahassee, Florida, and a sit-in in Chattanooga, Tennessee, sparked a race riot when whites attacked the protesters. By the end of 1960, 75,000 students, both blacks and whites, had staged sit-ins in seventy-five cities and towns, and 3,600 had been arrested. Two thousand more had been jailed in northern cities for forming sympathy picket lines at local branches of national chain stores with Jim Crow practices in the South.

All these factors helped the students to secure a victory. On July 25, 1960, the first blacks were served at the Woolworth lunch counter in Greensboro. Ironically, these first African Americans were not customers but black Woolworth employees. The counter manager instructed Geneva Tisdale and two other black kitchen workers to bring dress clothing to work with them, and, at the appointed time, they slipped away from their kitchen jobs, went to an upstairs room in the store, and

Protesters march in front of City Hall in San Antonio, Texas. Young blacks, following Martin Luther King Jr.'s call for "social change through nonviolent resistance," faced not only resistance from whites but sometimes outright violence—and often jail time.

changed from their uniforms into their "Sunday best." They returned to the store's shopping area, browsed for a few minutes, and then went to the counter to order a light lunch. Tisdale ordered an egg salad sandwich and a soda. They ate quickly, then left the counter, changed clothes again, and returned to their kitchen work. Tisdale later explained in the *News and Record* that few people ever knew "that it was Woolworth girls that was the first to sit at the counter to be served after they opened it up." By the time the press arrived to cover the history-making event, it was over.

It is not likely that any of those involved in the Greensboro sit-in realized at the time that they were participating in one of the most important events in twentieth-century civil rights history. Yet this sit-in not only spawned a national sit-in movement, but it also became the catalyst for broadening civil rights activism, which during the early years of the century had taken place largely in the courts. It also brought tens of thousands of college students into the movement. Ella Baker, one of the leaders of the Southern Christian Leadership Conference (SCLC)—a nonviolent direct action group founded in 1957 by Martin Luther King Jr. and others after the Montgomery bus boycott—set about organizing the energy of these students. Many of the SCLC's leaders saw an opportunity to work with the Greensboro students and other students in the region who were becoming increasingly active.

In mid-April 1960, just a few months after the initial Woolworth sit-in, Baker called a meeting "to share experience gained in recent protest demonstrations and to help chart future goals for effective action," according to the letter she sent to black student leaders. The meeting at Shaw University in Raleigh spawned a student-led direct action organization, the Student Nonviolent Coordinating Committee (SNCC). Less patient and more militant than the more traditional civil rights organizations, SNCC moved quickly to engage in the most dramatic protest action of the era. It not only galvanized young Americans, whites as well as blacks, it also inspired students around the world such as those in South Africa who were fighting racial apartheid and those in other parts of Africa, in parts of Europe, and in Asia who were struggling against class, religious, and ethnic injustice.

In the years since the original sit-in, the Woolworth store on South Elm Street in Greensboro has become a major symbol of the civil rights struggle. Twenty years after the event, on February 1, 1980, the state of North Carolina placed a marker at the corner of Elm and Friendly streets near the entrance to the store. No one would have predicted when the building was constructed in 1929 that it would become one of the most important civil rights markers of the twentieth century.

Built in the understated, clean-lined geometric architectural style of the 1920s and 1930s called Art Deco, it originally provided office and retail space for Greensboro's affluent white community during the years before the Great Depression. During those years, South Elm Street was in the heart of Greensboro's booming downtown. The building's architect, Charles Hartmann, was well known in the city as the designer of several important local structures. The Woolworth building was originally known as the Whelan Building, for its owner, the Whelan Drug Company, which operated a pharmacy in a corner of the building. Other businesses, including several women's wear shops, occupied the ground floor, while the upper floor was reserved for rental office space and storage. In 1939 Woolworth took over most of the building, and the store remained a popular downtown destination for thirty-three years.

In October 1993 the lunch counter stopped serving food, and within a few months the Woolworth closed its doors. By the 1990s, under heavy pressure from other discount stores such as Wal-Mart, the chain had been reduced to four hundred stores. In 1997 Woolworth went out of business. Soon thereafter, a local nonprofit historic group, Sit-in Movement Incorporated, bought the old Woolworth building for $700,000 with plans to make it a national landmark. For years, through a number of false starts and disappointments, Sit-in Movement Incorporated remained true to its purpose: to persuade the federal government to officially declare the former F.W. Woolworth five-and-dime store in downtown Greensboro a National Historic Landmark.

On June 26, 2001, at a sidewalk ceremony outside the former Woolworth store, the chancellor of North Carolina A&T State University, James Renick, and the county commissioner Melvin "Skip" Alston, co-founder of Sit-in Movement Incorporated, announced a partnership in the effort to re-open the Woolworth Building as the International Civil Rights Center and Museum. They also announced that U.S. Representative Mel Watt had introduced a bill in the House to study making the museum site part of the National Park system. They hope to raise ten to fifteen million dollars to fund the project.

A&T symbolized its full commitment to the venture by delegating David Hoard, its vice chancellor for development and university relations, as the museum's chief executive officer in charge of staff, fundraising, exhibits, and training. Hoard was at first uncertain about the task until his mother reminded him of the national importance of the project. Ironically, he had taken her to dinner in a restaurant that probably would not have served them in 1960. "Do you realize, that we are able to eat in this restaurant because of what those gentlemen did 41 years ago?" she asked. Of course he knew the answer, as will many more when the International Civil Rights Center and Museum opens its doors.

In January 1995 a section of the historic lunch counter of Greensboro's Woolworth store was moved to Washington, D.C., to become part of an exhibit at the Smithsonian's National Museum of American History. The lunch counter, with its Formica top and four rounded stools with padded plastic seats and metal backs, is typical of the 1950s style. It sits just yards away from the museum's display of the original Star-Spangled Banner that looms two stories above the exhibit hall. Perhaps it is fitting that the giant flag and the modest lunch counter share the same space in that museum dedicated to the history of this nation. Taken together they symbolize the hope and the contradictions of the American struggle for freedom and human dignity.

A historical marker outside the site of the Woolworth's store in Greensboro declares: "Sometimes taking a stand for what is undeniably right means taking a seat."

RELATED SITES

THE LINCOLN MEMORIAL

900 Ohio Drive SW
Washington, DC 20242
202-485-9880
www.nps.gov/linc/
NPS

The Lincoln Memorial was dedicated on May 30, 1922, in memory of the President who held office at the time of America's greatest national crisis, the Civil War. Most Americans see this place as a memorial to national strength and reunification. It has also become a symbol of national conscience and equal rights. To African Americans it is a place associated not only with the President who led the nation out of slavery, but one that served as a civil rights forum. When the Daughters of the American Revolution refused to allow Marian Anderson—one of the greatest internationally known opera singers of the twentieth century—to perform at Constitutional Hall simply because of the color of her skin, the federal government invited her to sing on the steps of the Lincoln Memorial. More than seventy-five thousand people were there on Easter Sunday in 1939 when she began her concert with the song "America."

Almost a quarter century later, in 1963, the Lincoln Memorial again took center stage for the most important statement on civil rights and racial justice made in twentieth-century America. With

more than one hundred thousand people in attendance, Martin Luther King Jr. delivered the keynote speech of the modern civil rights movement. He told the crowd that in spite of the tradition of racial injustice in America the nation would one day live out its promise of true equality and freedom. In words now familiar to every American, he predicted that "We Shall Overcome."

SELMA TO MONTGOMERY HISTORIC TRAIL

State Highway 80
Selma to Montgomery, AL
www.nps.gov/semo/
NPS

On March 7, 1965, six hundred civil rights marchers set out from Brown Chapel A.M.E. Church in Selma, Alabama, and headed toward

Montgomery, the state capital, fifty miles away. With their march they sought to highlight the injustice of the southern electoral system that routinely denied black people the right to vote. They walked east, along Alabama Highway 80, but they had traveled only six blocks when they were confronted by a force of one hundred state and local police. As the marchers crossed the Edmund Pettus Bridge that spans the Alabama River, the police attacked with clubs and tear gas. That day became known in the civil rights movement as "Bloody Sunday." Although police halted the march, television cameras broadcast pictures of the brutal beatings of the marchers as the nation looked on in horror. Two days later Reverend Martin Luther King Jr. led a second

At the Edmund Pettus Bridge, over the Alabama River, police attacked civil rights marchers on their way from Selma to Montgomery.

march from Brown Chapel. Again police halted the march, but this time without violence. Finally, on March 21, a third march departed from Brown Chapel, under the protection of the National Guard. After five days of walking it covered the distance to the State Capitol in Montgomery.

The demonstration and the violent police response aroused such public pressure that Congress passed a voter's rights bill that guaranteed the right to vote to all qualified Americans. On August 6, 1965, President Lyndon B. Johnson signed the Voting Rights Act into law. The Selma to Montgomery National Historic Trail runs fifty-four miles along Alabama Highway 80 from Brown Chapel A.M.E. Church in Selma to Montgomery. Trail markers, visible from the highway, commemorate this historic demonstration.

Martin Luther King Jr. was assassinated as he stood on the balcony of his room at the Lorraine Motel in Memphis. The New York Times *declared, "Dr. King's murder is a national disaster."*

THE LORRAINE MOTEL AND THE NATIONAL CIVIL RIGHTS MUSEUM

450 Mulberry Street
Memphis, TN 38103
901-521-9699
www.civilrightsmuseum.org/

The Lorraine Motel was built in 1925, and, like most southern motels of the period, served only whites. After World War II, as the Civil Rights movement gathered momentum, encouraged by President Truman's integra-tion of the U.S. armed forces, the owner was willing to rent rooms to blacks and it became a black establishment. Its guests included entertain-ers such as Cab Calloway, Count Basie, Nat "King" Cole, and Aretha Franklin and sports stars such as baseball players Roy Campanella and Jackie Robinson. In 1968, when 1,300 Memphis sanita-tion workers went on strike for better pay and working conditions, Martin Luther King Jr., Ralph Abernathy, Andrew Young, and other prominent black leaders came to lend their support. They stayed at the Lorraine Motel. After a day of bloody con-frontation between marching strikers and police, the federal court issued an injunction prohibiting further demon-strations. King was planning a march to protest the court injunction when, on April 4, 1968, James Earl Ray shot and killed him as he stood on the balcony of his room. The Lorraine Motel became part of the National Civil Rights Museum in 1991, and is now a major exhibit of that museum.

Chronology

1607
Founding of Jamestown, Virginia, first permanent English settlement in North America

1619
First Africans brought to British North American colonies land in Jamestown

1750
Crispus Attucks escapes from slavery in Framingham, Massachusetts

1758
Pennsylvania Quakers demand that their members not hold or trade slaves; Quakers elsewhere follow over the next few decades

1765
British Parliament passes the Stamp Act; blacks participate in anti–Stamp Act protests

1770
Boston Massacre

1775–1783
American Revolution; more than 5,000 African Americans serve in Continental Army

1777
Vermont constitution becomes the first to abolish slavery

1793
U.S. Congress passes the first federal Fugitive Slave Law

1808
United States prohibits the African slave trade

1816
American Colonization Society established

1821
American Colonization Society founds West African colony of Liberia for settlement of former slaves

1822
Denmark Vesey's plans for a slave revolt discovered in Charleston, South Carolina, and thirty-five blacks executed

1838
Frederick Douglass escapes from slavery in Maryland

1845
Narrative of the Life of Frederick Douglass published

1846
Dred and Harriet Scott sue for their freedom in St. Louis Circuit Court

1849
Harriet Tubman escapes from slavery in Maryland

1850
New federal Fugitive Slave Law makes recovering fugitives easier for slaveholders

1852
Harriet Beecher Stowe publishes *Uncle Tom's Cabin*

1857
The Supreme Court rules against Dred Scott in *Scott* v. *Sanford*

1859
John Brown, thirteen whites, and five blacks attack the federal arsenal at Harpers Ferry, Virginia

1860
Abraham Lincoln elected President

1861
Civil War begins; African Americans volunteer for military service but are rejected

1862
Slavery abolished in the District of Columbia, and slave owners are compensated for the emancipation of their slaves

1863
Abraham Lincoln issues Emancipation Proclamation; black troops enlist in the U.S. army; black troops of the Fifty-fourth Massachusetts Volunteers engage in battle at Fort Wagner

1864
Fort Pillow massacre

1865

Congress passes and ratifies Thirteenth Amendment to the Constitution abolishing slavery; surrender of Confederate General Robert E. Lee to General Ulysses S. Grant; Abraham Lincoln assassinated

1866

Congress passes Fourteenth Amendment to the Constitution giving blacks equal citizenship rights

1869

Congress passes Fifteenth Amendment to the Constitution guaranteeing blacks the right to vote

1877

Black town of Nicodemus, Kansas, founded

1896

U.S. Supreme Court establishes doctrine of separate but equal in *Plessy* v. *Ferguson*

1905

Black leaders establish the Niagara Movement

1909

The integrated National Association for the Advancement of Colored People founded as the successor to the all-black Niagara Movement

1917–1918

American involvement in World War I includes service by about 400,000 African Americans

1934

First live show staged at Apollo Theater

1940

Benjamin Oliver Davis Sr. becomes the first black general in the regular army

1941

First U.S. Army pilot training program initiated at Tuskegee, Alabama; President Roosevelt prohibits racial discrimination in war industries

1945

World War II ends; more than one million African Americans served in the armed forces during the war

1948

President Harry Truman ends segregation in the U.S. armed forces

1954

In *Brown* v. *Board of Education* Supreme Court declares public school segregation unconstitutional; White Citizens Council formed in Mississippi to resist racial integration

1955

The Montgomery Freedom Association, led by Martin Luther King Jr., begins bus boycott in Alabama

1957

Eighteen students protected by federal troops attempt to integrate Central High School in Little Rock, Arkansas; Congress passes Civil Rights Act of 1957 to form Civil Rights Commission and Civil Rights Division of the Justice Department

1960

Student Nonviolent Coordinating Committee

(SNCC) organized in Raleigh, North Carolina; students sit-in at Woolworth lunch counter in Greensboro, North Carolina, protesting segregation

1961

Integrated group of Freedom Riders attacked and beaten in Alabama

1963

President Kennedy sends federal troops to Birmingham, Alabama, to protect demonstrators from white rioters; Martin Luther King Jr. arrested and jailed; 200,000 join March on Washington to demand civil rights; bomb kills four young black girls attending Sunday school in Birmingham, Alabama

1964

President Lyndon B. Johnson signs Civil Rights Act of 1964, prohibiting racial discrimination in public accommodations, employment, and education; Martin Luther King Jr. is awarded the Nobel Peace Prize; three civil rights workers murdered in Philadelphia, Mississippi

1965

President Lyndon B. Johnson signs Voting Rights Act providing federal safeguards against voter discrimination

1967

Thurgood Marshall becomes the first African American to be appointed to the Supreme Court

1968

Martin Luther King Jr. assassinated in Memphis, Tennessee

Further Reading

General Sources on African American History

Berlin, Ira. *Many Thousands Gone: The First Two Centuries of Slavery in North America.* Cambridge, Mass.: Harvard University Press, 2000.

Franklin, John Hope, and Alfred A. Moss, Jr., eds. *From Slavery to Freedom.* 8th ed., New York: Knopf, 2000.

Hine, Darlene Clark, William C. Hine, and Stanley Harrold. *The African American Odyssey.* 2nd ed., Upper Saddle River, N.J.: Prentice Hall, 2002.

Horton, James Oliver, and Lois E. Horton. *Hard Road to Freedom: The Story of African America.* New Brunswick, N.J.: Rutgers University Press, 2001.

Kelley, Robin D. G., and Earl Lewis, eds. *To Make Our World Anew: A History of African Americans.* New York: Oxford University Press, 2000.

Jamestown, Colonial National Historical Park

Breen, T. H., and Stephen Innes. *"Myne Owne Ground": Race and Freedom on Virginia's Eastern Shore, 1640–1676.* New York: Oxford University Press, 1982.

Deagan, Kathleen, and Darcie MacMahon. *Fort Mose: Colonial America's Black Fortress of Freedom.* Gainesville: University Press of Florida, 1995.

McCartney, Martha W. *A Study of the Africans and African Americans on Jamestown Island and at Green Spring, 1619–1803.* Williamsburg, Va.: Colonial Williamsburg Foundation, 2003.

———, *Documentary History of Jamestown Island.* Williamsburg, Va.: Colonial Williamsburg Foundation, 2000.

Morgan, Edmund S. *American Slavery, American Freedom: The Ordeal of Colonial Virginia.* New York: W.W. Norton, 1975.

Price, David A. *Love and Hate in Jamestown : John Smith, Pocahontas, and The Heart of a New Nation.* New York: Knopf, 2003.

Wood, Peter H. *Strange New Land: African Americans, 1617–1776.* New York: Oxford University Press, 1996.

The Old State House

Horton, James Oliver, and Lois E Horton. *In Hope of Liberty: Free Black Culture and Community in the North, 1700–1860.* New York: Oxford University Press, 1997.

Kaplan, Sidney. *The Black Presence in the Era of the American Revolution.* Revised ed., Amherst: University of Massachusetts Press, 1989.

Littlefield, Daniel C. *Revolutionary Citizens: African Americans, 1776–1804.* New York: Oxford University Press, 1997.

Quarles, Benjamin. *The Negro in the American Revolution.* New York: W.W. Norton, 1973.

Zobel, Hiller B. *The Boston Massacre.* New York: W. W. Norton, 1970.

Kingsley Plantation

Landers, Jane. *Black Society in Spanish Florida.* Urbana: University of Illinois Press, 1999.

Schafer, Daniel L. *Anna Kingsley.* Rev. ed. St. Augustine, Fla.: St. Augustine Historical Society, 1997.

Stowell, Daniel W., ed. *Balancing Evils Judiciously: The Proslavery Writings of Zephaniah Kingsley.* Gainesville: University Press of Florida, 2000.

Stowell, Daniel W., and Kathy Tilford. *Kingsley Plantation: A History of the Fort George Plantation.* Jacksonville, Fla: Kingsley Plantation, 1998.

The African Meeting House

Cromwell, Adelaide M. *The Other Brahmins: Boston's Black Upper Class, 1750–1950. Fayetteville: University of Arkansas Press, 1994.*

Harris, Leslie M. *In the Shadow of Slavery: African Americans in New York City, 1626–1863.* Chicago: University of Chicago Press, 2002.

Horton, James Oliver. *Free People of Color: Inside the African American Community.* Washington, D.C.: Smithsonian Institution Press, 1993.

Horton, James Oliver, and Lois E. Horton. *Black Bostonians: Family Life, and Community Struggle in the Antebellum North.* Rev. ed. New York: Holmes and Meier, 1999.

Jacobs, Donald M., ed. *Courage and Conscience: Black and White Abolitionists in Boston.* Bloomington: Indiana University Press, 1993.

The Old Court House

Cheek, William, and Aimee Lee Cheek. *John Mercer Langston and the Fight for Black Freedom, 1829–65.* Urbana: University of Illinois Press, 1989.

Fehrenbacher, Don E. *The Dred Scott Case: Its Significance in American Law and Politics.* New York: Oxford University Press, 2001.

Finkelman, Paul. *Dred Scott v. Sandford: A Brief History with Documents.* New York: St. Martin's, 1997.

Fleischner, Jennifer. *The* Dred Scott *Case: Testing the Right to Live Free.* Brookfield, Conn.: Millbrook, 1997.

Harpers Ferry National Historic Park

Anderson, Osborne P. *A Voice from Harper's Ferry.* 1861. Reprint, New York: World View, 1974.

Finkelman, Paul, ed. *His Soul Goes Marching On: Responses to John Brown and the Harpers Ferry Raid.* Charlottesville: University Press of Virginia, 1995.

National Park Service. *John Brown's Raid.* Washington, D.C.: Government Printing Office, 1990.

Quarles, Benjamin. *Allies for Freedom: Blacks and John Brown.* New York: Oxford University Press, 1974.

Cedar Hill, Frederick Douglass National Historic Site

Blight, David W. *Frederick Douglass' Civil War: Keeping Faith in Jubilee.* Baton Rouge: Louisiana State University Press, 1989.

Douglass, Frederick. *Narrative of the Life of Frederick Douglass.* Ed. David W. Blight. Boston: Bedford, 1993.

Green, Constance McLaughlin. *The Secret City: A History of Race Relations in the Nation's Capital.* Princeton, N.J.: Princeton University Press, 1967.

Hutchinson, Louise Daniel. *The Anacostia Story, 1608–1930.* Washington, D.C.: Smithsonian Institution Press, 1977.

McFeely, William S. *Frederick Douglass.* New York: W.W. Norton, 1991.

Nicodemus, Kansas

Chu, Daniel, and Bill Shaw. *Going Home to Nicodemus: The Story of an African American Frontier Town and the Pioneers Who Settled It.* Morristown, N.J.: Julian Messner, 1994.

National Park Service. *Promised Land on the Solomon: Black Settlement at Nicodemus, Kansas.* Washington, D.C.: Government Printing Office, 1986.

Painter, Nell Irvin. *Exodusters: Black Migration to Kansas after Reconstruction.* New York: W.W. Norton, 1976.

Redkey, Edwin S. *Black Exodus: Black Nationalist and Back-to-Africa Movements, 1890–1910.* New Haven, Conn.: Yale University Press, 1969.

Sweet Auburn Historic District

Ayers, Edward L. *The Promise of the New South: Life after Reconstruction.* New York: Oxford University Press, 1992.

Carson, Clayborne, ed. *The Autobiography of Martin Luther King, Jr.* New York: Warner Books, 1998.

Grossman, James R. *Land of Hope: Chicago, Black Southerners and the Great Migration*. Chicago: University of Chicago Press, 1989.

Litwack, Leon F. *Trouble in Mind: Black Southerners in the Age of Jim Crow*. New York: Knopf, 1998.

Pomerantz, Gary M. *Where Peachtree Meets Sweet Auburn: A Saga of Race and Family*. New York: Penguin, 1997.

The Apollo Theater

Cooper, Ralph, with Steve Dougherty. *Amateur Night at the Apollo: Ralph Cooper Presents Five Decades of Great Entertainment*. New York: HarperCollins, 1990.

Lewis, David Levering. *When Harlem Was In Vogue*. New York: Oxford University Press, 1979.

Osofsky, Gilbert. *Harlem: The Making of a Ghetto*. 2nd ed. New York: Harper and Row, 1971.

Peretti, Burton W. *The Creation of Jazz: Music, Race, and Culture in Urban America*. Urbana: University of Illinois Press, 1994.

Schiffman, Jack. *A Pictorial History of Modern Black Show Business and the Apollo Theater*. New York: Prometheus, 1984.

USS *Arizona* Memorial

Bailey, Beth, and David Farber. *The First Strange Place: The Alchemy of Race and Sex in World War II Hawaii*. New York: Free Press, 1992.

Clarke, Thurston. *Pearl Harbor Ghosts: The Legacy of December 7, 1941*. New York: Ballantine, 1991.

Fletcher, Marvin E. *America's First Black General: Benjamin O. Davis, Sr., 1880–1970*. Lawrence: University of Kansas, 1989.

Trotter, Joe William, Jr. *From a Raw Deal to a New Deal? African Americans, 1929–1945*. New York: Oxford University Press, 1996.

Wynn, Neil A. *The Afro-American and the Second World War*. New York: Holmes & Meier, 1993.

Brown v. *Board of Education* National Historic Site

Burns, Stewart, ed. *Daybreak of Freedom: The Montgomery Bus Boycott*. Chapel Hill: University of North Carolina Press, 1997.

Harding, Vincent, Robin D. G. Kelley, and Earl Lewis. *We Changed the World: African Americans, 1945–1970*. Oxford University Press, 1997.

Haskins, James. *Thurgood Marshall: A Life For Justice*. New York: Henry Holt, 1992.

Kluger, Richard. *Simple Justice: The History of* Brown v. Board of Education *and Black America's Struggle for Equality*. New York: Vintage, 1975.

Patterson, James T. Brown v. Board of Education: *A Civil Rights Milestone and Its Troubled Legacy*. New York: Oxford University Press, 2001.

The F.W. Woolworth Building, Downtown Greensboro Historic District

Carson, Clayborne. *In Struggle: SNCC and the Black Awakening of the 1960s*. Cambridge, Mass.: Harvard University Press, 1981.

Hampton, Henry, and Steve Fayer. *Voices of Freedom: An Oral History of the Civil Rights Movement from the 1950s through the 1980s*. New York: Bantam, 1990.

King, Mary. *Freedom Song: A Personal Story of the 1960s Civil Rights Movement*. New York: William Morrow, 1987.

Williams, Juan. *Eyes on the Prize: America's Civil Rights Years, 1954–1965*. New York: Penguin, 1987.

Index

References to illustrations and captions are in bold.

The National Register of Historic Places, National Park Service

The National Register of Historic Places is the official U.S. list of historic places worthy of preservation. Authorized under the National Historic Preservation Act of 1966, the National Register is part of a national program to coordinate and support public and private efforts to identify, evaluate, and protect America's historic and archeological resources. The National Register is administered by the National Park Service, which is part of the U.S. Department of the Interior.

Properties listed in the National Register include districts, sites, buildings, structures, and objects that are significant in U.S. history, architecture, archaeology, engineering, and culture. Places range from ancient Indian pueblos, to homes of writers or philanthropists, to bridges, to commercial districts. Among the tens of thousands of listings are: all historic areas in the National Park System; National Historic Landmarks; and properties nominated for their significance to communities, states, or the nation. The public can find information about these places on the web from the National Register Information System (NRIS) or request copies of documentation files.

For more information about the National Register of Historic Places, visit our Web site at www.cr.nps.gov/nr; phone 202-354-2213; fax 202-371-2229; e-mail nr_info@nps.gov; or write National Register of Historic Places, National Park Service, 1849 C Street, NW, Washington, DC 20240.

Teaching with Historic Places

The Teaching with Historic Places program (TwHP) uses places listed in the National Register to enrich and enliven the study of history, social studies, geography and other subjects. Historic places have the power to make us more aware of our connection to the people and events that preceded us. It is possible to experience that "sense of place" whether or not site visits are possible. By actively investigating places and documentation about them, students can develop enthusiasm and curiosity while they enjoy a historian's sense of discovery and learn critical skills.

A series of lessons based on places around the country forms the cornerstone of the TwHP program. It includes Revolutionary and Civil War battlefields, presidential homes, churches that hosted Civil Rights meetings, places where women made history, and much more. Each lesson plan includes an activity that leads students to research the history and historic places in their own communities. TwHP lessons are free and available online, where they are indexed by state, historic theme, time period, and the National Standards for History.

For more information about the award-winning TwHP program or to acquire the lesson plans, visit the TwHP Web site at www.cr.nps.gov/nr/twhp; phone 202-354-2213; fax 202-371-2229; e-mail nr_twhp@nps.gov; or write Teaching with Historic Places, National Register of Historic Places, National Park Service, 1849 C Street, NW, Washington, DC 20240.

Gilder Lehrman Institute of American History

Dedicated to collecting, preserving, interpreting, and promoting interest in the history of the United States, the Gilder Lehrman Institute of American History advances the study of history by offering public lectures, conferences, and exhibits; research fellowships for scholars to work in the Gilder Lehrman Collection and other archives of American history; summer seminars and enrichment programs for public, parochial, and independent school teachers; books, essays, journals, and educators' guides in American history; electronic media projects for students, teachers, scholars, and the general public; history-centered high schools and Saturday academies for New York City students; and prizes for the most outstanding books on Lincoln, the Civil War Era, Slavery, and Abolition. Founded in 1994 by businessmen and philanthropists Richard Gilder and Lewis E. Lehrman, the Institute's Advisory Board is made up of leading figures in the study and public presentation of American history. The Gilder Lehrman Institute may be contacted at:

19 W. 44th Street, Suite 500
New York, NY 10036-5902
646-366-9666
fax 646-366-9669
http://www.gliah.uh.edu/index.cfm

Picture and Text Credits

Pictures

14 Beacon Street, Suite 719 Boston, MA 02108: 59; Alabama Bureau of Tourism: 190; American National Historic Site: 53; Atlanta Public Library / African American Research Library: 126; Courtesy of the Apollo Theatre: cover, 141; Courtesy of the APVA Preservation Virginia: 14, 16, 18, 22; Boston Athenaeum: 50, 52, 76; Chicago Historical Society: 31; Chicago Landmarks Commission, Bob Thall, Photographer, 1997: 136; City of Augustine Church: 118; Collection of the New-York Historical Society neg. #48163d: 44; Photo by David T. Gilbert: 80 top; Documenting the American South (http://docsouth.unc.edu), The University of North Carolina at Chapel Hill Libraries: 56; © Ernest C. Withers. Courtesy, Panopticon Gallery, Waltham, MA: 133; Florida State Archives: 47; Annie Straith Jamieson Fonds, University of Western Ontario Archives: 81; Frank Driggs Collection: 137 bottom, 143, 145, 147; Frederick Douglass Papers, Moorland-Springarn Research Center, Howard University, Washington DC: 96; Courtesy Frederick Douglass National Historic Site, National Park Service: 92, 102, 104; Georgia Department of Economic Development: 132, 135; The Gilder Lehrman Collection, On Deposit at the New York Historical Society, New York: 32; GLC 2917. Print: The fifteenth amendment celebrated May 19th, 1870, 1870 (The Gilder Lehrman Collection, courtesy of The Gilder Lehrman Institute of American History, New York): 88; GLC 5111.01.1318. Photograph: Portrait of Frederick Douglass [cabinet card] (The Gilder Lehrman Collection, courtesy of The Gilder Lehrman Institute of American History, New York): 90 top; GLC 5762. Object: Twenty Star American "Abolitionist Flag", 1859 ca. (The Gilder Lehrman Collection,

courtesy of the Gilder Lehrman Institute of American History, New York): 55; GLC 6117. Book. Narrative of the Life of Frederick Douglass, Written by Himself. (The Gilder Lehrman Collection, courtesy of the Gilder Lehrman Institute of American History): 93; GLC 6132. William Nell. Book. The Colored patriots of the American Revolution; with sketches...1855 (The Gilder Lehrman Collection, courtesy of The Gilder Lehrman Institute of American History, New York): 26, 86; Courtesy of The Herndon Home: 128, 130; Courtesy of Historical New England/SPNEA: 35, 58; Jack Kidd: 106; Jefferson National Expansion Memorial/ National Park Service: 63, 64, 72, 73; Jim Steinhart and www.PlanetWare.com: 25, 36, 191; Kansas State Historical Society, Topeka, Kansas: 107, 108, 111, 175 ; Karen Schaefer: 89; King Memorial Baptist Church: 180; Library Company of Philadelphia: 82, 85; Library of Congress: 29 bottom, 30, 67, 68, 70, 76-77, 78, 80 bottom, 90 bottom, 112, 115, 119, 123, 153, 170, 173, 176, 178, 181; Courtesy of The Library of Virginia: 15; Madison County Historical Society, Oneida, NY: 94; The Mariners' Museum, Newport News, VA: 17; Courtesy of the Massachusetts Historical Society: 28, 33, 54; memphistravel.com: 149; Missouri Historical Society, St. Louis: cover, 61; National Archives: frontis, 150, 151, 154, 163, 165; © National Maritime Museum, London, Greenwich Hospital Collection: 19; National Museum of American History Smithsonian Institution Behring Center: 183; National Park Service: 24, 29 top, 37, 38, 40, 41, 43, 49, 65, 109, 116, 117; National Park Service, Colonial National Historical Park: 23; National Park Service, Harpers Ferry National Historic Park: 87; Courtesy National Park Service, Museum Management Program and Frederick Douglass National Historic Site, FRDO 246, Anna Murray Douglass, Painting by O.W. Brooks, http://www.cr.nps.gov/museum/exhibits/douglass/246.htm: 101; Courtesy National Park Service, Museum Management Program and Frederick Douglass National Historic Site, Violin, FRDO 2505 / Photograph by Carol Highsmith / http://www.cr.nps.gov/museum/exhibits/dou-glass/2505.htm: 99; Courtesy National Park Service, Museum Management Program and Tuskegee Airmen National Historic Site, Hangar No. 1, Morton Field 1999, http://www.cr.nps.gov/museum/exhibits/tuskegee/lgimage/air13.htm: 167: NPS- Photo Collection: 152; NPS Photograph by Jody Cook: 122; Oberlin College Archives: 83; Oberlin Heritage Center/O.H.I.O. Resource Center, Oberlin, Ohio: 74; Philadelphia Convention and Visitor's Bureau: 75; Photographs and Prints Division, Schomburg Center for Research in Black Culture, The New York Public Library, Astor, Lennox and Tilden Foundations: 137 top, 139, 140; The San Antonio Light Collection UT Institute of Texan Cultures at San Antonio, No. L-6175, Gift of the Hearst Corporation: 186; Photo: By Scott Hoffmann. Greensboro News and Record: 184, 189; Topeka Chamber of Commerce: 168, 171; Tuskegee Airmen National Historic Site: 160; University of Florida - Special Collection: 39; Virginia Historical Society, Richmond, Virginia: 21, 124; Yale Collection of American Literature, Beinecke Rare Book and Manuscript Library: 142

Text

p. 27: Boston Gazette, October 2, 1750.

p. 81: Osborn Perry Anderson, A Voice from Harper's Ferry Boston: TK publisher, 1861, p. 3.

p. 84: Virginia. Calendar of Virginia State Papers and Other Manuscripts (1652-1869), (Richmond, 1875–1893), vol. XI, p. 310.

p. 31: Sidney Kaplan. The Black Presence in the Era of the American Revolution, 1770–1800. Washington, D.C.: Smithsonian Institution Press, 1973, p. 20.

p. 42: Stowell, Daniel W., ed. Balancing Evils Judiciously: The Proslavery Writings of Zephaniah Kingsley. Gainesville: University Press of Florida, 2000, pp. 23–25.

James Oliver Horton is the Benjamin Banneker Professor of American Studies and History at George Washington University and director of the George Washington University Center for Public History and Public Culture. Horton has been honored with many awards for excellence in scholarship and teaching, as well as an appointment by President Clinton to serve on the Abraham Lincoln Bicentennial Commission. He has served as historical expert for First Lady Hillary Rodham Clinton on the White House Millennium Council; acting chair of the National Park System Advisory Board; Senior Advisor on Historical Interpretation and Public Education for the Director of the National Park Service; and historical advisor to museums throughout the world. In addition to consulting on film and video productions, he has himself been the subject of an episode in The History Channel series "Great Minds in American History." His numerous books include *Free People of Color: Inside the African American Community, The History of the African American People* (coedited with Lois E. Horton), and *In Hope of Liberty: Culture, Protest, and Community Among Northern Free Blacks, 1700–1860* (coauthored with Lois E. Horton). In 2004, Horton will assume the presidency of the Organization of American Historians.